S0-BIF-723

CATASTROPHE!

HOW PSYCHOLOGY EXPLAINS WHY GOOD PEOPLE MAKE BAD SITUATIONS WORSE

Christopher J. Ferguson

Prometheus Books

Essex, Connecticut

Prometheus Books

An imprint of Globe Pequot, the trade division of
The Rowman & Littlefield Publishing Group, Inc.
4501 Forbes Boulevard, Suite 200, Lanham, Maryland 20706
www.rowman.com

Distributed by NATIONAL BOOK NETWORK

Copyright © 2022 by Christopher J. Ferguson

All rights reserved. No part of this book may be reproduced in any form or by any electronic or mechanical means, including information storage and retrieval systems, without written permission from the publisher, except by a reviewer who may quote passages in a review.

British Library Cataloguing in Publication Information Available

Library of Congress Cataloging-in-Publication Data

Names: Ferguson, Christopher J., author.
Title: Catastrophe! : how psychology explains why good people make bad
    situations worse / Christopher J. Ferguson.
Description: Lanham, MD : Prometheus, 2022. | Includes bibliographical
    references and index. | Summary: "This highly original book examines the
    personal and collective psychology behind the breakdown of rational
    decision-making during times of crisis and offers solutions to how we
    can be better prepared"— Provided by publisher.
Identifiers: LCCN 2022013304 (print) | LCCN 2022013305 (ebook) | ISBN
    9781633887954 (cloth) | ISBN 9781633887961 (epub)
Subjects: LCSH: Decision making. | Crises—Psychological aspects. |
    Emergency management—Psychological aspects.
Classification: LCC BF448 .F47 2022 (print) | LCC BF448 (ebook) | DDC
    153.8/3—dc23/eng/20220321
LC record available at https://lccn.loc.gov/2022013304
LC ebook record available at https://lccn.loc.gov/2022013305

♾️™ The paper used in this publication meets the minimum requirements of American National Standard for Information Sciences—Permanence of Paper for Printed Library Materials, ANSI/NISO Z39.48-1992.

To my wife, Diana:
Our marriage is at least one thing in this world
that hasn't been a catastrophe.

CONTENTS

1   DISASTER!   1

2   WHEN TOILET PAPER BECAME LIKE GOLD   23

3   DO/DON'T PANIC (PICK ONE)   39

4   NUKED!   57

5   TERROR IN THE SKIES   77

6   SCHOOLS ABLAZE   95

7   A RACIAL RECKONING?   113

8   JUMPING THE SHARK   141

9   FIRE!   159

10   BARBARIANS AT THE GATE   171

11   THE END OF REASON   187

12   DOES EVERYTHING END IN CATASTROPHE?   205

NOTES   215

INDEX   243

DISASTER!

On May 31, 2009, Air France flight 447 rolled onto the tarmac in Rio de Janeiro, Brazil. On board were 12 crew members and 216 passengers, most of them French, Brazilians, or Germans. These included eight children, one of whom was an infant. Perhaps some were French citizens returning from vacation in Brazil or, conversely, Brazilian citizens enjoying a trip to Paris to see the Louvre and the Eiffel Tower. Others were traveling on business or attending conferences. One was a Turkish harpist, returning from playing at a festival.

The plane had an experienced crew of three: Captain Marc Dubois, copilot David Robert, and copilot Pierre-Cédric Bonin. The extra co-pilot allowed each of the flyers a chance to rest during the grueling thirteen-hour flight. The plane hugged the coast of Brazil, traveling north, then broke out across the Atlantic.

Here, about four hours into the flight, several fateful decisions were made. First, the flight path took the plane directly through a thunderstorm, even though other planes had flown around it.[1] Second, the captain left the cockpit to take his scheduled nap.

Modern commercial jets are designed to fly largely by themselves. Using external data fed into computer systems, modern planes can handle much of their own flying. However, they sometimes fail or become confused, and human pilots must take control. Flying through the thunderstorm—exposure to the elements—caused the autopilot to fail.

Based on the investigation report,[2] the thunderstorm caused ice to accumulate on one of the plane's external sensors, called a pitot tube. This confused the plane's computers, which disengaged the autopilot, shifting control back to the pilots.

Here control reverted to humans, humans who have to make decisions as a crisis begins to develop. Airline pilots are trained to handle crises, but they are still humans. And despite all the training in the world, crises are often like snowflakes: each one unique in its way.

Pitched about in the thunderstorm, the plane began to roll and copilot Bonin, who was at the controls, attempted to control the plane in the turbulence. According to reports, despite thousands of hours of experience, he had not been through a situation like this one before. Perhaps perceiving that the plane had lost altitude, he pitched the plane's nose up. This was a critical mistake.

We all like to think of ourselves as rational people. Our perceptions of the world, and the decisions we make based on them, are objective and based in data. We think we are open to change if our behavior fails to initially produce the outcome we want. Surely it is *others* who are irrational, emotional, prone to perseverative errors in the face of calamity. Yet too often we are wrong. Our responses to crises—personal, environmental, and occupational—are often catastrophically bad. It's easy to see in others precisely because we are not emotionally invested. But emotion—fear, anger, despondency—can be a critical intrusion in good decision making.

By pulling the nose up, copilot Bonin put the airplane into a stall, a condition in which the angle of the wings is too high to retain lift and gravity pulls the plane back to earth. When a stall occurs, the best response* is to put the nose down, so the wings can reacquire lift. However, it may be instinctual to point the nose up, away from the ground, when a plane is losing altitude. Surely, the engines should propel it higher. Combined with faulty or confusing information from the plane's sensors, pilots may struggle to comprehend the crisis unfolding.

Copilot Bonin and copilot Robert now became thoroughly confused, a situation the official report notes may have been compounded by their inability to see what the other was doing with the stick controls, each potentially undoing the other's efforts. The report notes that they did not

---

* I'm no pilot, so I'm basing my comments here on various reports.

engage in the expected maneuvers to fix the stall, possibly due to their confusion. Worse, Bonin continued to pull back on the stick, nosing the plane upward, which was entirely the wrong thing to do.

As the plane continued to plummet, copilot Bonin exclaimed, "I don't have control of the plane at all!" Copilot Robert gave the call to take over control, "Controls to the left" (referring to his position). However, co-pilot Bonin continued to pull up on the stick, undoing copilot Robert's efforts to resume control of the plane. Apparently, copilot Robert was unaware of Bonin's actions, confusing Robert as well. Overall, voice recordings suggest that by this point, the copilots were panicking and not communicating well with one another.[3]

At this juncture Captain Dubois returned to the cabin and found the copilots in a state of discombobulation. Confused and terrified, they were unable to tell him what had gone wrong, only that "We tried everything." What ensues is a distressing exchange of incomprehension and indecision among the three crew. Dubois struggles to diagnose the problem, but he is confronted with poor information from the airplane systems and two terrified copilots.

Finally, Bonin informs Captain Dubois that he has been keeping the airplane's nose pitched up for most of this descent. Only then does Dubois realize the error, commanding the copilots to pitch the nose down to avert the stall. By then, however, the realization comes too late. The plane is critically out of control and spiraling toward the sea below.

Bonin exclaimed, "Fuck, we are going to crash. . . . [I]t can't be true!" To which Robert responded, "We are dead!"

Seconds later the plane crashed into the Atlantic Ocean in a belly-flop position, traveling at 200 kilometers per hour. All passengers and crew on board were killed instantly.

—⁂—

My intent in detailing this tragedy is not to place undue criticism on the pilots in this situation nor to stoke people's fear of airplanes (more on this in a bit). Indeed, quite the contrary—the pilots in this case were well-trained and competent individuals. However, when presented with incomplete data in a crisis environment, emotion overtook them, creating confusion and causing them to engage in unhelpful behaviors that ultimately led to the plane's demise. There were other failures, such as the icing of the pitot tubes and the cockpit design such that the pilots couldn't see what the other was doing. But human error compounded by emotion was not a trivial element of what went wrong with Flight 447.

In this case, the behavior of copilot Bonin is indicative, not of some unusual personal failing, but of the frailties of normal human cognition. Bonin continued pulling up on the stick, nosing the plane up, even though that effort was clearly a failure. This is what we, in the field of psychology, call a *perseverative error*. A person perseveres in continuing the exact same behavior despite that evidence suggests the behavior is ineffective in obtaining one's goal. Far from being a sign of madness, persistence in a behavior and expecting it to obtain different outcomes than before is a normal human response to high pressure and panic. One can imagine Bonin thinking, "This *has* to work; it just *has* to!" We've likely all been there, just fortunately not while at the controls of a plane.

A large part of the problem is simply that of emotion. Emotionally driven decision making tends to result in a higher proportion of errors. That's not necessarily true only for negative emotions such as anger, fear, or depression.* Even positive emotions such as love or excitement can cause us to make errors, though their relationships with negative outcomes are a bit more complex. Training for crises in professions that must contend with them—emergency services, military, airline pilots—to a large degree often attempts to navigate around the paralysis that can come with heightened emotions by making crisis response a routinized, cognitive process. But the reality is that it's difficult to escape the degree to which we can become ruled by our emotional responses.

In the story of Air France flight 447, we can see how an immediate crisis can paralyze human cognition. Communication breaks down, decision making erodes, impulsivity increases, perseverative errors emerge. These are, to some extent, likely a function of preprogrammed biological responses to extreme stress. We are programmed for flight or fight, a set

---

* There is, interestingly, the concept of depressive realism which, in short, suggests that depressed people are more likely to accurately perceive negative information than nondepressed people who are too optimistic. Nonetheless, there appears to be little evidence this results in better crisis decision making. See: Moritz, D., & Roberts, J. E. (2020). Depressive Symptoms and Self-Esteem as Moderators of Metaperceptions of Social Rejection versus Acceptance: A Truth and Bias Analysis. *Clinical Psychological Science*, 8(2), 252–65. https://doi-org.stetson.idm.oclc.org/10.1177/2167702619894906.

of instinctual panic responses that served our ancestors well twenty thousand years ago but serve us less well when flying a plane, taking a test, or receiving an IRS audit in the mail. When confronted with a hungry puma, flight or fight may work rather well (or at least as well as anything), but in the modern largely puma-free technological world, slower, more methodological cognitive responses may be more efficient. We're just not exactly programmed that way.

That said, not all crises are acute, and chronic problems can bring their own set of decision-making errors. These can happen both at the individual level and, perhaps more critically, at the level of entire societies.

I typically hate the role of Kassandra and, generally, my view of the world is quite optimistic. By most metrics, we are living in a remarkably golden age of humanity: homicides are way down, poverty is the lowest it's ever been, issues related to inequalities are more positive than ever.[4] This is not to say everything is roses and unicorns: injustices still exist, massive gaps among the wealthiest and poorest exist, poverty and war still exist. But it's impossible to name any other epoch in history when it would be better to be alive on any rung of the social ladder. Even if we accept that the abysmal year of 2020 was the worst in our living memory, I challenge anyone to pick *any* year in, say, the fourteenth century that would have it beat.

Yet reading our news media, watching the hyperbole on social media, or listening to many professors in academia, it would be hard to know the truth of the world in which we live. Instead, we are told that things are as bad as they have ever been and are getting worse, despite considerable data to the contrary. Why is this happening? Is there some kind of negativity bias that is infectious to humans, and to what degree is it leading us to make critical mistakes?

A NATIONAL DEPRESSION

If we allow that 2020 was certainly a remarkably bad year, most national indicators suggest that things have *generally* gotten better over time in a practical sense. Yet if you look at data about how people *feel*, things look pretty bad.

An interesting data point came in just as I was working on this chapter. According to a new Gallup poll, religiosity in the United States has dropped precipitously, hitting historical lows.[5] For the first time, a majority of Americans don't affiliate with any major religion. That's not unusual for Europe, which has been highly secularized for a long time. However, that's quite strange for the United States. This decline began about twenty years ago, with the majority of it occurring just in the last ten.

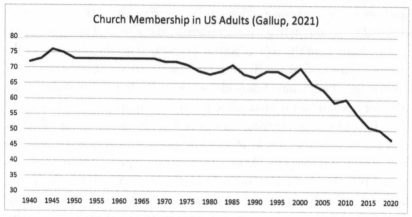

Graph created by the author using Gallup Data (2021).

Now, whether this is particularly bad news or not, in and of itself, is subjective. If you're religious, this may seem like a terrible trend; if you're not, this may get a shrug. Fair enough. But interestingly enough, it mirrors other trends in our society. For instance, consider Gallup data on race relations. Through most of the early 2000s, perceptions of race relations among both black and white adults were quite positive, with solid majorities saying that race relations were very or somewhat good. But beginning around 2014 (roughly the same time as the plummet in religiosity), race relations began to decline precipitously, despite little evidence that racial injustices had worsened in the United States (more on this in a later chapter).

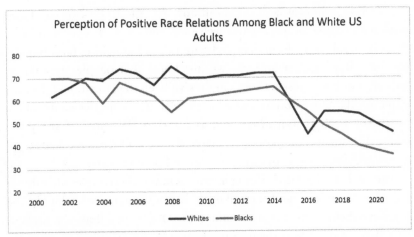

Graph created by the author using Gallup Data (2021).

Of course, we can simply look at suicide rates as an index of how people are doing. Here, in contrast to other social data such as violent crime, which has been plummeting for decades (at least until 2020), suicide rates have been increasing. This data is compiled from CDC data on suicides.[6]

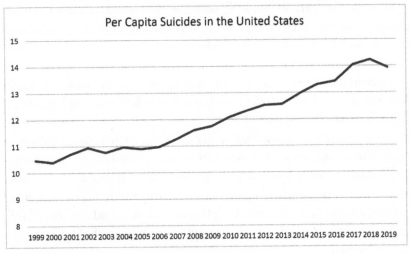

Graph created by the author using CDC Data (2021).

Other data, such as faith in institutions, the opioid epidemic, and pessimism about the future, suggest we've entered a broad societal malaise. It's important to try to understand why this is happening (and frankly, we don't have a clear answer—we just know that people are angrier, sadder, and more pessimistic than they've been in generations). But it's also critical that we understand what this can do to our decision-making processes, both as individuals and as a society. We may be at a point where the rate of error in our national decisions is likely to escalate as our decisions ping-pong between two polarized political extremes.

Part of this is because, during moments of social crisis, people's thinking, both the masses and societal leaders, can begin to look a lot like the cognitive distortions that are common to some mental illnesses, particularly depression. These distortions or biases can cause us to misperceive evidence, dismiss evidence that conflicts with the biases, respond incoherently (or not at all) to crises, and make wildly misinformed decisions.

COGNITIVE BIASES DURING CATASTROPHE

The idea that certain thinking patterns characterized certain mental health disorders such as depression was demonstrated by psychologist Aaron Beck back in the 1970s.[7] The exact list of cognitive biases common to depression varies, but they are generally marked by a tendency to interpret evidence in the most negative way possible, which we might call a negativity bias. A few of the major biases follow (though this list is by no means exhaustive).[8]

Generalization: Generalization occurs when we perceive a pattern of negativity from one or a few incidents. In other words, if one thing is going wrong, everything is going wrong. We can each probably remember doing this at times when something really frustrating happens. For instance, our car gets a flat tire. We get out, look at it, and exclaim, "Well, great, this whole day has been crappy!" even though the day had been pretty normal.

Catastrophizing: Catastrophizing occurs when we exaggerate the impact of a fairly minor negative incident. I see this a lot with college students. A student will get a bad grade then show up in a faculty member's office crying, "If I get a D on this paper, I'll flunk your class, then I won't graduate, I'll never get a good job, then I'll die penniless and homeless on the street, thrown away like so much garbage." Bad events are rarely as bad as they seem in the moment. Perceiving them as catastrophic can cause us to overreact to them.

Mind reading: Mind reading occurs when we make assumptions about the intent of other people, usually in the most negative or least charitable way possibly. This has become increasingly frequent in internet disagreements wherein any disagreement with a desired position is taken as evidence of the other person's moral turpitude. It's normal to try to infer intent in other people, but we also have to remember we tend to filter those judgments through our own expectations.

Dichotomous thinking: Dichotomous thinking occurs when we perceive something as either totally good or totally bad, never nuanced. We see this in a lot of political debates in which one side advertises a policy as the doorway to utopia and the other side rages that it will end civilization as we know it.

Personalizing: Personalizing occurs when we assume that something random or innocuous was specifically targeted to harm us. I can use a non-internet example for myself for this one. Once when dining with my then girlfriend/now wife, I held the door open for her. Behind her, another woman entered the restaurant and I held the door for her as well. She blew past me without so much as a nod. A bit irritated by this rudeness, I pointed it out to my wife once we were seated. She, being wiser than me by far, noted that the woman might be distracted with something on her mind or simply having a bad day. In other words, there were multiple explanations for the woman's behavior, but I had personalized it as a direct insult to myself when likely it was not meant as such.

Inability to disconfirm: Inability to disconfirm occurs when we adopt a belief about the world but then become resistant to any evidence that would disconfirm that belief. There's an idea that people tend to act as amateur scientists, testing assumptions against reality, but with inability to disconfirm, we cease doing so. Our beliefs no longer need evidence to support them; indeed, we may view evidence as the product of some kind of conspiracy theory. This thought pattern is one source of many moral panics, conspiracy theories, and dangerous partisan divides.

Affective forecasting: Affective forecasting involves making predictions about how an event will influence us in the long term. We can see teenagers do this when their heart is broken for the first time: "I'll never love anyone else again!" Typically, our ability to foretell the future in such a way is wildly inaccurate.

Blaming: Blaming involves the tendency to look for a bad guy who is the source of our problems. In some cases, this may be us, "I never do anything right!" or it may be someone else who seems to be impeding our goals, "You never help me!" In partisan political battles, this can lead to demonizing the other side.

To consider how these work in the context of making crises worse, let's take a look at World War I, one of the most destructive and simultaneously dumbest wars ever fought. We'll look at it particularly from the perspective of the Central (Germany, Austro-Hungarian Empire, Ottoman Empire) powers and their decisions that led to the war.

WHOOPS! WE ACCIDENTLY STARTED WORLD WAR I!

Even by the standards of dumb wars, World War I was a pretty dumb one. Alas, poor World War I, vastly overshadowed by its sequel, with fewer cartoonish bad guys to hate or a clear narrative of good and evil. Nonetheless, this massive war resulted in the death of nine million soldiers and perhaps six million civilians (although some figures put it higher). One author ranked it as the eleventh worst atrocity in history in terms of deaths.[9] It would almost certainly get more attention if not for looming under World War II and the disturbingly evil figure of Hitler and his Nazis.

World War II also has the benefit of a clear good-versus-evil narrative, thanks to those same Nazis and other fascist regimes that fought on the side of the obvious bad guys. The narrative for World War I doesn't quite have the same good-versus-evil feel (despite the propaganda of the day, which portrayed Germans as King Kong–like apes). Mostly, people were just dumb and a war that killed fifteen million (give or take) people was the result.

Sometimes called the "War to End All Wars" (it wasn't), World War I was one of the most foolish and destructive military engagements up until that time. By foolish, I mean that the countries involved stumbled into it: they had no clear megalomaniacal plans for conquest nor were they battling for freedom as the Axis and Allied powers did in World War II. Discussing the advent of World War I in detail would and has taken volumes, but here is a brief sketch of what happened and how we can relate this to at least some of the cognitive distortions I mentioned earlier.

The epicenter of the origins of World War I would prove to be the sclerotic multiethnic state of Austria-Hungary.* This empire encapsulated multiple ethnic groups from the named German Austrians and Hungarians, to Czechs, Italians, Poles, Serbs, Romanians, and a multitude of other groups. Multiethnic states commonly experience tension over sharing of rights and which groups have preeminence, language customs, nationalism, and so on, and Austria-Hungary was no exception. The empire tried to deal with this by promoting linguistic rights within the empire, though this may have inadvertently contributed to their citizens' tendency to view themselves as distinct ethnic groups.[10] But tensions remained high, particularly among the Austrians and Serbian Slavs within their state.

There also was a separate Serbian state, conveniently right next door, which didn't get along with Austria-Hungary at all. Serbia hoped to break away portions of the Austro-Hungarian Empire with Serbian majority populations and incorporate these into its own nation. Naturally, this was not the sort of thing likely to go over well with the Austrians.

Enter into this picture one Archduke Franz Ferdinand. Franz Ferdinand (the archduke, not the Scottish rock band), was known as a reformer. He hoped to expand the rights of Serbian minorities within the Austro-Hungarian Empire and, by doing so, make them fully integrated citizens. This predictably pleased no one, not the Austrians (who liked being the big cheese) nor the Serbians (who, remember, wanted to break away parts of the empire to form their own megastate, because that's what folks did in the early twentieth century). However, as heir to the throne of Austria-Hungary, Franz Ferdinand was likely to have significant sway

---

* Note, I will use the terms Austria-Hungary, Austro-Hungarian Empire, and Austria somewhat interchangeably here. I suspect only people with narrowly focused PhDs will care much.

over future events. Unfortunately, despite what we now recognize as some generally good ideas, Franz Ferdinand doesn't really come across as the most charismatic figure (getting a title like "Archduke" probably doesn't foster modesty), and he ruffled a lot of feathers. His uncle, the Emperor Franz Joseph (himself no teddy bear), seems to have loathed him. Even in photos, he doesn't exactly look snuggly.

So Franz Ferdinand (the Austrians sure did love the name Franz) had to go. A conspiracy between Serbian nationals in Austria-Hungary and some elements of the Serbian military secret services led to Franz Ferdinand's assassination in June 1914.

We now recognize this as the event that touched off World War I, but nobody thought so at the time. Even Franz Ferdinand's uncle Franz Joseph (are you keeping track of all these Franzes?) seemed largely unconcerned.[11] At the time it wasn't clear if the Serbian state was involved (it was) or whether it was purely a homegrown amateur effort that had succeeded. It was a crisis, but not one that anyone thought would kill fifteen million. Why would it? Nobody even liked the guy.

Franz Ferdinand. *Wikimedia Commons by Ferdinand Schmutzer—Österreichische National-bibliothek, Bildarchiv Austria, Inventarnr.*

As a quick diversion, it's also important to understand why this one event touched off an absurd cascade of bad decisions. European countries at the time were hardly the panoply of espresso-sipping and military-obligation-avoiding countries they are today. European countries were hostile toward each other, and those hostilities regularly degenerated into dumb and expensive wars. This eventually led to an alliance system that obligated countries to come to each other's defense. These alliances tended to shift with the political fortunes. By 1914 they had evolved such that Austria-Hungary was on one side and France and Russia were on the other. Italy was supposed to be in alliance with Germany and Austria-Hungary but quietly slipped away when fighting broke out, only to join with France and Russia in 1915. The United Kingdom and Ottoman Empire were technically outside this system but ultimately joined opposing sides for reasons of their own (briefly, the United Kingdom was suspicious of German navy buildup and outraged when Germany invaded Belgium on the way to France as one does, whereas the Ottoman Empire was suspicious that France and the United Kingdom wanted to carve up the Ottoman Middle East empire, which they did). But amid all this, Russia was obligated to defend Serbia, despite Serbia touching all this off with the stupid plot to assassinate Franz Ferdinand.

So, Franz Ferdinand's dead. That sucks for him, but it was not as if there wasn't a dry eye in the house, so how did things go south from there? At this point, most folks agreed that Serbia would have to engage in some form of restitution to Austria-Hungary even if the Serbian government wasn't clearly involved in the assassination (though, remember, we now know it was). Even if the Austria-Hungarian government wasn't exactly put out by the loss of Franz Ferdinand, the assassination of an archduke was still a major affront to the nation's honor. So, some form of payback was to be expected. And here people began to make incredibly stupid decisions.

Remember, in June 1914, almost nobody wanted or expected a big war, but by August 1914, World War I had begun. It began with Emperor Franz Joseph (gah, too many Franzes!) and the Austrians overplaying their hand, egged on by Germany. The Austrians delivered what was called the July Ultimatum to Serbia, a series of ten harsh demands that all but crippled Serbia's integrity as a sovereign nation. The demands were intended to provoke war. Nobody was fooled and the sympathy initially offered to Austria-Hungary began to ebb. Surprisingly, Serbia accepted most of the demands, except for two that would have allowed Austria-Hungarian military and police entities to function with impunity within Serbia's borders. Now sympathies began to swing toward Serbia who, despite instigating the assassination (which, again, wasn't clearly known at the time), now seemed surprisingly reasonable. Austria-Hungary was having none of that.

But why? It had gotten remarkable concessions from Serbia. And it had certainly saved face in regard to the insult to its national honor from the assassination of Franz Ferdinand. Why not take their winnings and go home? Let's look at this in terms of cognitive distortions.

The most obvious one in relation to the July Ultimatum is dichotomous thinking. The Austrians had gotten *most* of what they wanted from the Serbians but not all of it. In reality, if we ignore the tragedy of a few deaths (Franz Ferdinand's wife was also assassinated), which nearly everybody did at the time, Austria-Hungary had made out rather well vis-à-vis Serbia regarding the death of Franz Ferdinand. But it had difficulty seeing it that way. *Any* recalcitrance on the part of Serbia could not be accepted and war could be the only proper solution.

Other cognitive distortions are relevant to Austro-Hungarian's decision making. Though few wept over the death of Franz Ferdinand, the Austrians nonetheless *personalized* his assassination as an affront to the empire. *Blaming* is, of course, at the root of many irrational conflicts. It becomes easy to see one's foes as entirely at fault for a crisis without recognizing one's own contribution. With *affective forecasting*, decision makers perceive the need to find an immediate, dramatic, and somewhat impulsive decision to fix a crisis in the belief that it will worsen rather than ease over time.

So, the Austro-Hungarian Empire declared war. So far this was a regional conflict and the outcome wasn't much in doubt. Austria-Hungary had many times greater a population and resources than the Serbian nation. However, Russia, ethnically Slav like the Serbs, felt compelled to defend the little nation and began to mobilize its army. This kicked into action a series of interlocking alliances that would pull Russia, France, Germany, the United Kingdom, and, due to some savvy diplomacy by

Germany and poor diplomacy by France and the United Kingdom, the Ottoman Empire as well as multiple smaller states (poor Belgium got overrun mainly because it was geographically in the way). But how the hell did that happen? Surely some saner heads could have seen that a regional conflict over the death of one unliked man couldn't possibly be worth pulling all of Europe and the Middle East* into a massive war?

If you think that, you don't know people. You could just as easily say endless culture war on the part of American Democrats and Republicans is clearly bad for the United States (it is) and saner heads should get their act together and work toward compromise (they won't, at least not until incentivized to do so). We can pretty much see how that is going. So began a foolish slide toward a massive war in August that, back in June, nobody really wanted or expected.

Everybody likes to blame the Germans—and let's just admit it, they have a historical tendency to break things: the Roman Empire (they invaded initially through Gaul, modern-day France), the Thirty Years' War (during which the Germans mostly broke Germany at least), the Franco-Prussian War, both World Wars. . . . One gets the sense the Germans see something in France that the rest of us don't see. But if we acknowledge that everybody screwed up leading to World War I (they did), the Germans still deserve a lion's share for nudging their allies in Austria toward war, then leaping into war with Russia when they might have worked to cool things off. Oh, and then the whole invading-Belgium thing, a poor little confused nation that wasn't even involved in any of this other than having far too many "This way to Paris" signs on their roads. What the hell were they thinking?

Germany ended up snared between France and Russia. France already had a bone to pick with Germany, Germany having grabbed several territories from France during the Franco-Prussian War a generation or two back. Germany, Austria, and Russia had together picked Eastern Europe clean and now butted up against each other. Germany became worried that, in the future (affective forecasting), Russia would become more powerful, and this would reduce Germany's influence. That

---

* Japan joined as well on the side of the Entente powers but mainly gobbled up German-owned islands in the Pacific. Germany's clumsy attempts to try to convince Japan to switch sides ultimately would play a small part in drawing the United States into the latter part of the war.

Russia might become more powerful one day than Germany was perceived as *catastrophic* for Germany. In that catastrophizing mind frame, it made sense to go to war *now*, when Germany was still ascendant, rather than *later*, when it might be too late. Though German leadership in 1914 was marked by conflict, hesitancy, confusion, as well as aggression,[12] ultimately this overarching concern about losing influence put Germany very much in the mind of stumbling toward a war it thought was inevitable anyway.

There was also a fair amount of *mind reading* in Germany's view (it was assumed Russia had the goal of dominating Germany in some future) and *inability to disconfirm* (despite czarist Russia's overtures toward deescalating tensions, Germany remained convinced they were locked in an existential struggle). Although Germany pushed the continent toward war, descriptions of thinking among German leaders highlights the panic, indecision, waffling, and stress among political and military commanders as they tried to decide what to do as the crisis unfurled.[13] The issue was less that German leaders were aggressive monsters and more that they were alarmed and unable to see past their own cognitive biases. Certain that war must come at some point, it seemed better to fight the war now than in an uncertain future.

Monday-morning quarterbacking the decisions of historical leaders can be illustrative and a bunch of fun. But just like with the Air France flight 447 pilots, my intent here is not to suggest that the actions of pretty much everyone in charge of Europe in 1914 were uniquely foolish, but rather to note how common it can be for people, both ordinary and ordained by history, to fail in moments of crisis.

A century or so on, it's easy to look back and think, "I'd be the adult in the room. I'd swagger on in there and point out to everyone, 'Look folks, nobody here even liked old "Frank-Ferdy," so how's about we dial it back a bit, everybody shakes hands, and we try not to wipe a baker's dozen or so million people off the planet?'" It's easy to think we'd make rational decisions when we're calmly uninvolved in the situation at hand. Then again, even if we're right about our own level-headedness, it might not make a difference. Unfortunately, too often our personal decision making is constrained by a bunch of other idiots; namely, our family, friends, coworkers, and fellow citizens.

EVERYBODY, LOOK AT HOW MODEST I'M BEING

To review the discussion so far, I've noted how fear and panic during a crisis can overcome rational decision making. I've also looked at how, perhaps a bit more long term, cognitive distortions similar to those experienced by people with depression can lead to poor crisis management by both individuals and at the societal level. There's another factor that leads to bad decision making. That is to say, most of us (the grumpy old guy waving his cane at kids walking on his lawn* being the exception) are social animals who worry about what other people think of us. This means we tend to *conform* to those around us, even if what those around us are doing is kind of dumb.

To show how this works, consider a classic series of experiments by psychologist Solomon Asch in the 1950s. Asch brought male college students into a room where they were asked to make judgments about the length of a line. They were given a target line and three answer choice lines of differing lengths. They were asked to select which of the answer choices were the same as the target line. A pretty easy task.

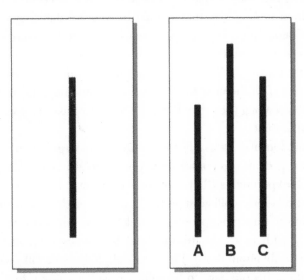

Asch Experiment. *Creative Commons. Attributed to "Fred the Oyster."*

---

* I have been this guy.

Easy except that the participant wasn't the only one in the room. Eight men did the task together, each of them vocally calling out their answers. Only what the real participant didn't know was that the other seven were confederates (people in on the experiment, not the folks who fought at Gettysburg) who were instructed to purposefully give the wrong answer. What Asch wanted to know was whether the real participant would change his answer from the obviously correct answer to the wrong answer that was the consensus of the rest of the group. Very often, people did.[14]

Most people conformed at least some of the time. A good one-third or so conformed most of the time. Only about a quarter of people (the world's fearless curmudgeons, and I salute you) declined to conform at all. By contrast, those in a control group with no social pressure failed to guess the correct response only about 1 percent of the time. In the glass-is-half-full category, most participants defied conformity at least *some* of the time (only about 5 percent of respondents conformed on every single trial). So there is some nuance to the results, but they do suggest that we have at least some tendency to become uncertain of our convictions in the face of the convictions of those around us.

Asch also interviewed participants about their decisions. For those who declined to conform, they tended to respond that they either had great confidence (i.e., they felt the social pressure but were confident in their answer) or were socially withdrawn (i.e., they didn't care much about social approval). By contrast, conformity was related to both lack of confidence (i.e., the view that the majority must be right) or desire to go along to get along (i.e., they knew the majority answer was wrong but didn't want conflict).

There are lots of debates still about exactly what's going on in people's heads when it comes to conformity. There are also some fair critiques of the Asch experiments (they were pretty artificial; it's hard to general-ize from 1950s male college students to pretty much anyone else, etc.). Yet we can say this: most people feel at least *some* pressure to conform, particularly with in-group attitudes and beliefs, even when they may have some doubt about those. There are definitely some folks who don't, although these people have to be willing to suffer some ridicule, anger, and shame when groups employ these tactics to enforce conformity (and they do).

Keep in mind that deciding the length of a line is a pretty innocuous task. Conformity issues can become worse when there's a moral component to a societal question and people don't want to be labeled as being on the wrong moral side. People can become so obsessed with being on the "right side of history" that they become utterly unconcerned with being on the right side of facts. This can bring us to a constellation of related terms: moral panic, availability cascade, bandwagon effect, witch hunt, moral grandstanding, social contagion, etcetera. These terms have some differences among them, and I'll discuss them throughout the book. Yet, in common is the sense that, for many people, moral reasoning and the desire to maintain moral social capital can override rational thinking. This is, of course, the moral of the old play *The Crucible* about the Salem witch trials of 1692 and 1693. The whole thing was made up, and some folks kinda *thought* it was made up, but most people didn't want to say anything out of fear of appearing in cahoots with the devil and getting caught up in the panic themselves. Even as people were killed, reputational management and fear kept most people silent.

We can look back on the events of the Salem witch trials and shake our heads in disbelief (indeed, we use the term *witch hunt* pejoratively). But that doesn't mean people have become immune to the same mistakes. Indeed, in some twist of irony, *The Crucible* itself has come under criticism for being problematic, mainly in not conforming to twenty-first-century "woke" ideals of what stories are OK to tell (or at least to tell to young students[15]). But the social pressures to conform—including public shaming, job loss, even lawsuits (and in other parts of the world, imprisonment or death)—are not trivial.

A MODERN-DAY WITCH HUNT

We tend to like to believe that we and other human beings—or at least those on *our side*—base actions and decisions in clear thinking and analysis of data. But unfortunately, that is seldom the case. Most people are emotional thinkers, too easily convinced by poor evidence (like anecdotes) and tend to prefer evidence that supports their prior beliefs and to ignore or condemn evidence that does not (something called confirmation bias, which I'll talk about elsewhere in the book). To make this even worse, there's another kind of important bias called myside bias. This means people tend to have an easier time spotting faulty or irrational thinking among sociopolitical opponents than among allies on one's own side. If you're a Democrat, say, or pro-life, or pro-gun control, the flaming idiocy of the other side (Republicans, pro-choice, pro–Second Amendment) is clear as day. Simultaneously, it can be hard to identify lunacy on one's own side until it eventually comes for you (as it often does).

We just mentioned *The Crucible* and its lessons about witch hunts and moral panics. Reading or watching it, it can be easy to breathe a sigh of relief that we don't live during such irrational times. But not so fast—there are plenty of witch hunts in the modern era. Sometimes they take real problems and make them worse. Other times they misdiagnose a problem and condemn the wrong cause. At other times they invent a problem out of nothing and still punish people for it.

An example of a modern witch hunt might be the satanic ritual abuse panic of the 1980s and 1990s. Based mainly on the belief in recovered memories of child abuse, a largely discredited idea,[16] many elements of society, including news media, law enforcement, and many therapists, believed children were being kidnapped and abused as part of satanic practices.[17] People were arrested and jailed; lives were ruined until lawsuits eventually revealed that the science behind the idea was bunk and the memories were largely false.

One of the most famous episodes from the satanic panic was the McMartin Preschool case. Beginning in 1983, seven teachers, including elderly women, working at the preschool were accused of sexual abuse of children at the day care. This began with a single accusation by one mother, the estranged wife of teacher Ray Buckey, but mushroomed when overzealous investigators used leading and demanding questioning of impressionable children. Reports eventually suggested that Buckey's wife, the first accuser, had paranoid schizophrenia.[18] She claimed her son told her, among other things, that bestiality was occurring in the preschool and the devil had given Ray Buckey the power of flight.

The police sent out a notice to other parents of children at the preschool. Terrified parents brought their children in to be interviewed.

The interviewers were leading, pressuring the children to make allegations, which eventually many did, including fantastical stories of underground tunnels, the killing of a horse, and day trips by plane to an isolated farm. Despite the obviously nonsensical nature of many of the extraordinary claims, the accusations progressed to trial. Ray Buckey and his mother Peggy endured years of court proceedings as well as the loss of their business and reputation. Ray Buckey would spend five years in jail without ever being convicted of a crime.[19] Most now view this case as a travesty of justice, with Ray and Peggy Buckey as victims of a moral panic and irresponsible justice system.

This situation is often referred to as a moral panic, and it has a few characteristics that are common to these sorts of social phenomena. For instance:

- It relates to an issue most people (thankfully) don't have direct experience with: childhood sexual abuse.
- The issue of child sexual abuse is frightening to people in society, particularly parents.
- Most people must rely on secondary sources of information, such as news media, which tend to hype the panic rather than provide objective information.
- There is a moral component such that skeptics can be accused of not "believing the children." This creates social pressure to support the panic.
- People grossly overestimate the prevalence of the feared behavior.

Combined, this sort of scenario can result in people exaggerating the significance of a phenomenon and, as a consequence, responding to it in ways that ultimately do more harm than good.

Like the Salem witch trials, it's rather easy *in hindsight* to look back upon the satanic ritual abuse panic as a kind of weird anomaly. Surely people are smarter now, right? Nope. Controversially, I'm going to suggest that many of the banners around which people wave their flags today—everything from the panic over masks being tyranny on the right, to systemic racism that seems everywhere and nowhere at once on the left—fit into this same pattern of basic human failure to process complex information efficiently and to avoid relying on emotion, moral grandstanding, and social pressure.

MANAGING CATASTROPHE

So, are there ways we can learn to manage catastrophe better? Yes, but they take practice. But the good news is that there are both individual and societal steps we can implement to manage crises better. But we'll save all that happy, feel-good news for the end. That's just what books do (no skipping ahead!). That's not *really* what you're here for anyway, is it? Mainly you want to learn about all the ways we've screwed up and why. And that's excellent because, in the pages ahead, I hope to enlighten you on how we've all gone nuts. Let's start with the COVID-19 epidemic and see how it reveals the frailties of human cognition. Buckle your seatbelts, folks, we're going on a wild ride into the chaos of the human mind.

2

WHEN TOILET PAPER BECAME LIKE GOLD

By early March 2020, I began to get the sense that the COVID-19 plague was going to be something more than yet another overhyped local epidemic. Before then, like many folks, I wondered if this might have been like the 2009 swine flu, estimated to have killed roughly 12,500 people in the United States.[1] In 2009, I'd been living with my family in Laredo, Texas. Hand sanitizer dispensers went up everywhere. People were encouraged to use them liberally. We worried about swine flu, but it didn't shut down the country, the economy, nor lead to widespread social unrest. Eventually it went away and so, strangely enough, did the hand sanitizer dispensers. Presumably the dispensers would be useful for preventing other more routine diseases but, alas, those weren't making the news.

But in March 2020, it was beginning to hit home that this wasn't "just" another swine flu. One afternoon, my son had the day off from school, so we decided to take a short drive to Winter Park, a suburb of Orlando where the posh live. There's a trendy spot called Park Avenue with boutique restaurants, candy stores, ice cream, as well as clothing and shoe stores for people who like that sort of thing.* On that day it was dead. This was during the early March gray zone before mask mandates and social distancing, but after people had started canceling air flights. Advice from the government and health agencies was confusing. There

---

* There's also a cigar shop, which pollutes the air with the noxious odors of tobacco and entitlement.

was still the sense that maybe the plague would just blow over, be another swine flu, though the optimism for that outcome was winnowing by the day.

It was a nice afternoon (we live in Orlando, after all, where March is like early summer everywhere else) and I was struck by the absence of other people. It felt like watching gray storm clouds looming in the distance, rolling in with lightning, wind, and rain. In that sense, it was almost wondrous, as it was hard to escape the feeling that something historic was about to happen. But, like a storm cloud, it portended danger and disaster. Nonetheless, we got our lunch and ice cream and took a walk to view all the mansions of the rich, wondering if we might be able to indulge our hopeful pretentiousness and afford such a home one day.* My son asked if we'd still be able to go on a planned father-son trip to Texas. I had to answer him that I wasn't even sure he'd be going back to school.

THE GREAT TOILET PAPER PANIC OF 2020

On that warm but ominous day in March, I wasn't yet aware that my family's toilet paper supply was about to come into serious jeopardy. That warning would come from a video clip making the rounds on social media, as such things do. Two women were captured on camera fighting over toilet paper. One woman had loaded her shopping basket full of multiple packages of toilet paper effectively stripping the shelves clean. Another woman was understandably upset by this, and the whole episode degenerated into screaming and punching. Meanwhile, a bemused male manager tried to break them apart, largely without success.†

Admittedly, I was still slow to catch the warning inherent in this video, even as a psychologist. This is because I thought rationally, which, it would turn out, was a serious mistake. Indeed, the women in the video seemed kind of silly, or at least the one doing the hoarding. I could understand grabbing all the hand sanitizer or disinfectant or facemasks

---

* We appreciate you, dear reader, for contributing to this cause by buying this book!

† I do not provide the link to the video not only because I'm too lazy to look it up, but also because I do not wish to humiliate two random individuals for behavior most of the world ultimately engaged in.

(though again, this was still in the days when we were being told not to wear masks by health officials). Those were all products that had direct relevance for a plague. But toilet paper?

Toilet paper is easy to make, and there are robust supply chains in the United States for producing and distributing it. There's no good reason to think that toilet paper would suddenly vanish in an epidemic. Unless, of course, somebody panics. A first wave of panicking people hoarding toilet paper got noticed by a second wave of people who, reading the tea leaves, decide they'd better stash it too before the third wave noticed and started stockpiling, and so on and so on. Pretty soon—poof!—no toilet paper. Those of us thinking about supply chains and the irrationality of it all were left with our pants down, figuratively and literally.

As a Floridian, I should have known better. Hurricanes are a real deal, so I don't want to downplay them. But people can get hung up on details, like the need for bottled water, during emergencies. There they will stand, rending their clothes in the empty bottled water aisles, when not one aisle away are rows and rows of perfectly good bottled soda and juice, entirely untouched. Is it gauche to drink carbonated beverages during a cyclone?

So, what's up with toilet paper and why did people panic over it?

I pondered this one day, soon after I realized my mistake in dismissing the individuals fighting in that video. Driving around Orlando, I found, sure enough, not a single store had a roll of toilet paper. Not even the frou-frou stores catering to rich people who wanted their toilet paper hand-woven from gossamer strands of silkworm taffeta while an angelic children's choir sang to soothe the weavers at their work. Online, price gouging went to work and soon it seemed it might be just as well to get one's toilet paper straight from an ATM machine.

Part of the panic is that there's not exactly a lot of palatable options when the paper runs out. The history of bottom care is strangely fascinating. Before toilet paper became mass produced in the mid-1800s, toilet hygiene was, ahem, a sticky issue. It's thought that the Romans, one of the historical cultures most like modern Americans in many ways, used sponges on a stick for cleaning. These sponges were kept in a bucket of salt water or vinegar, and it seems unlikely the bucket was changed between uses. Let that thought percolate for a moment. Other cultures used bits of pottery—ouch!—although one could inscribe the names of folks one didn't like on the pottery, which had a certain appeal. The ancient Chinese used cloth-covered sticks resembling spatulas, although they seem to have happened upon the first variant of toilet paper that came into fairly widespread use in the 1300s, though mainly for the upper social strata.[2]

Americans would have to wait until the 1800s. Before this, corncobs were used, then newspapers and magazines (famously, the Sears catalog gets some mention). Apparently, toilet paper wasn't entirely "splinter free" until the 1930s. Another point to ponder.

All this having been said, it is quite understandable that people feel a bit protective of their toilet paper, particularly in industrialized countries where we're a bit prudish about bathroom stuff and squeamish in regard to poo. Nonetheless, the irrationality of the toilet paper panic is obvious: there was no reason to worry about a shortage of toilet paper until people started panicking and hoarding, creating the very shortage they were worried about in the first place. News reports documented people lining up at stores early in the morning to get toilet paper, like concert goers used to do for premium tickets. There was even at least one armed robbery of toilet paper in Hong Kong![3]

COVID-19 didn't create the United States' first run-in with toilet paper panic. Back in 1973 US Congressman Harold V. Froelich put out a press release warning that paper pulp production was down, which might cause a shortage of toilet paper. He raised the specter of rationing and declared this "no laughing matter." Talk show host Johnny Carson disagreed and made a joke about it on his show. Panic ensued for several months until people slowly realized that the panic created the shortage itself, not decreased production of toilet paper.[4] The whole sequence was not unlike that of 2020. Why do we do this to ourselves and why is it so hard to learn from history?

AVAILABILITY CASCADES AND SOCIAL CONTAGION

There are lots of reasons why people hoard. To some degree, collecting resources in advance of a perceived famine is evolutionarily adaptive. It can also give us a sense of control over situations (like a plague) in which we have little real control. Both individual and social factors play a role as well. People generally process information and data rather poorly and tend to respond emotionally to things. And, in some situations, particularly novel situations, people may feel pressured to respond in ways that other people respond, perceiving there to be both practical and social costs in not doing so.

As such, I'd like to introduce two concepts from psychology: the availability cascade and social contagion. They have some overlap as concepts, so it makes sense to talk about them together here.

Let's start with availability cascades, a cognitive theory about how myths are formed in public consciousness. One academic paper defined an availability cascade as "a social phenomenon where empirical data are ignored by groups in favor of information that is more available to them through examples of dramatic individual cases."[5] We appear particularly likely to apply availability cascades to disasters or other alarming situations like, say, airplane crashes.[6] In effect, we are presented with a scary situation about which we know little. We don't have any direct experience with the thing in question. As such, we rely on two of the worst possible sources of information: anecdotal stories and national news media. Both of these sources tend to hype the dangerousness of the phenomenon, increasing our anxiety and causing us to overestimate the frequency by which an event occurs. Then, as those around us in our social circle come to believe the myth, we begin to conform to the myth ourselves. Availability cascades thus spread from person to person, fueled by cherry-picked anecdotes and misinformation and eventually even becoming resistant to or skeptical of actual good empirical data. Some availability cascades can take on moral components (panics about violent video games and youth violence, for instance), making them even more resistant to conflicting data.

Availability cascades often arise from a cognitive bias called the availability heuristic. The availability heuristic basically suggests we are likely to overestimate the frequency of an event that is easy to remember and underestimate the frequency of an event that is more difficult to remember. Once again, the information source here is typically anecdotal. Famously, people's fear of airplane disasters is based in the availability heuristic. When a plane crashes, that tends to get tremendous news coverage, making such events easier to remember. By contrast, car crashes tend to get much less coverage overall. Because anecdotal cases of airplane disasters are easier to remember, people have historically perceived airplane travel as more dangerous than car travel, despite a wealth of data suggesting the opposite is true.[7] In terms of passenger deaths per billion miles traveled, planes are the safest. Buses also are apparently fairly safe, whereas ferries are floating coffins. Think of that next time you cross the waters! But cars are hands down the worst.[8]

Now, a few people may instinctively know that. Typically, these are people who have direct knowledge, either because they've actually been in a serious car crash or work somewhere in the automobile safety industry and are well aware of the numbers. But most people don't have direct information. Instead, they rely on news media reports that hype disasters and replay them over and over. Then they talk to their friends, who also mostly don't know anything, and the fears get reinforced. Or they tell their friends to check out the story about the latest disaster, spreading the cascade further.

Over time, the message that cars are more dangerous than planes has *sort of* sunk in to the general populace, but only after decades of the data being publicly shared over and over. This doesn't happen with most availability cascades, and this long effort also shows how difficult it can be for data to compete with availability cascades. People just ignore the data because it doesn't *feel* right to them.

Perhaps an even better example is that of mass homicides, an area of research I'm involved in. Mass homicides remain extremely rare in the United States, but people tend to vastly overestimate their prevalence.[9] This is because they get dramatic news coverage, most people don't have any direct knowledge of these crimes, and they are used for a variety of moral agendas, whether gun control or censorship of video games. As such, they are often the focus of numerous myths. One famous example is the discredited belief that violent video games are associated with mass homicides. Although this belief has been thoroughly debunked for decades, it nonetheless resurfaces from time to time. In fact, evidence suggests that mass homicide perpetrators consume *fewer* violent video games than other males their age. But that empirical data doesn't *feel* right to people amid an availability cascade, so they ignore it, going with their emotions instead. Other folks have tried to wrap mass homicide into racial justice issues, claiming that mass homicide perpetrators are all white. Just as with the claim about video games, this belief is false; in fact, mass homicide perpetrators are about as ethnically representative as the US population from which they come. Ultimately, the availability cascade causes people to overestimate the prevalence of mass homicides and make faulty assumptions about who commits them and why.[10]

So, let's think of an availability cascade as occurring under certain conditions:

- A dramatic or frightful threat is perceived, whether real or imagined.
- Most individuals do not have direct information or experience with the issue at hand.
- Secondary sources of information (i.e., news media) rely on anecdotes or other poor sources of data.
- As individuals communicate the cascade with each other, they create social incentives to support the cascade rather than be skeptical.
- The threat often has a moral component to it. This isn't always required (e.g., airplane crashes), but it can worsen the cascade.
- Actual data that conflicts with the cascade is discounted, underreported, or (falsely) considered less important/more biased than the anecdotes or other dubious data used to support the cascade.
- The cascade results in severe overestimates of the prevalence or severity of the threat in question.

We can see this process with toilet paper. Most of us have no idea how it's made or distributed. When a few nincompoops start howling about toilet paper shortages, the rest of us panic, having no personal relevant data with which to confront those panics. A few people, industry insiders or whatnot, may try to hold up some analyses with actual numbers on them, but by that point, it's too late. They'll get trampled by the rest of us stampeding to the supermarket to get first in line.

If I'm making it sound like we're all kind of gullible, well—that's true—and I'm not discounting myself from that! But, even worse, we can work to make one another dumber. This brings us to the notion of social contagion.

The idea of social contagion is nothing new, going back at least a century. In short, the theory suggests that we are likely to adopt the behaviors or beliefs of those around us even when those behaviors and beliefs may be absurd.[11] This is a form of conformity but tends to exist under certain situations, namely:

- There is some form of conflict being experienced by the imitating individual.
- The imitating person feels a heightened degree of stress or dissatisfaction related to the conflict area.
- The imitating person feels some impulse toward a resolving behavior, but also may feel some inhibition.
- The modeling individual (the person the imitator imitates) openly engages in the target behavior without fear or guilt.

The concept of social contagion is controversial insofar as it's not always clear as to what circumstances it applies and when it does not apply. One of the classic examples is the "june bug" incident from 1962 wherein sixty-two workers at a dressmaking factory reported being bitten by a nonexistent "june bug" and developing symptoms like nausea and numbness.[12] It has also been applied to the notion that suicide-themed shows such as *13 Reasons Why* might provoke imitative suicides in youth, although this notion is largely debunked through good science.[13, 14]

One more recent and controversial example has been the debate about whether a rise in the number of young girls identifying as trans boys might be due in part to social contagion. This hypothesis was raised in 2020 by journalist Abigail Shrier in her book *Irreversible Damage*.[15] The basis of her argument is that some girls, particularly those with mental disorders such as borderline personality disorder, a condition prone to identity confusion and impulsivity, may misinterpret their identity confusion as transgenderism, particularly when group dynamics create social capital around marginalized identities. She isn't saying that *every* youth who identifies as trans wouldn't benefit from transition but argues for better screening and avoidance of the affirmative approach wherein merely stating a trans identity is automatically accepted without screening. Her argument is that medical interventions such as puberty blockers carry significant side effects, which may be irreversible should those individuals change their minds when older.* Anecdotes abound about exactly this phenomenon, but remember, anecdotes aren't evidence and can lead us to availability cascades. However, some evidence does suggest trans identification is more common among youth with borderline and other personality disorders[16] as well as autism spectrum disorders.[17] Shrier's thesis isn't entirely outlandish.

That having been pointed out, it's also important to acknowledge that many trans individuals are upset by the book and consider it to be transphobic. Shrier's use of phrases like "trans craze" likely didn't help that perception. From my own reading of the book, I did worry she strayed from good science in multiple areas, such as overemphasizing the impact of social media on mental health (itself arguably an availability cascade panic) and ignoring considerable data that gender identity is biological, not social, originating in the hypothalamus in the brain.† Of course, it's entirely plausible that *most* youth who identify as trans are indeed trans and may benefit from medical transition, while *some* youth may have other issues and would benefit from a different approach. We need to be sensitive not to stigmatize marginalized populations while also allowing science the nonideological room to objectively analyze important issues such as these.

It's important to note that even if we are alert to these as irrational processes of availability cascade or social contagion, there's no real way to win. We might say, "Hah! This toilet paper hoarding is part of an availability cascade! I refuse to participate!" That feeling of intellectual superiority lasts only as long as it takes to start wondering what things lying around the house—newspaper, tissues, the cat, and so forth—could substitute for toilet paper. Availability cascades are like runaway trains. Recognizing you're in the middle of one doesn't stop you from careening along with it.

---

* The proportion of individuals who detransition, as it is called, remains poorly understood.

† Shrier isn't alone in this. The anti-science mantra, "Gender is a social construct," is a common saying in the humanities and social sciences despite a wealth of data to contradict it. It appears to originate, at least in part, with second-wave feminism, which may explain why its successors, "gender critical" feminists (such as J. K. Rowling), and trans activists find themselves locked in nasty debates over sex and gender and the definition of "woman."

BASKETBALL CLOSES ITS DOORS

We can probably think of numerous historical and contemporary examples of availability cascades (the word I'll mainly stick with for simplicity moving forward). But we can use an example from COVID-19 itself: basketball.

In the early days of the pandemic the general populace (abetted by some politicians, medical groups, and even psychologists) downplayed the significance of the disease. In early March 2020, Utah Jazz player Rudy Gobert made light of COVID-19 during a press conference, taking time to purposefully rub his hands all over press microphones to show his disdain for the emerging disease. A few days later the NBA made the decision to suspend the rest of the season after a player tested positive for COVID-19. Which player, you ask? Why, the universe being what it is, Rudy Gobert, of course! This meant his goofy act of touching the microphones had potentially exposed many reporters to the virus as well.[18]

However, once the NBA made this decision, it opened the floodgates of cancellations. In remarkably rapid succession, most other sports leagues canceled their seasons, new movies stopped being released and theaters closed, restaurants and bars shut down, beaches and parks closed, travel ceased, schools closed—pretty much everyone was thrown into effective isolation. It's important to note at this juncture that although there were good reasons to suspect social distancing could be effective in limiting the transmission of the disease, there wasn't clarity on which activities may be safe and which were dangerous. For instance, evidence gradually emerged that schools probably were not COVID-19 hotspots and, with proper safety protocols, could likely safely reopen.[19] Similarly, as long as social distancing, mask wearing, and other safety protocols were observed, beaches, parks, and other outdoor spaces were likely safe.[20]

This is not to say the NBA was wrong to cancel its season, quite the contrary. However, in doing so, it established a palpable moral pressure for others to follow suit, setting up a cascade of cancellations that were as much fear based as they were evidence based. No one wanted to be caught flat-footed, taking too long to cease operations when most assuredly they'd be subsequently blamed for lost lives. This was a fascinating phenomenon to watch and, indeed, feel in real time. Once the NBA had made its decision, it created a moral stampede of others moving in the same direction.

In the case of cancelling crowded meetings of sports fans, this almost certainly was the correct decision, although as that cascade spread to other places, such as schools and open spaces like beaches and parks, it's less clear that the cascade was beneficial. But these types of cascades aren't necessarily benign and are just as likely to send society careening down a bad and dangerous path as they are a good one.

To examine this, we can look at the societal reaction to another epidemic, this one human immunodeficiency virus (HIV) as it emerged in the 1980s. Unlike COVID-19, HIV was transmitted by direct contact with bodily fluids such as blood or semen. Although there were several routes of transmission for the disease, including blood transfusions, unprotected sexual contact and intravenous drug use were particularly risky. Until the development of effective antivirals in the 1990s, HIV was typically fatal. Understandably, this created considerable fear and anxiety about the disorder.

In the comparatively homophobic culture of the 1980s, there was a lot of confusion about how to communicate public health messages about HIV. Although both heterosexual and homosexual individuals could contract HIV through sexual contact, it became particularly associated with gay men. And, coupled with intravenous drug users, this invited some commentators to mix in HIV with moral grandstanding about sexuality and other issues. Public health messages also deferred from addressing issues of safe sex and the gay community directly out of fear of condoning homosexuality.[21] This may seem absurd now, but these moral issues impeded messaging about safe sex and stigmatized individuals with HIV.

This situation has many of the characteristics of an availability cascade. For instance:

- It relates to an issue most people don't have direct experience with: a novel epidemic disease.
- The issue of contracting a fatal illness is frightening.

- Most people must rely on secondary sources of information such as news media, which tend to hype the panic rather than provide objective information.
- There is a moral component, in this case involving homosexuality.
- That moral component puts pressure on even government officials to frame the situation in particular ways including, in this case, ignoring the gay community and failing to directly fight stigma.
- People can overestimate their personal risk, in the case of HIV, such as by contracting it via casual contact.

In hindsight, our desperate quest for toilet paper can seem comical. But availability cascades such as that which occurred with HIV can do real damage. Can they be avoided?

WHEN THE LIGHT AT THE END OF THE TUNNEL IS A FREIGHT TRAIN HEADED YOUR WAY

If you believe that your country or culture is barreling toward an availability cascade, what can you do to stop it? In a word: nothing. Nobody's listening, and if you try to get in front of it, you'll be shouted down as an immoral, callous individual. It's sort of like standing in front of a dam that burst, holding your hands up and ordering the water to "Stop!" At least in the short term, availability cascades are virtually unrelenting. Possibly, were the scientific community to unite against one, that could put on some brakes, but that rarely happens, and more often the scientific community gets caught up in it, too.

Availability cascades tend to crescendo then fade over time as gradually more data come to light to call them into question. Unfortunately, there isn't a predictable time line for how this happens. Even looking at different examples, we see varying patterns. The toilet paper panic appears to have had a fast half-life. It came on fast, was annoying for some months, then largely disappeared once production and distribution caught up with the increased demand due to hoarding. This gave people the emotional and cognitive space to realize the whole thing was a bit silly.

By contrast, misinformation and fear about HIV went on for decades and, arguably, stigma attached to the disease continues to the present day. Panics over video games peaked in the 1990s and early 2000s, and for a while the scientific community happily collaborated in promoting the panic by foisting low-quality studies on the public. Eventually better-quality studies confirmed that there is no link between video game violence and societal aggression or violence, and fears have subsided over time, although they have not gone away entirely. Some professional guilds such as the American Psychological Association continue to mislead the public even as the science has clearly swung against their public statements.[22] Fear of airplanes provides one last data point: in this case, pretty much every secondary source, whether news media or transportation officials, has gotten behind the message that air travel is safe. Nonetheless, any high-profile crash has the potential to resurrect our fears.

This may sound a bit depressing, but in fact, most of these cases are success stories. Despite resurgences in stigma, HIV is neither the killer nor focus of bigotry it once was. Fears about video games are much reduced from twenty years ago, even if they haven't fully gone away. We generally *know* that airplanes are safe, even if we clutch our seats with white knuckles. Perhaps we can never slay the beast of our emotions, but we can keep it at bay. So, what *can* we do during an availability cascade? Here are a few thoughts.

1. *Don't stand in front of it*: At least during an availability cascade's early stages, nobody is really listening to evidence. If the populace is suddenly determined to believe that space aliens are abducting children, standing in front of that wave with datasheets only gets you steamrolled. Particularly if there's a ferocious moral component to that cascade, you'll be accused of not caring for children and ostracized, perhaps losing your job in the process (it does happen). That initial wave won't last forever, but you'll want to be strategic about how and when you bring better information to bear.

2. *Don't be snarky or sarcastic*: Availability cascades can seem silly in retrospect. We might even laugh at them with the 20/20 hindsight of history. But in the moment, nobody's laughing. And people can become *extremely* defensive of their availability cascades (perhaps

because, unconsciously, they may realize there's something inherently irrational at play). More broadly, nobody's more likely to listen to your evidence after you just called them an idiot.* Pointing and laughing at someone for their beliefs only makes them believe those things *more*, not less. Keep all conversations civil and data based. This also will reduce (but not eliminate) any risk of getting socially ostracized if you're off-message with the cascade.

3. *Acknowledge the issue*: Child abductions are bad whether aliens are doing it or not. We do want to reduce youth violence whether video games contribute or not. It's important to worry about the side effects of medications for our children even if the risks of vaccines are less than the diseases they prevent. If you acknowledge that it's OK for other people to have the fears that they have, they'll generally be more open to data that might actually assuage those fears.

4. *Focus on good data*: It's an unfortunate element of human nature that people are more convinced by anecdotes and emotional appeals than they are by statistics. And, sure, some statistics are pretty bad anyway. But good data *can* win out over time. In fact, as time progresses, people can become attracted to the countervailing narrative. The idea that we all freaked out over something, but it turns out that something isn't true, is itself an interesting story, and people gradually will respond to it. Be prepared to make well-informed arguments.

5. *Hold leaders accountable*: Picking on the populace for being irrational will work against you. But if politicians or scientists are spreading false information (as often happens), they can and should be called to task for doing go. Do be civil about it, but pointing out bad information and its source can help the public realize when they're being misled.

6. *Be persistent and patient*: Combatting availability cascades is very often a grueling, many-year project. You'll need to be ready to repeat your data-focused message over and over, every chance you

---

* This has been consistently one of the worst strategies I've seen "elite" people apply, whether to anti-vax movements, global warming denialism, QAnon, or whatever else. Ridicule is not an effective persuasion strategy.

get. You'll need to be prepared to get negative feedback from those who don't want to believe the evidence. There will be moments—lots of moments—when you'll feel you're not making any progress. And, yes, there can be risks to your friendships, even to your career. Keep at it anyway. In my experience, availability cascades *do* eventually fade in the face of good evidence. But you'll need to be brave and persistent. Don't get into mud fights, but if you keep presenting the data, calmly and rationally, gradually people will start to listen.

Ultimately our quest for toilet paper reveals something about ourselves. We like to think of ourselves as rational and evidence focused. But often we're not. Perhaps a bit more alarming, even if you or I happen to see an availability cascade for what it is, we still may get swept into it, bouncing around the rapids, sighing wistfully the whole way. But we can take comfort that sooner or later rational heads will prevail, and smoother sailing awaits—at least until the next cascade!

3

DO/DON'T PANIC
(PICK ONE)

A bit of whimsical self-deprecation about how COVID-19 sent us all scrambling for toilet paper is one thing. Yet, there's little question that COVID-19 has been devastating for many. As of this writing, the official US death toll for COVID-19 hovers around 914,000. Countries such as India are seeing massive spikes (and deaths may be underreported there), many countries in Latin America have been devastated, Europe remains in a quagmire. The worldwide death toll is approximately 5.79 million and likely to rise significantly before this book is published. At the same time there have been remarkable success stories. Some east Asian and Pacific countries remained comparatively untouched, such as Taiwan, South Korea, Singapore, and New Zealand. Companies in the United States, United Kingdom, Russia, and Germany produced vaccines in record time.* COVID-19 created numerous economic problems and many people, particularly in the service industry, continue to struggle with unemployment. Yet it appears not to have created a new Great Depression, at least not yet, as some had feared. As I write this, the current US unemployment rate is about 6 percent, hardly the best ever, but down from pandemic highs that topped out around 14 percent.

There's a general sense that during moments of crisis societies should come together, set aside their differences, and work toward the common

---

* I've left China off this list as, currently, there have been concerns about the effectiveness of the Chinese vaccine.

good. For instance, those old enough to remember may recall the flag waving and patriotism that followed the 9/11 attacks. This produced widespread support for the government and presidency of George W. Bush (which perhaps wasn't such a great thing in many ways, as we'll see in chapter 5). Yet it did provide a sense of cultural solidarity that can be useful if directed toward good goals.

Nothing like that happened for COVID-19. In the United States, and to a lesser extent other Western democracies, COVID-19 became part of broader culture wars. Those on the right wailed about attacks on civil liberties while those on the left used this as evidence that those on the right were uneducated hicks. Messages from the World Health Organization (WHO) and Centers for Disease Control (CDC) were muddled, contradictory, sometimes politicized, and they were accused of sometimes shading the truth, for instance regarding the effectiveness of masks or the numbers required to achieve herd immunity.[1] Many politicians didn't much help, notably US President Trump's seesawing messages, which failed to rally the right to embrace mask wearing in particular and sometimes flirted with odd treatments for the virus, such as using UV light or injections of bleach.[2] Whatever else we may say of it, for the most part, COVID-19 was not a crisis well-managed by most of the world. How did we goof this up so comprehensively?

PSHAW! HOW BAD COULD IT BE REALLY?

For public health messages to function, several key components must be in place. First, public health officials need to have some efficient mechanism of communicating with the broader public. In today's hyperconnected world, that's really not a major problem (albeit there's so much communication it's possible health officials might get crowded out by a ton of other garbage). Second, public health officials need to have the trust of the public. However, to a large degree, for reasons both good and bad, that's increasingly no longer the case. Some of this is due to various culture wars and suspiciousness regarding experts (particularly from the political right, given most health experts tend to lean to the political left), but public health officials have a fair number of self-inflicted wounds as well. Third, public health officials need to have a clear, actionable, reasonably consistent (data does sometimes change), and *truthful* message for the public. I'd argue they should almost never lie or obscure the truth for the public, even if this seems to be good for short-term gains (see point 2). Here, the public health community flubbed the COVID-19 response, particularly in early months.

Problems began right from the start. The COVID-19 pandemic originated in the Chinese city of Wuhan in December 2019. From there, the virus would spread via human-sprayed airborne droplets to pretty much the whole world. Being a repressive, authoritarian regime, the Chinese government initially sought to downplay international attention to the disease.[3] The Chinese government even punished doctors who tried to spread word of the pandemic. Once again, we might not expect much different from the communist government of China. The Chinese government spreading falsehoods isn't likely to damage public confidence in health officials, as no one in their right mind thinks the Chinese government tells the truth in the first place.

Trouble came when the WHO (not to be confused with the much cooler British rock band) largely and uncritically repeated the official Chinese line. On January 14, 2020, the WHO tweeted "Preliminary investigations conducted by the Chinese authorities have found no clear evidence of human-to-human transmission of the novel #coronavirus." On January 22, the WHO declined to declare a public health emergency.[4] Only at the end of January did the WHO declare COVID-19 a global emergency, though it still offered effusive praise to China,[5] lauding its "extraordinary measures" and discouraging any restriction in trade with or travel to China. The WHO wouldn't declare COVID-19 a pandemic until March.[6]

If the WHO initially treated COVID-19 with less seriousness than it ultimately deserved, in fairness, it was hardly alone. But the question is why the WHO seemed to stick so close to the official party line of communist China? To help understand this, it bears acknowledging that organizations that are ostensibly "science" often are no such thing, but are either political organizations (like the WHO) or professional guilds that exist to promote those professions (like the American Psychological Association, American Psychiatric Association, or American Academy of Pediatrics).

These organizations are notoriously loose with the scientific "truth," instead promulgating convenient narratives as "sciency" so long as they promote their organizations or sociopolitical goals.[7] They're human endeavors, in other words, with axes to grind. That doesn't make them evil empires, but it doesn't make them arbiters of objective truth either.

Many of the problems for the WHO revolve around the influence of its member states, particularly powerful nations like China.[8] Put simply, the WHO has a dual problem: it relies on information from member states but also does not wish to offend them. The WHO has had similar problems with other outbreaks, but it's not just diseases where we see this. For instance, the WHO recently included the controversial diagnosis "gaming disorder" in its classification of diseases, despite little clear research evidence to support the existence of this disorder. In an email exchange I had with WHO officials, they acknowledged being under pressure from "Asian countries" (their words) to make the diagnosis happen.[9] In other words, the WHO has a pattern of making health decisions based on politics rather than good science.

The decision by the US Trump administration to ban travel from China in January 2020 also became the subject of confusing messaging. Once again, public health officials, including the WHO, largely condemned the move.[10] Granted, their points about potential backfire and unanticipated downstream effects are well taken. Indeed, steps that seem intuitive at first can often make a situation worse rather than better. And I'm certainly in no position to say what the best epidemiological course of action is. However, this early reticence may have harmed the credibility of these organizations when they later endorsed lockdowns. Planes traveling from the viral origin point are fine, but I can't get a pizza delivery without spraying the pie down with bleach before eating? Hmmm. Ultimately, evidence suggests that travel restrictions can indeed work to *slow* the spread of disease, though these should be thought of as mainly a means for buying time to implement other procedures such as testing and contact tracing.[11]

In fairness, my own discipline wasn't exactly showering itself in glory during these early days. Psychologist Stuart Richie had documented several cases during the early days of COVID-19's spread into the United States and Europe in which prominent psychologists took to the press to say, in effect, "Covid? Meh. We tend to panic too easily."[12] Turns out we psychologists have a wee tendency to try to inject ourselves into topics we know little about. This seems to be a disciplinary reaction to the perception we're not a "real science." We feel an irrational need to show just how important we are (usually by trying to point out how stupid everyone else is). Unfortunately, a good deal of our research really is junk. I'm not just saying that as an opinion; this has been empirically demonstrated.[13] Some psychologists had, in effect, taken studies conducted in artificial laboratory settings, some of which may have experienced statistical nudging to make their results interesting,* then tried to apply them to a real-world pandemic. Unfortunately, many of these comments appeared to minimize the impact of what would become a massive pandemic. Who listens to psychologists anyway, right? Well, now we see why. Jokes aside, it's issues like this, wounds inflicted by research psychologists, not pop psychologists, that harm the credibility of our field. If this were just a one-off, it might be easy to excuse, but it is not. Unfortunately, our field and our professional guilds such as the American Psychological Association have a long history of making misleading statements to the public.[14]

I'd argue that part of psychology's problem is its bias toward a kind of outcome trope that is basically of the "look how stupid you are" variety. Granted, particularly as they hit newspaper headlines, these findings were wrapped in a kind of counterintuitive coolness, basically, "You think X causes Y, but actually the opposite is true!" Coupled with shoddy science and a pressure to publish cool, headline-grabbing results, at least some portion of psychology's subsequent replication crisis can be attributed to this culture. Even better, of course, is if the "stupid" people were conservatives,[15] whom psychologists regularly smear,[16] with little acknowledgment of the conflict of interest in doing so, given most psychologists are liberals.[17]

In this sense, I suspect psychology fell into the trap of trying to capitalize on the narrative that emerged in leftist circles that concerns about the 2014 Ebola outbreak in Africa spreading to the United States were "racist."[18] To be fair, if an outbreak is associated with a particular group, ostracism of that group can result. This may be both evolutionarily

---

* To be clear, I am making a statement about common practices in the field that have been well demonstrated, not singling out any particular studies for this accusation.

adaptive and, at the same time, socially ugly, resulting in isolation, prejudice, or even violence toward that group.* But the urge to condemn those reactions as irrational may itself be the result of tribal left-versus-right virtue signaling. Given that most outbreaks like the 2014 Ebola crisis didn't translate to massive problems for the United States, psychologists may have experienced a kind of extrapolation bias, assuming that pattern would hold for COVID-19, with the extra dash of, once again, pointing out how dumb the frightened masses were and, of course, seeming not racist, given COVID-19's own connection to China. In other words, people tend to adopt beliefs under the bias that previous patterns will hold indefinitely, particularly when the expression of those beliefs is likely to increase their social capital.

TO MASK OR NOT TO MASK?

COVID-19 didn't create the political sectarianism in the United States and elsewhere—the roots of that go back decades, and there is blame on both right and left. But COVID-19 did become a kind of weird cultural lodestone for 2020, exacerbating other culture war debates (including race and policing, which I'll examine in chapter 7, as well as "cancel culture," or the general tendency to not debate issues, but instead to try to destroy the lives of those who disagree), but also becoming a focal point of debate itself. To wit, was mask wearing a key hygiene practice slowing the transmission of COVID-19 and protecting millions or was it a lever for increased government intrusion into personal lives and decisions?

Lost in this debate is the potential that it could be both, of course. Let me start by saying clearly: I'm no epidemiologist; I generally believe what eventually became the medical consensus that masks, particularly N-95 or KN-95, were one of the most helpful strategies in preventing the spread of COVID-19, and I certainly wore masks myself in any public spaces where they were either wise or required. So, my general nonmedical expert opinion is: yeah, we should have been wearing masks. But, if we're to be fair, did government authorities arguably trample on individual rights and

---

* In the United States, for instance, the treatment of gay men during the early years of the HIV epidemic.

take a heavy-handed approach at times that may have exacerbated people's annoyance? Probably so.[19] These things aren't mutually exclusive, and if we were able to look at things rationally (apparently, we can't), we might be able to have a reasonable discussion about how to best manage the competing interests of public health and personal freedom and persuade those who may have more concerns. Certainly, greater authoritarianism and the ability to brutally enforce mandates can be incredibly effective at stopping the transmission of epidemics (China being a key example after its initial fumble). Presumably we don't want *that*, so we need to find a better means of getting everyone in a rowboat together on a sound policy that saves lives while recognizing the legitimacy of some concerns.

Look, I live in Orlando and have had to stick sweaty masks on my face in the hot sun, so nobody needs to convince me that mask wearing is rather a bummer. But, on balance, the best evidence we have suggests that particularly N-95 or KN-95 masks were probably one of the most effective means of slowing the spread of COVID-19.[20] So why did this become such a cultural lodestone, sometimes prompting angry protests, coming mainly from the political right? I argue two things occurred. First, health officials blew an opportunity for early and clear messaging on the effectiveness of mask wearing (and have continued to fumble right up until this writing). Second, people don't really assess "science" anymore as a clear-headed, stoic analysis of data, but rather as a kind of tribal virtue signaling. So the left will "believe the science," at least until that science runs up against taboos on the left, such as that biological sex differences exist or that race may not play a major role in police shootings; and the right will "believe the science" until it runs up against their own proscriptions, such as on global warming or gun control.

Speaking as a scientist, the whole idea of "believe the science" or "science is real" is goofy anyway. Science isn't an immutable and flawless set of facts one is supposed to adhere to like a religious dogma. We should scrutinize it. It is ever changing, much of it is seriously flawed, scientists do have biases, even widespread cultural ones (though there are discipline-specific differences, scientists tend to be on the left of the political spectrum), and much of it is just wrong. On the other hand, it is still better than "other ways of knowing"; that is, anecdotes, "lived experiences," narratives, or, frankly, indigenous wisdom, whether we're talking about Christian creationism or the folk tales of a remote tribe. We can certainly offer respect to these other modes of thinking—we need not be dismissive, disrespectful, or cruel—but science and a stoic, dispassionate look at data remains by far the best way of obtaining the most objective information about how the world works. So, it is good to be a skeptical consumer of science, but not to treat it as one among many equal buffet options about how to know the world.

The reality is that most people (even many scientists) are shite at being critical consumers of scientific data. If you see someone with a "in this house, we believe science is real" sign on their lawn, you can almost *guarantee* they are not scientifically informed. What does it even mean to say "science is real" anyway? What is the proportion of people arguing that science is a fairy tale like dragons or Santa Claus (sorry kids, this book was meant for adults, so blame your parents for letting you read this)? People can have legitimate arguments about the quality of scientific evidence and be dead-ass wrong about their conclusions, but that's still different from suggesting that some people think science is pixie dust.

The thing about "believing the science" is, once again, that our belief in science tends to be contingent upon several things, namely:

1. Does the science confirm what I already think is true?
2. Do other people in my cultural "tribe" agree with the science on this matter?
3. Does the science contradict my own perception of my own experiences?

In general, people on both the political left and right tend to "believe science" when it makes them feel good to do so and reject science when the science does not. What they're doing isn't science at all, but rather using "science" as a convenient bludgeon for their own social-political worldviews.

As to the first point, this is a kind of human bias called confirmation bias. Confirmation bias occurs when we tend to trust or approve of data that confirms our beliefs about the world but ignore or distrust evidence that does not. This is a widespread and common bias and we all basically do it. This itself can take many forms.

Part of confirmation bias reflects in the way we use anecdotes, which is to say, badly. Anecdotes are *not* evidence; indeed, they are largely useless as sources of information. There are several reasons for this (for one thing, the reliability of anecdotes is pretty low—you're likely not hearing the full story, but more on that in a minute). But we generally pay attention to or pass along anecdotes that support our worldview and ignore those that do not. So do documentaries, by the way, one reason that documentaries are a very poor source of information, particularly the more they rely on anecdotal stories. For instance, a common misuse of anecdote in my own area of research on violence in video games was to look for evidence that action games were associated with mass homicides. When people had a preexisting belief that such games were "harmful" to kids (they, in fact, are not[21]), they would look for an anecdote about a young person who'd done something horrible, shake their heads, cluck their tongues, and say, "Lookie there, dagnabbit. It was them thar vidja games what done it for" (somehow these people always speak like this when I imagine it—probably one of my own biases!). But when the perpetrator is a sixty-four-year-old man, such as for the October 2017 shooting that killed sixty at a country music festival in Las Vegas or even a middle-aged woman such as forty-four-year-old Amy Bishop, who shot up her biology department after not getting tenure (tenure is a big deal to us academics), nobody points and says, "Look, those folks didn't play video games!" Yes, the reasonable people somehow drop that 1930s undereducated accent (see how I'm manipulating your biases?). This also persists in the belief some people have that some killers, such as those who perpetrated the Virginia Tech (2007) and Sandy Hook (2012) massacres were avid action game players, when official investigation reports concluded they were not.[22]

Things like anecdotes and "lived experiences" are also misleading at best, due to one other common bias, the self-serving bias. This bias occurs when we attribute the cause of our successes to be ourselves and our own abilities, yet the cause of our failures to be external factors beyond our control. Thus, when telling stories about events we're involved in, we tend to narrate them in such a way as to make ourselves appear to be the good guys (or victim if something bad happened), whereas others involved are potentially bad guys. Ever notice that, among your friends, you always seem to be friends with people who are the victims of bad relationships, but never the ones who made the relationship bad in the first place? This is why all the recent talk about "lived experiences" and believing people's stories at face value is the devil's road to nonsense.

Our tendency to employ confirmation bias doesn't end with anecdotes, of course. We can use it with scientific studies as well. Once again, we tend to believe scientific studies at face value when they confirm our prior beliefs and either ignore or harshly criticize studies that fail to support them. This isn't an uneducated person thing—scientists themselves are just as inclined to do this as anyone else.

This brings us to the second point, and the tendency to weigh how those in our social circle believe in different forms of evidence. This is a phenomenon called *myside bias* (which I introduced in chapter 1). This is, again, something we're all prone to, given there are social advantages (what I'll call *social capital*) wound up in agreeing with people in our peer group as well as disagreeing with groups that are acrimonious toward our own. Here, too, intelligence is not a protective factor in these types of cognitive biases, and very smart people do it just as often as those who are less cognitive.[23] Nor is it a political thing. Liberals tend to like to think that they are the guardians of objective truth (hence all those yard signs about believing science is real), yet research indicates that they are just as likely as conservatives to engage in science denial when data challenges their worldview.[24]

We tend to form what are called *echo chambers* along sociopolitical lines, and that appears to be even more true in recent years.[25] In these echo chambers, the same beliefs are echoed back and forth among all members of the group such that they can seem like facts, even when they are utter garbage. Those who don't believe the "facts" can seem woefully out of touch, and any evidence contradicting those facts ultimately can seem heretical. In some cases, members of the group simply parrot the beliefs even if they themselves don't, in fact, believe them. A recent example of this came to light in the case of Paul Rossi, a teacher at an elite school who challenged that school's increasing focus on critical race theory (CRT). CRT promotes the belief that racism is everywhere and racial identity is essential to who we are and how we interact with each other. Rossi argues this influence on teaching may be harmful to kids (it probably is; more on this in chapter 7). In a public letter, he claimed that his principal agreed with him that this theoretical approach was harmful but promoted it anyway. The principal denied this, but unbeknownst to the principal, Rossi had recorded their conversation and was able to prove that, indeed, the principal had real concerns about CRT yet exposed hundreds of kids to it in their school.[26] That's just one "gotcha" example, and it's easy to condemn the principal for not standing up for his beliefs but, frankly, why would he? In the world of education, adherence to CRT is like a kind of quasi-religion. Standing up to it is a great way to lose your job, so people don't. Put simply: people regularly get up in public and claim absolute adherence to ideas they know are bullshit. They do it because they think it's to their advantage to do so.

This can relate to another factor called *bullshit asymmetry factor*, which, quickly for now, says that once bad information becomes public, it's actually much harder to convince the public that bad information is wrong—people's concerns about vaccines, for instance, or once again, the belief that violent video games cause aggression (despite a wealth of newer, better-designed studies showing they do not). But I'll return to this when I discuss the public health messaging on masks.

As to the third point, people tend to view their own experiences as unquestionable. If you had itchy toes and you took Magical Wort Mix for your itchy toes and your toes got less itchy, you'll tend to attribute that change to Magical Wort Mix rather than coincidence, no matter how many studies come out saying Magical Wort Mix is garbage. People regularly misattribute the cause of changes in their environment, including their own behavior, misremember things, purposefully distort them, unconsciously distort them (see the self-serving bias above), and, in general, are incredibly poor sources of information, including about their own lives. It has been known for decades, for instance, that eyewitness testimony, even for individuals who are the victims of crimes, tends to be unreliable.[27] But people can be stubborn and, even in the face of data, can adhere to their belief that their memories or perceptions of an event trump any other source of data.

Now, having convinced you that everything you think you know or agree about with your peer group is probably rubbish, let's return to the issue of masks. We've covered how convincing people of stuff with the science, such as it is, can be difficult. But it also helps if public health officials don't drop the ball and then fumble and trip all over it like a bunch of three-year-olds learning how to play soccer. But that's largely what public health officials and politicians did *and continue to do even as I write this* on the issue of masks.

The initial error came in public health officials downplaying the use of masks by the general public. Early advice from the WHO[28] and CDC[29] downplayed the use of masks by the general public. The WHO stated, "If you are healthy, you only need to wear a mask if you are taking care of a person with suspected 2019-nCoV infection," whereas the CDC stated "CDC does not recommend that people who are well wear a facemask to protect themselves from respiratory diseases, including COVID-19." In retrospect, this advice seems to have been disastrously wrong. In fairness, this mostly came in the early months of the epidemic when the utility of masks may not have been as clear, but there also seems to have been some cultural and practical aspects at play. For instance, mask wearing by healthy individuals in the general public was already culturally normative in parts of the East but was largely unheard of in the West. I'm not the sort of person who sees racism hiding behind every bush (too common these days), but all cultures have a tendency to be parochial and resistant to absorbing habits of other cultures. For instance, it's entirely possible that the habits of European men to wear yellow and orange pants may have some imperceivable benefits we Americans just can't see, who knows? People get locked into their cultural habits and there's not necessarily anything more sinister than that.

However, preservation of masks for healthcare workers may also have been a factor. Indeed, the CDC site alludes to this, as did the WHO.[30] This may have understandably (and correctly) confused people. If masks are so useful for health workers, wouldn't they protect me, too? Turns out, yes, they would. As a consequence, some have speculated that public health officials may have *deliberately* misled the public about the effectiveness of masks in order to prevent the public from gobbling up the limited supply, saving them for health workers.[31] I can't be sure how much of the misinformation was *intentional*, but if it was, this was a catastrophic mistake. Deception by public health officials corrupts the public trust. The public depends on public health officials to give them information to protect themselves and their family. If, instead, public health officials dispense advice that works *against* this, even for an otherwise worthwhile cause, trust in public health officials will plummet quickly.

About a year later, public health officials stirred controversy by moving in the other direction. In May 2021, the CDC issued new guidelines that vaccinated individuals could resume all activities without masks, so long as it was legal in that jurisdiction to do so.[32] This was based on the latest evidence that vaccinated individuals were at very low risk of contracting or transmitting the virus. This caused a sense of whiplash for some people, the new guidelines being a major change from a few weeks earlier when the CDC only allowed that vaccinated people could ditch masks outside when not in crowds.[33] This advice about outdoor masks had surprised a lot of people who seemed unaware they were supposed to be wearing masks outside when not in crowds, that message having never filtered well to the general populace. These sudden changes in mask suggestions ultimately threw people off and left many uncertain about the quality of the CDC guidelines.

As for the lifting of restrictions on the vaccinated, some folks worried that the honor system meant that unvaccinated folks would cheat the system, going maskless without being vaccinated. That's probably true, although I suspect the joke would be mainly on them. Granted, there may be a few folks who remain high-risk despite being vaccinated, and the goal of herd immunity is definitely worthwhile. At the same time, the idea the CDC should *lie* to the general public or sit on data that the vaccinated are no longer at risk is itself a really bad idea. Ultimately, the CDC and other public health officials need to provide the most honest information. If people misuse it, I get it, that's bad, but that's also on them.

MASKS ARE TYRANNY!

It's easy (and fun) to become an armchair critic with 20/20 hindsight. My main concern is not so much that public health officials got things wrong. I think most people understand that this will happen, and advice will update as new information comes in. Rather, I am concerned that some decisions by public health officials may have appeared deceptive (as with downplaying masks to spare them for health workers). This later became an issue for public health officials when 1,288 uncritically bought into the sudden 2020 narrative that systemic racism is widespread in the United States and signed an open letter to support mass protests against "white supremacy" during COVID-19 social distancing, even though these protests were largely based on misinformation regarding police violence (more on this in chapter 7). Later, the CDC endorsed the policy of prioritizing essential workers like healthcare workers, grocery store workers, public service workers, etcetera ahead of elderly people for vaccines. The logic appeared to be that ethnic minorities were more highly represented among essential workers, whereas white people were overrepresented among the elderly. However, elderly people are more highly susceptible to death resulting from COVID-19. Had this policy gone fully into effect, the deaths of elderly people of all races would have been much higher. One professor of ethics (!!!) suggested this approach to "level the playing field a bit" on race. This is an excellent example of the ghoulish (and racist) kind of decision that smart people can make in the guise of a moral principle ("equity" in this case[34]). These examples reduce public trust that public health officials are neutral, dispassionate experts attempting to provide the best advice to everyone based on the latest data. When that happens, people stop listening.

Yet, in fairness, despite these stumbles, public health officials did achieve clarity on the issue of mask wearing once masks' utility to the public (and the potential toll of not passing on that advice) became clear. By contrast, the messaging on masks was often undone by politicians in some countries, including President Trump in the United States or Jair Bolsonaro in Brazil, who appeared blasé about COVID-19 in general and, at least early on, mask wearing. Most of this ultimately split along a conservative/liberal line with more conservative folks evincing greater skepticism of masks. But how did this happen?

If we are to learn one lesson of psychology from COVID-19, it is the degree to which people, even smart people, irrationally contort their opinions on matters of fact around who else holds those views and who holds the opposing view. This is, as we discussed earlier, myside bias but with the added bit that we often assess the value of a line of argument not by the data to support it, but rather by the people making it. Indeed, rather than just a fringe observation, this appears to be a primary driver of decision making at present, infecting both sides of the political aisle and leading to nonsense even in science journals (which tend to skew to the political left).

Put bluntly, people aren't always bright (I don't exclude myself from this), and when they get angry, they get even less bright. Both the views that masks are tyranny and that racism is hiding behind every bush are products of building polarization and anger, which have been sitting about like a bunch of dry tinder, waiting for a match like COVID-19 to set it aflame.

BETTER MESSAGING

If public health officials and politicians flubbed much of the messaging on COVID-19 and the general public turned into rabid hordes of irrational rubes, how can we learn from this for future pandemics? In truth, the history of pandemics doesn't exactly shine a positive light on people's faith in science as the beacon to lead them forward. Pandemics generally lead to chaos and COVID-19 suggests this trend hasn't stopped in the modern era.

Pandemics also tend to divide people, often driving them to racism or prejudice toward other types of outsiders. Consider the most famous of all pandemics, the black death of the fourteenth century. One of history's worst outbreaks, the disease is estimated to have wiped out roughly a third to half of the population of Europe and North Africa. Generally thought to be carried in fleas transported by migrating ground rodents, the fleas basically vomited the contents of their gut into hosts when attempting to feed (gross, I know), hence spreading the disease.[35] But back then, nobody knew how the disease spread. So it became common to expect that outsider groups, particularly (though not limited to) the Jews, were poisoning wells or otherwise spreading the disease. This in turn led to massacres of these groups of people.[36] We can see echoes of this in anti-Asian discrimination in Western countries during COVID-19 and, tellingly, racism against Africans in China, given concerns among some Chinese that Africans had spread the disease to their country.[37]

So, anxious and bereft of good information, we search for obvious answers—often based on flimsy observational data and our tendency to see correlations where they don't exist—and take aggressive action once our minds are made up. The consequences can be tragic.

The public needs health officials in whom they can place their trust. Unfortunately, trust has been breaking down between the public and almost all institutions, whether the government, academia, journalism, or health officials. To be frank, much of this is self-inflicted, as even academia and science organizations become increasingly ideological and polarized. How can public health officials restore public confidence?

Don't get political. Public health officials are hardly isolated from politics. I once attended a meeting of the Institute of Medicine on gun violence in which a panelist suggested to the group that gun violence research be shielded from politics. This generated considerable laughter from the audience. But, ideally, his point was on target.

It can be tempting for public health officials to start advocating for policy, particularly if the data seem to point a particular way. But this is a bad idea. It politicizes science. The organization develops sunk costs: having gone out on a limb advocating for policy can make it difficult for public health officials to acknowledge if the science later changes. And dipping toes into politics creates political enemies, which public health officials don't need. Back in the 1990s, the head of the CDC came out advocating for gun control, given data linking guns to higher homicide rates in the United States compared to other nations (compared to Europe, the United States does not have a higher assault rate but does have a much higher homicide rate). His doing so basically caused Republicans in government to shut down federal funding for gun research ever since. Were the Republicans cynical to stop research they didn't like? Absolutely. But the CDC head was wrong to take a policy stance that made the CDC an effective wing of the Democratic Party. Public health officials need to simply communicate facts and do so objectively and without policy goals. Policy advocacy and science simply do not mix.

Tell the truth. For the public to listen to health officials, they must believe those officials are honest. As we saw with the mask issue, it can sometimes be tempting for health officials to bend the truth in service to worthwhile short-term goals. But long term, this reduces confidence in public health officials' honesty. And if the public thinks that health officials are trying to game the system by releasing false information, the public will stop listening. Public health officials need to always tell the truth, as best as it is understood given the current evidence, even if the short-term consequences of this may be undesirable.

Admit when you're wrong. Among professional guilds such as the American Psychological Association, there appears to be a reflexive aversion to acknowledging mistakes. The APA still tries to tell the public that violent video games are linked to aggression, despite that studies refuting this continue to roll in. This is the classic "sunk costs" mode of thinking. The APA put its reputation on the line with dramatic claims—the science changed and shifted from under them—and admitting failure on this score would be humiliating. Rather than face the short-term embarrassment, the APA has dug in its heels. This may seem satisfying in the short term but undoubtedly is contributing to reduced confidence in their organization and psychology in general. The same holds for actual public health organizations like the WHO or CDC. Sometimes, they're simply going to get things wrong. It's best to be honest about this and to explain how mistakes occurred and how procedures will be improved to make them less likely in the future.

Don't pick sides in culture wars. The open letter signed by 1,288 health officials in 2020 endorsing mass racial protests amid a pandemic, particularly as it was based on the dodgy "systemic racism" narrative, can only be a difficult blow to public confidence in health officials' objectivity. It was so obviously a moral grandstanding statement that went against what was known about both COVID-19 and the complexities of race and policing at the time. Particularly, as health officials had been only recently condemning (and fairly so) protests from the right complaining about lockdowns, this statement made it painfully clear that, far from being neutral, objective purveyors of truth, public health as a field is politically on the left, perhaps even the far left. Protests for me but not for thee.

It's irrational to signal your allegiance to one political tribe then wonder why the other political tribe doesn't listen to you. Granted, in a perfect, rational world, there wouldn't be political tribes. But moves like this only dig them in further. Public health officials need to find it in themselves to rise above the partisan sniping and political pressure (WHO, I'm looking at you). Granted, they are human and none of us manages this all the time. But particularly since public health officials tend to lean toward one side of the political spectrum, it would help for them to understand how this can create social pressures within their community that can lead to bias and bad messaging. Or perhaps put another way: Don't try to be "cute" on Twitter. You're not.

It's fair to note that COVID-19 does provide examples of amazing success. Most notably, science managed to set unbelievable records for bringing safe, effective vaccines into production, allowing people to return to some semblance of normality earlier than we might have hoped for. Like the black death, COVID-19 may be with us for some time, mutating and reoccurring. But we can have confidence that science will now keep up with this, perhaps requiring booster vaccines yearly or every several years, keeping infections manageable, and reducing the direst consequences of infections when they do happen. But the early months of COVID-19 represent a catastrophic failure of humankind's ability to tame nature. The epidemic was worsened by poor decision making by leaders and individuals at every turn. Looking at the history of pandemics, much of this should have been expected. But hopefully we can learn from this latest example. Much of the world, as I write this, still struggles with COVID-19. Despite the development of vaccines, countries such as India are seeing worse outbreaks than ever. Hopefully that will change by the time this book comes to print.

But enough about COVID-19. Now let's take a look at why we still joke about the dangers of microwave ovens and how that is almost certainly hurting the environment.

4

NUKED!

Sometime back in the early 1980s my family joined what was then the modern age* by getting a microwave oven. Microwave ovens were not exactly new. Prototypes had existed since at least the 1940s, and in 1955 the first commercial home-use microwave became available. This little beaut went on sale for a fairly stiff $1,295,[1] stiffer still if one remembers that this was 1955 dollars, which would be worth somewhere around $13,000 as I write this in 2021. So not exactly intended for college dorm rooms. Reasonably priced microwaves became widely available by the 1970s and, in typical form, my folks waited another decade before they allowed me to realize that there was a whole wide world of food out there that didn't involve boiled vegetables from a can.

The thing about these ovens was that nobody really knew if they were safe. Theories started to abound that the microwave radiation emitted by these handy little machines would be akin to keeping a nice chunk of uranium in the home. These fears got passed down from dumb old people to dumb kids. We worried that too much exposure might cause our nibblets to fall off or our bones to glow. Still, the promise of quickly reheated pizza made it worth the risk.

For a while there, people really worried these things would cause cancer (they still used them though—there's some fundamental lesson about human behavior here somewhere). After several decades of

---

* At least in part: the joys of cable TV were to be deprived of me until I was in my twenties.

research, it turns out they are entirely harmless so long as you don't do foolish things that make it such that you deserve to die, like trying to dry off your cat in the microwave. Actually, pet microwaving is almost always an act of deliberate cruelty. One defendant tried to blame the death of a kitten on other cats, saying they had shut the kitten in the microwave.[2] I've known enough cats to be tempted to believe this, but that's another story.

Microwaves do "leak" a bit of radiation (indeed, our "smart" TV gets goofy when the microwave is on), but it's well below the amount that is dangerous to humans. The British charity Electrical Safety First assures us that the leakage from a microwave "would result in a mild warming effect, if anything." Hmmm . . . so we're only *slightly* being cooked like a bag of popcorn. Reassuring. But no, seriously, folks, these things are totally safe.

Now, most people don't really worry about microwaves. Five decades of society just cooking along (Ha ha, get it? Sorry, no refunds on the book) have mostly assured people of their safety. But we still sometimes use the technopanic language of those woebegone days when these machines seemed like space-age technology. When we heat up some poor unloved leftover, we still say we *nuked* the thing as if we'd set off Big Boy or Fat Man. We just can't quite shake our fear of anything even vaguely associated with nuclear power, even if microwave ovens and nuclear power plants are worlds apart.

The funny thing is, at least for the near future, if we're really serious about reducing climate change by replacing carbon-emitting fossil fuels, nuclear power is likely going to need to be part of the mix. No form of power is without risks, and I'll discuss some of the disasters involving nuclear power, but compared to the toll of fossil fuels, nuclear power looks positively rosy. So why are we so frightened of it?

KEEP THE COAL FIRES BURNING

During the mid-twentieth century, most homes in London were heated by burning coal in stoves. This is the origin of the Santa myth (this is not a book friendly to childhood fantasies), wherein the bad kids got coal for Christmas. Coal, in this case, being easy for lazy Santa to find in the fireplace or stove and stuff in the naughty kid's shoe or stocking as a sign of disgrace. Why go to the effort of hauling gag gifts all over the world in your sleigh, when people have left cheap garbage in their own homes?

As a heating source, coal had the benefit of being cheap and (particularly in the United Kingdom) plentiful. On the downside, it also coughs up tendrils of toxic greenhouse gases and soot. When this stuff mixes with water vapor in the air, it converts fog to *smog*, for which many cities became famous in the twentieth century.

Smog sounds like an ugly nuisance, but it's actually quite dangerous. This became clear one winter in 1952 when, during a cold snap, Londoners fired up their coal stoves to keep warm. An unlucky weather convergence then occurred, trapping cold air around the city in a kind of bowl, allowing smog to collect without being dispersed by winds. This Great Smog of 1952[3] choked the city with noxious fumes for five days. The fumes were so thick they blinded people, stopped traffic, and left a greasy film on sidewalks and exposed surfaces. They also were deadly, particularly to elderly people, those with respiratory problems, young kids, and heavy smokers whose lungs weren't in such great shape. Hospitals became clogged with people suffering the ill effects. Estimates suggest that four thousand people died as an immediate consequence of the Great Smog, with perhaps as many as twelve thousand dying as the result of long-term consequences of exposure to the deadly fog.

Following the Great Smog, London gradually switched from coal-burning stoves to other methods of heating, such as oil, gas, and electric, though these too depended mainly on burning fossil fuels. Nonetheless, these methods released fewer plumes of smoke directly into residential areas. But, overall, burning fossil fuels is a deadly business. There is, of course, the whole climate change thing, a source of endless culture war. Here, I think climate activists shoot themselves in the foot by declaring the end of the world every decade like some kind of doomsday cult.[4] This is not to say I don't take climate change seriously, but rather the all-hyperbole, all-the-time model of activism eventually just exhausts the public.

Yet, aside from climate change, there is the degree to which the burning of fossil fuels contributes to premature deaths. The numbers can sound startling, so it's important to put them into context. By premature deaths, this doesn't mean that someone was in perfect health, hit a wall of smog, then turned green, got those X eyes, and keeled over. Rather, people with a preexisting problem—let's say emphysema, which reduces lung capacity—are exposed to particulates in the air, which then worsen their condition. So they had a chronic condition that was likely going to kill them, but air quality issues worsen the condition and kill them faster. Premature deaths can be estimated by examining the degree to which death rates increase or decrease under certain circumstances. Let's say evil television executives release the reboot of the 1990s saccharine catastrophe *Full House* as *Fuller House*. That year, the US death rate increases over prior years. When those TV executives finally come to their senses with the blessed wisdom of God and cancel *Fuller House*, the death rate goes down again. Examining this, we could estimate the number of premature deaths inflicted on the United States by the toxic awfulness of *Fuller House*.

One recent study suggested that air pollution may account for as many as ten million premature deaths each year, particularly in China and India.[5] Even if that number is off the mark, almost no one who studies this disagrees with the central conclusion that the burning of fossil fuels plays a role in millions of deaths every year. Yet, we continue doing it, barely blinking an eye.

By contrast, nuclear energy has been estimated to have caused five thousand deaths between 1971 and 2009 and to have *saved* about 1.8 million lives each year that otherwise would have been lost due to fossil fuel emissions.[6] So, to repeat, fossil fuels contribute to the deaths of millions every year, whereas nuclear fuel saves millions every year. Nonetheless, fossil fuel burning remains common whereas some countries are moving to *close down* their nuclear power plants, potentially replacing them with fossil fuel sources (although the stated goal is to ramp up renewable energy sources).[7] How did we become so suspicious of nuclear energy, even as fossil fuel burning continues to seriously damage the planet?

NUCLEAR POWER'S BAD PR

Right from the start, nuclear power faced an uphill battle in the court of public opinion, being associated with the two big bombs that ended World War II and decades of Cold War that always seemed to promise the end of all life on the planet. After all, there's no *coal bomb* that leaves massive areas uninhabitable by humans and causes cancer years later in people who were too near the blast. Even outside nuclear weaponry, people became quickly alert that radioactive material exerted a creepy, quasi-magical, death ray–like effect on people. Walk around with a lump of coal in your pocket all day and you just have a dirty pocket. Walk around with a lump of plutonium in your pocket all day and you dissolve into a puddle of goo. Safety protocols around the handling of radioactive material were a bit lax early on, and the stories of Harry Daghlian and Louis Slotin, two government researchers who died from acute radiation exposure, can set your skin crawling.[8] Put briefly, this kind of exposure can cause a person to progress from feeling some tingling, burning, and initial nausea, to their body literally falling apart within days. Other beliefs, such as those popularized in the film *The China Syndrome* suggested a nuclear meltdown at a power plant could burn its way through to the center of the Earth. Who wants *that* just down the street?

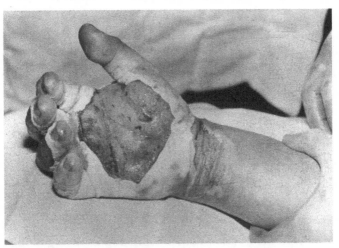

Burns to Harry Daghlian's hand following fatal radiation exposure.
Wikimedia Creative Commons.

These types of concerns have been fueled by three major nuclear incidents, namely those at Three Mile Island in the United States, Chernobyl in the former Soviet Union, and Fukushima in Japan. We'll consider each in turn.

The Three Mile Island accident occurred in March 1979 near Middletown, Pennsylvania.[9] In this situation, a mechanical failure caused a valve to get stuck open, releasing nuclear coolant in the form of steam. Without proper coolant, the nuclear reactor began to overheat. Chaos then ensued. The human workers inside the plant didn't know what was going on and were unaware that a loss-of-coolant problem was in progress. Thus, their decisions compounded the initial issue, causing one of the nuclear cores to overheat, triggering a partial meltdown.

The problems that led to the accident were twofold. First, the design of the instrumentation and indicators in the control area were poor, giving operators insufficient or misleading information about what was happening. This led to them making improper decisions that worsened rather than alleviated the initial problem. Second, plant staff also were not adequately trained and supervised, leading to poor decision making.

The good news regarding this accident is that nobody died and at least the official government word is that the damage was contained to the site, and there was no noticeable effect on the general populace in terms of cancer or other health outcomes. The radiation exposure estimated to have been experienced by residents nearer to Three Mile Island was said to have been less than a typical chest x-ray. One study suggested a very slight elevation in cancer rates in the area around Three Mile Island in the years after the accident, but it was unclear if this was due to the accident, stress related due to the accident, or changes in health surveillance caused by the accident.[10] Cleanup of the site was officially completed in 1993. I probably wouldn't go for a casual stroll through the interior of the structure myself nonetheless. As of 2019, Three Mile Island's second power-generating station, which was not involved in the accident, discontinued operations, apparently because producing power using fossil fuels is cheaper.[11]

Perhaps the most famous nuclear accident occurred several years later at Chernobyl in the Soviet Union in April 1986.[12] Being in high school at the time, I can remember this one and the attention it got. Many

Three Mile Island. The non-operational cooling towers to the left were the site of the accident. *Wikimedia Creative Commons, Z22.*

Soviet nuclear reactors weren't exactly the best designed, and Chernobyl was no exception. Poorly trained staff and unclear safety guidelines also contributed to the accident.

Reactor personnel had been conducting a maintenance and safety check (ironically enough), but in doing so, reduced the water coolant flow to the reactor. A nuclear chain reaction ensued and steam built up in the coolant pipes, ultimately exploding and destroying Reactor 4 and causing a fire. The fire pumped radioactive fumes into the atmosphere for about nine or ten days before it was finally contained. Two people were killed in the explosion, and twenty-eight other workers would succumb to acute radiation poisoning while valiantly fighting the fire.

Thirty-six hours later, Soviet officials began evacuating the nearby town of Pripyat, though residents already had begun complaining of the effects of radiation poisoning. Ultimately, an eighteen-mile zone around Chernobyl would be closed off, displacing over 220,000 people. A United Nations report on the accident from 2018 found that radiation exposure from the accident was likely responsible for some increase in thyroid cancers in the nearby region (radioactive iodine settles in the thyroid and taking regular iodine "fills up" the thyroid gland so it won't absorb radioactive iodine, which is why you see characters in movies drinking iodine when they've been exposed to radiation—not something I'd suggest without a doctor's advice if you're getting nervous about your microwave).[13] Fortunately, although the larger impact on cancer for the region is difficult to fully estimate and certainly shouldn't be downplayed, it appears to have been less than initially feared. Nonetheless, estimating the number of premature deaths caused by the Chernobyl disaster in the decades since has been controversial.

The Soviets were also slow to inform other nations of the disaster. Only when radiation levels began to increase in Sweden did the larger world become aware of the accident. As for the local area, the initial radiation exposure temporarily wiped out a nearby pine forest and is reported to have caused deformities in local fauna. However, freed of human interference, the area around Chernobyl now teems with wildlife (though levels of radioactive substances in their bodies remains high). Most famous is the abandoned town of Pripyat. It remains radioactive (and will for an estimated twenty thousand years), although the doses are low enough that one-day touring expeditions are now offered in Pripyat to visit the abandoned buildings and amusement park.

So, let's state the obvious: making a chunk of real estate (about one thousand square miles) uninhabitable for humans for twenty thousand years is hardly a consequence to wave off as unsignificant, even if the human death toll for nuclear power is low. Even if accidents like Chernobyl are rare, they could certainly add up over twenty thousand years! Granted, most reactors in the United States and Europe aren't Soviet clunkers like Chernobyl was, but concerns about this kind of damage aren't made up. Were this to happen in a more densely populated area, the consequences could be an exponential nightmare.

The failings of the human response to catastrophe are evident in one other corollary to Chernobyl. Some evidence suggests that the proportion of abortions rose in the Soviet Union, Eastern Europe, and even as far away as parts of Italy, which appear to be a consequence of panic among the general population and physicians alike that fetuses of pregnant women exposed to the European atmosphere after the accident would be at increased risk of experiencing birth defects.[14, 15] It should be noted that the evidence appears country specific, with no evidence for this in some countries, such as Austria.[16] The amount of radiation

Pripyat, abandoned since 1986. *Wikimedia Creative Commons, Keith Adams.*

released would not have been enough to significantly raise the likelihood of birth defects among pregnant women. However, many abortions may have resulted (and the number appears to still be in dispute). This would have been a tragic and unnecessary response to nuclear phobia.

The last of the major nuclear disasters is the Fukushima crisis in Japan, in which a nuclear reactor was stunningly taken out by a tsunami. Though there were concerns about failures in safety protocols as with other disasters, the Fukushima incident has a true hand-of-God feel to it. Here's what happened.[17]

In March 2011, an undersea earthquake triggered a massive tsunami wave on the Japanese coast near the Fukushima nuclear power station. The station survived the earthquake reasonably intact, but problems with the power supply caused emergency generators to turn on to maintain cooling of the reactors (like most reactors, these used a circulating water/steam system). Unfortunately, the station was submerged by the forty- to forty-five-foot tidal wave from the tsunami, and this caused the emergency generators to fail. This set up the now-familiar situation of overheating cores and meltdown.

The result, despite valiant efforts by the reactor engineers and crew, was multiple explosions blowing radioactive steam into the atmosphere. More than 150,000 residents had to be evacuated by authorities from the area around Fukushima, an effort made more difficult by the tsunami itself, which was reputed to have caused slightly fewer than 20,000 deaths (the deaths caused by the tsunami, as opposed to the nuclear meltdown with only a single death so far attributed to radiation exposure, likely contributed to the perception that the mortality of the accident was much higher than it was). Plant workers and emergency personnel worked valiantly to contain the disaster despite many having lost homes and family in the tsunami. Radioactive emissions were released into the air, although these appear mainly contained within the evacuation zone around the plant itself. Fortunately, a report by a scientific committee of the United Nations concluded that exposure to radiation for the general public around the nuclear plant was minimal and unlikely to have major health implications.[18]

HOW DEADLY IS NUCLEAR ENERGY?

The idea of having a big puff of radioactive gas moving through the neighborhood is undeniably frightening. But we tend to have an unrealistic perception of the cost in human lives of nuclear energy as compared to coal, natural gas, and other fossil fuels. The good news is that we have some reasonably good data estimating the death rates as well as greenhouse gas emissions from these energy sources. By any standard, despite all our concerns about nuclear power generating Godzillas, giant ants, and epidemics of cancer, nuclear power is closer to renewables in safety than fossil fuels.

The data I'll present are compiled by Our World in Data, a collaborative project of the University of Oxford and nonprofit Global Change data lab. They compile data from academic and scholarly sources and make it freely available for public consumption. Using data from scientific studies, their analyses examine energy source deaths due to accidents as well as air pollution using a term called *death per terawatt hour*. This is a way of allowing for direct comparison between energy sources

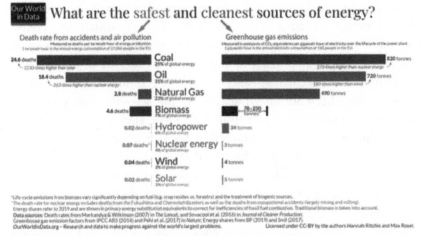

Death tolls by energy source. *Our World in Data, Creative Commons.*

by controlling for how widely they are used. Otherwise, we might expect that a widely used energy source might be related to more deaths even if it is safer, simply because it is in wider use. By controlling for relative levels of energy output (i.e., use), we can get a comparable sense of the relative toll of each energy source.

As the Our World in Data numbers make clear, nuclear power is a remarkably clean and safe energy source, on par with renewables such as hydro, wind, and solar power. The main difference is that nuclear power isn't intermittent, meaning that nuclear power is continually available, whereas sometimes the wind stops blowing and the sun is covered by clouds. Again, I am not promising that bad things *never* happen, and accidents like Chernobyl make clear that nuclear disaster can be significant. But by eschewing nuclear power given our nervousness, instead we're relying primarily on harmful fossil fuels, doing more damage than good.

Nonetheless, much of the opposition to nuclear power comes from environmentalists! For instance, the environmental group Green America states of its efforts to transition the US power grid away from fossil fuels, "But all of that work will be wasted if we transition from fossil fuels to an equally dangerous source—nuclear energy."[19] The concerns range from nuclear waste, to the possibility of nuclear energy being used for weapons or targeted by terrorists, to the difficulty for poorer countries to set up nuclear power plants. Variants of these basic concerns are echoed on other activists' sites. Some of these concerns, albeit reasonable, are cause for risk mitigation rather than outright dismissal (for instance, of course we should worry about terrorist attack, but as an eventuality to prepare for rather than as an alternative that terrorists preclude us from using). Concerns about accidents, cancer risk, and greenhouse gas emissions seem to have been addressed already by the scientific data suggesting that nuclear power is safe and clean. Of course, applying nuclear energy to the climate change issue shouldn't deter us from seeking ways to better harness renewables. This kind of thinking is a classic all-or-nothing cognitive error: if we embrace nuclear, that will detract us from investing in renewables. But there's no evidence we couldn't do both. They're not really competing—the competition is with fossil fuels—and multiple alternatives could have a positive impact. Faced with a worthy mission (enhancing our use of renewables), it can become easy to slip into stubbornness and see anything else as a zero-sum game pulling society away from our own goals.

But if, on balance, nuclear power is safer and cleaner than fossil fuels and, for the moment at least, potentially easier to implement than renewables, why is there so much opposition to it? Part of this comes from difficulties we have in assessing risk. Let's take a look at why that is.

HOW WE (BADLY) ASSESS RISK

Let's start this with a bit of humility. In the previous chapter, I mentioned how psychologists during the early stages of COVID-19 often argued that people were overestimating the risk of the disease. Boy, were they wrong! Some things *really do* turn out to be major risks. If a nuclear power plant blows up and burns a hole through to the center of the Earth, I'll probably really regret this chapter (look for a slightly abridged second edition to come out soon after). I can't promise you that if you step outside you won't be struck by a meteorite, though the odds are vanishingly small.[20] The point isn't that people are *never* right when attempting to assess risks; rather that our ability to do so isn't always reliable and can cause us to become both overly concerned about relatively small risks and indifferent to relatively high risks.

At the most basic level, we are afraid of many things because we have evolved to be. Early humans who were nervous about certain situations tended to survive better than the dumb oafs who thought it would be fine to pet the wild bear. The survivors then passed these fears onto their young and—voilà!—a kind of evolved fear becomes common in the species. A fairly obvious example of this is that some degree of fear of the dark is quite common among young children (and darkness is still perceived as threatening even into adulthood, hence most great horror movies don't take place under upgraded lighting). Why do young children think that monsters lurk in the dark? Well, because historically they did. Humans don't see well in darkness, and young hominids (various early human species) wandering away from safety at night tended to end up as puma snacks.

The same thing is true with many animal species. Though not all snakes are venomous, many are, so a fear of picking up or handling snakes is quite normal. I lived in Laredo, Texas, for eight years, where rattlesnakes are quite common, and it can be nerve-wracking to walk outside at night during their mating season (still, your average diamondback has more generosity and forbearance than your typical keyboard warrior on Twitter). Some spiders and almost all scorpions are also venomous, and even some bugs carry disease, so phobias about insects and arachnids also became common. Fears of things like heights (humans don't swing through trees like some other apes), water (we suck at swimming), enclosed places (can't escape), and blood (if you're seeing it, this can't be a good sign, not to mention how many germs get passed along by it) also became common. The simple reason is that running away from these things generally was more advantageous for early hominids. Lifetime prevalence of phobias ranges from 3 to 15 percent around the world, with fears of animals, heights, and some of the other aforementioned things being among the most common.[21] Remember, in our not-too-distant evolutionary past, many of these were outright deadly.

But modern society is quite different, and many of these threats have receded. Do you know of anyone (or are you that person) who is deathly afraid of, say, cockroaches? Few people outside of university biology departments outright love them, but I'm talking about people who get visibly panicky and run screaming from the room, as if that cockroach might at any moment whip out an Uzi? Probably most of us know at least one person, perhaps many. By contrast, how many cockroach-related deaths were there in the United States? I mean specifically the killings of humans by errant palmetto bugs and their ilk? I actually looked this up and the only case I could find was a 2012 event in which a man choked to death while binge-eating cockroaches in a contest to win a python.[22] I didn't make that up, I swear. But just don't do that. Beyond that, Healthline informs us that cockroaches can transmit some diseases like salmonella if they come into contact with our food and can trigger allergies or asthma for some people.[23] These aspects are probably a hint about why we're afraid of them in the first place—the disease-carrying thing. Don't leave your pizza boxes out (yes, they're having a nibble while you sleep), have the house sprayed from time to time, and you'll probably be OK. But there's no roachmageddon in effect in the United States. Nor should you try to snuggle a cottonmouth, but death or serious injuries due to venomous critters in the United States (Australia is a different story*!) is fairly uncommon. According to one study, roughly 157 people in the United States are killed by animals annually.[24] The biggest offenders are wasps, hornets, and bees, followed by "other specified animal" (one suspects these involve people getting attacked by bears, panthers, alligators, even deer, etc.), and then dogs. During the time period of the study, even rats managed to kill two people!

If you're one of those 157 people in any given year, that obviously sucks. But compare that to something that isn't a common phobia: motor vehicles. Some people may have PTSD-type anxiety after having been in an accident but, barring that, specific phobias of automobiles are pretty rare. However, compared to the paltry efforts of animals, roughly thirty-six thousand people were killed by vehicles in the United States in 2019.[25] And that's a *decline*; that's *good news*! Data on electrocution deaths in the United States every year are a bit trickier, as they're divided into workplace and consumer deaths, but government estimates suggest between forty and seventy consumers[26] and perhaps three to four hundred workers[27] are electrocuted each year. That's not nearly as high

---

* I'm not kidding about this—snake and insect/arachnid bites remain a real problem, not just in Australia but also in other parts of the tropics and in less-developed nations in particular. See White, J. (2000). Bites and Stings from Venomous Animals: A Global Overview. *Therapeutic Drug Monitoring*, 22, 65–68.

as car accidents but still at least twice the rate of animal deaths. So why aren't we afraid of electricity and, particularly, cars? The short answer is that these are recent innovations and not enough time has passed for us to evolve species-wide phobias of these things. So some of our fear is simply evolutionarily derived. This includes our fear of other people (other hominids having been a historically common source of death), which I'll return to when I discuss race issues.

If biology primes us to be more afraid of some things than others, our cultures sometimes can as well. One theory that has tried to explain how this occurs, at least in modern media-rich societies, is cultivation theory. As we'll see in chapter 6, media-effects theories are controversial and, in general, fictional media has much less effect on people, kids included, than we often assume. Cultivation theory has crashed against some of the same rocks. It doesn't appear that, for instance, watching a bunch of *Law and Order* makes us think crime is more common.[28] But information does get transmitted to individuals through social groups, and here there seems to be some distinction between nonfictional media (whether we're discussing village elders or news media) versus fictional media (tall tales across the ages).

The basic gist of this is that *in the absence of any other source of information* we rely on what appear to be sources of expertise to form opinions about novel things we know nothing about. So if something new pops into our environment, we look to the experts to tell us if we should be afraid of that thing or not. The only problem is that sometimes we misidentify idiots as experts and even real experts get things wrong sometimes.

Consider the case of genetically modified organisms (GMOs). I, like most people, know exactly zilch about GMOs in terms of personal expertise. I don't do research with them, I have not read research reports about them, I am not a chemist or botanist. But I do read the paper (mostly online these days, to my shame). If you're not aware, GMOs are typically plants or animals used as food that have been engineered using some form of rapid DNA-altering technology to acquire traits that make them more disease or drought resistant, more nutritious, grow faster, and so forth. The idea is basically a good one: more crop efficiency could address food scarcity, make food more nutritious, etcetera.

Technically most of our food has been "genetically modified" over hundreds or thousands of years of selective cultivation. What, you thought turkeys looked like that in the wild?* But the new GMOs can be made by editing genes, removing or adding them, putting the genes of one critter into another critter, and so forth. You might have heard the tale of scientists who created glow-in-the-dark mice by inserting firefly bioluminescence genes into them.[29] Pretty cool stuff!

But once again, this probably runs at least a bit against some natural fear inclinations. Our food shouldn't glow in the dark, so if scientists are doing this weird stuff to mice, what are they doing to these GMOs we are supposed to eat? Being wary and not knowing much about GMOs, we turn to experts—or at least that's the idea. Part of the problem is that we have to decide who is an expert. We look for credentials, but we also tend to be impressed by confidence. As such, we may sometimes be tricked by bloviating idiots who appear supremely confident as opposed to the more naturally hesitant scientists† who appear less sure of themselves.

The case of GMOs is on point. There are plenty of experts out there online, in news media, giving talks, warning us about the dangers of GMOs. To quote one example from Green America[30] speaking about GMOs, "The increase of cancer in humans, strange illnesses and infertility is alarming and everyone keeps wondering why. Perhaps we don't have to look too far to find a probable cause, we only have to take another look at what types of foods we are putting into our bodies." By contrast, research evidence has found that, by and large, GMOs are safe and not linked to substantial health concerns.[31] Of course, GMOs are an entire category, and the safety of each product must be individually tested. But it appears that GMOs offer a general net positive, despite our concerns about them causing cancer, infertility, etcetera.

The trick here is that GMOs already seem kinda weird and unnatural, and it's not too hard for us to find loud voices warning us about their imminent dangers. Put simply, fear can easily drown out rational, nuanced thinking based in evidence.

---

* In fairness, chickens more or less still look like the red junglefowl from which they were domesticated, if certainly fatter than their wild cousins.

† Don't get me wrong, the categories of "bloviating idiots" and "scientists" are not mutually exclusive.

That said, cultivation effects don't appear to be very strong. They tend to work only in situations in which a person has no prior knowledge of the thing in question and no real ability to check claims made by authorities. People who are prone to nervousness or who have already had a bad experience with the thing in question (such as exposure to crime) are also more prone to cultivation effects. The source of the information must appear to be authoritative; fictional media just won't do. Nonetheless, within the United States, we can see cultivation effects progressively as news media informs us to be afraid of, say, the Russians, then gang violence, then GMOs, then video games, then the police, then President Trump/Biden (depending upon which news you consume), then the Russians again. Most of these things we know nothing about (except violent video games in my case), so we have to trust that the news media know what they're talking about even when, more often than not, nothing could be further from the truth.

However, news media aren't a neutral, unvarnished source of truth. They make money from ratings and are increasingly polarized. But, ignoring the polarization for a moment, news media tend to latch on to novel, flashy stories as opposed to mundane ones. Couple that with the availability heuristic I've already discussed, and this can distort people's perceptions of danger. One nuclear plant melting down in a radioactive cloud but killing very few people still gets more attention than the quiet deaths of multitudes due to coal-fired plants and air pollution. And, in fairness, nuclear power was announced to the world with a bomb, so it's little wonder that nuclear power's mascots were a horde of giant ants, spiders, crab monsters, and lightning-breathing lizards from the 1950s.

I DARE YOU TO CHANGE MY MIND

Remember, in terms of threat identification, our decision-making power is largely left over from the days of, "Is that striped thing with fangs something I should run from?" It's not really meant to deal with nuclear power or a host of other modern-day issues. Thus, our eyes tend to glaze over when presented with empirical data, but we're excited by anecdotes and quick to see patterns in isolated events. The other issue is that our beliefs are often attached to emotions, and this makes even dumb ideas remarkably resilient in the face of evidence against them.

You can see these kinds of irrational responses to fear. Let's say there's a thing, I'll call them Pazoozles, that are fairly common and easily available. Kids love Pazoozles and beg their parents to get them all the time. But wait! Some dude in Kansas died mysteriously and there was a Pazoozle in the room. Another woman died in China, and she was a well-known Pazoozle enthusiast. Coincidence? *Yes!* But promoted by news media, people tend to assume a pattern in these isolated incidents with no clear causality. People get upset and call for investigations or even bans.

Then a bunch of eggheaded scientists like me get together to study the impact of Pazoozles. Unfortunately, this takes a few years because science is often slow (and when it's rushed, there are more mistakes, unsurprisingly). But after a few years of data crunching and peer review, the conclusion is published: Pazoozles are absolutely harmless and safe for children. Everyone breathes a sigh of relief, right?

Well, some people do. But you'd be surprised by the proportion of people who become *angry* about this conclusion. The scientists must be in league with Big Pazoozle. Someone's kid isn't doing well in school and at some point in the past, they bought that kid a Pazoozle (or even better, a grandparent did), so there must be a link, right? What else could it be? People don't need science to tell them what they can see with their very own eyes!

Once people form beliefs and become emotionally invested in those beliefs, shaking them loose, even with data, becomes very difficult. It can happen, but it takes patience and persistence, and most people don't have that. Look at debates on vaccines, for instance, in which pro-vaccine people quickly resort to calling anti-vaccine people stupid and selfish. Whether that's fair or not, it's definitely a poor way to persuade people. In fact, confronting people head-on with the wrongness of their belief or shaming them for it makes them *more* likely to persist in that belief. It is more effective to listen to why people believe something and provide them with evidence without putting them on the spot to change their belief right there and then. People need the opportunity to save face or else they tend to become stubborn as a shame-reducing strategy.

So, if the risks of nuclear energy are fairly minimal—not zero by any means and certainly recognizing that a nuclear accident can cause a lot of trouble locally at least—compared to the damage of using fossil fuels, why do so many folks persist in opposing nuclear? Fundamentally, it's because they *want* to believe it's bad. It simply makes sense that something that is also a bomb must be terribly dangerous. Or they've invested considerable moral certitude or, in the case of activists, even years of time in that particular belief. There are what we call *sunk costs*, meaning a person's time, energy, money, reputation, or moral identity have become tied to the belief and abandoning it would create significant personal disruption for the individual. This fundamental aspect of human belief is a large part of why misconceptions persist even in the face of considerable evidence.

THE CATASTROPHE OF NUCLEAR POWER

Three Mile Island, Chernobyl, and Fukushima were three major catastrophes involving nuclear power. Fortunately, their death toll either directly or indirectly appears to have been fairly few. But the true catastrophe of nuclear power is how our emotional aversion to this weird energy source may have cost far more lives lost to the pollution of fossil fuel plants, something most people just shrug off. That sucks, right, but what is one to do? There's also something about the law of good intentions in here, wherein well-meaning environmentalists may have actively worked to block an energy source that could have reduced climate change, holding out instead for clean renewables that never quite gear up (whether due to tech issues or simple politics) and replace fossil fuels.

That doesn't mean that there are any bad guys. This is just normal human decision making coming to a predictably bad end. We don't want Kaiju stomping through our backyards, nor radioactive waste turning our teenagers into raging sludge monsters (though with some of their hygiene habits, aren't some of them already?). Once we're afraid of something, we can become stubbornly so, even becoming angry if someone tries to bring the good news that the frightening thing isn't really so bad with reasonable regulation and protection.

If climate change is a catastrophe, our aversion to nuclear power is probably making that catastrophe worse. Yet I don't see any momentum toward moving forward with building more nuclear power plants. Fear is simply getting in our way. Fear can make us do really stupid things. With that in mind, we'll take a look at the 9/11 attack and its disastrous aftermath.

5

TERROR IN THE SKIES

I can still remember* the morning of September 11, 2001, the event that is likely *the* defining event of my lifetime. I was still in graduate school at the time, living in a one-bedroom apartment in Winter Park outside of Orlando. My now wife was then my girlfriend (somehow, I'd convinced her that marrying me was a good idea, so we were engaged by this point). I'd woken probably around 8:30 a.m. EST, having become expert in minimizing my morning preparation time to maximize my sleep time. I didn't even eat breakfast (I still don't), doing a quick routine of showering, brushing teeth, dressing, and checking email, an indulgence that remains my earliest morning activity.

Back in the 1990s, having an America Online (AOL) email account was cool, and even though it now marks one as a social pariah, I've been too lazy to change it. AOL was always good about throwing important news in front of you while you check email, and the news of the morning, probably by now around 9:00 a.m., was that a plane had struck one of the World Trade Center Twin Towers. Initially, I'd assumed it had been a small, private plane. There had been one or two incidents like that recently, small planes striking large buildings, probably a suicide by the pilot. Small planes generally didn't do a lot of damage except to

---

* I say this with full acknowledgment that human memory—even for so-called flashbulb vivid memories—is actually quite poor. So take any recollection with a grain of salt!

themselves. Thinking it was a tragedy, but a small one, I got into my car and made the fifteen-minute drive to campus for my first class.

In that time, the whole world had changed. In one of the buildings I walked through on my way to class, there was a public big-screen TV with people clustered beneath it. It turned out the small plane wasn't a small plane at all, but instead a passenger jet filled with people. A second plane had, by then, already struck the other major tower at the World Trade Center and both were now burning. Soon, another passenger plane would crash into the Pentagon and a fourth would crash in a field in Pennsylvania after passengers tried to regain control. Terrorists from the fundamentalist Islamic group Al Qaeda had been responsible for the horrible attack that ultimately killed just under three thousand US citizens.

It's difficult to overestimate the impact of this single event on the United States in terms of politics, war, international relations, psychology, and public policy. Even having lived through the end of the Cold War, I suspect 9/11 has more impact on our struggles today. And the story of 9/11 is really one of two catastrophes: first, the decision by a small group of men who believed that a violent assault on the United States would somehow improve conditions in the Middle East (at least in alignment with what they saw as a desirable outcome) and then the flailing, often irrational and destructive response of the United States. The latter has led to significant expenditures of money and resources, countless deaths, the erosion of our international standing, and public policies that have eroded individual rights. I consider each of these catastrophic failures of decision making in turn.

WHAT WERE THEY THINKING?

In this section, I'll try to get in the head of a terrorist. Of course, in so doing we must acknowledge that not all terrorists are the same, either in goal or in their role in terrorism. For instance, since we'll focus on Al Qaeda, the fundamentalist organization responsible for 9/11, there are undoubtedly significant gulfs in psychology between organization leaders such as Osama bin Laden and the individual terrorists who actually committed suicide during the 9/11 attacks (something bin Laden himself appeared decidedly disinclined to do). To what degree is terrorism an effective means of reaching the goals of the organizations that employ it?

That's a big question and the easiest answer is, "it depends." Generally, terrorism is employed to create fear and passivity in a population of individuals and, by doing so, to increase the power and control of the organization. This *can* be effective in the short term, of course, but can also create resentment and backlash. For Al Qaeda, the movement arose out of the guerilla war in Afghanistan against the Soviet Union back in the 1980s. Having successfully pushed the Soviet Union out of Afghanistan, bin Laden and his allies sought to expand this effort and expel all outside influences, particularly the United States, and the corrupt local regimes supported by the West from predominantly Muslim areas as a kind of global jihad.[1] Simplifying things for the sake of this argument, we can say that, basically, Al Qaeda sought to eliminate the US presence in the Middle East. It did so through a series of bombings and terrorist attacks, including the 1998 suicide truck bombings of US embassies in Kenya and Tanzania, and the 2000 suicide boat bombing of the navy destroyer USS *Cole*, which killed seventeen sailors.[2] The 9/11 attacks were the dramatic follow-up to this.

To worry "a foreign power has too much influence over my country" isn't in and of itself remotely unreasonable (though the fundamentalist vision Al Qaeda had for the region would have been a horror show). Middle East politics isn't remotely my specialty, so I won't opine about whether the region would be better or worse off with less US investment (I suspect most others with strong opinions aren't much better informed either). But we can look at whether Al Qaeda's tactics ultimately achieved its goals. After two major wars (Iraq and Afghanistan), countless drone strikes, the ongoing survival of most US-supported (whether enthusiastic or not) regimes in the area,[3] increased Islamophobia worldwide, hundreds of thousands of deaths, the involvement of not just the United States but also Russia in the Syrian civil war, the death of bin Laden and crippling of Al Qaeda itself, etcetera, etcetera, can we honestly say Al Qaeda has achieved anything like its ostensible goals? We can say the same for the United States, if on a lesser scale, whose vision of a peaceful, democratic Middle East following military intervention has also proven largely fruitless and at the cost of significant money, reputation, and lives.

If Al Qaeda's goal had simply been to provoke the United States like an angry bull in a porcelain shop, then mission achieved, but Al Qaeda's strategy, we can safely say, has done not one bit of good for the people of the Middle East.

Its strategy involved a fundamental misread of both history (Pearl Harbor?) and human psychology. When attacked, people tend to lash out, often stupidly, not become cowed and submissive. Provoking people can be a great strategy for online flame wars but not for real-life politics. I won't claim that violence is never successful in achieving goals—we know that it can be—but it is a risky strategy likely to accelerate resistance from the "other side."

So why did Al Qaeda make a fundamental miscalculation in thinking that a dramatic terrorist strike on US civilians would somehow lead to a betterment (at least in their vision) for the Middle East? Again, we need to look at what drives the personalities of both the leaders of terrorist organizations, as well as the rubes who actually carry out terrorist attacks.

Let's start with suicide terrorists themselves. It's hard to motivate me to get off the couch at night and go to bed, so how do you convince someone normal to fly a plane into a building or detonate a bomb strapped to his or her body? The short answer is, you don't. Suicide terrorists, it turns out, are specifically recruited by terrorist organizations based on preexisting mental health issues that terrorist groups can exploit.

Let me make one diversion and note that terrorist groups sometimes exploit nonconsenting individuals. Children or cognitively impaired individuals may sometimes be fitted with bombs then sent into public areas. This is a cruelly effective strategy, as people tend not to suspect children and cognitively impaired individuals who don't know they're carrying a bomb and thus may not show the behavioral signals that police, soldiers, or security may otherwise look for. But for the moment, this isn't the group we're talking about. Instead, we're focusing on individuals who *knowingly* and *purposefully* commit suicide as part of a terrorist act.

Suicide isn't a typical behavior. That is to say, we are generally programmed for survival, and self-destruction is, largely, not the direction in which we are genetically programmed for survival. Although depressed animals sometimes refuse food or engage in other behaviors that lead to their demise, true suicide largely appears to be a uniquely human phenomenon.[4] Not all suicide in humans occurs due to mental illness; for instance, cultures ranging from Imperial Japan to Soviet Russia have allowed it as a means of restoring honor when facing shame. There is considerable evidence that shame is one key component to self-injury and suicide,[5] though the evidence is clearer for self-injury than for suicide.[6]

When it comes to conflicts, there are examples of self-sacrifice resulting in the death of an altruistic individual. Parents may die to save children from danger, or there's always the 1950s war movie cliché of the heroic soldier throwing himself on a grenade to save his comrades. These behaviors aren't really suicide, though, as the intent is not specifically to die, but rather to spare the lives of others. Presumably if that grenade turned out to be a dud, that heroic soldier would be rather thrilled.

So, why, instead of fighting soldiers on a battlefield—a dangerous but reasonable response to intergroup conflict (assuming war is ever "reasonable")—do some people die while also blowing up a school bus filled with children? Well, it turns out that there's another group of individuals who engage in similar behaviors, ending their own lives in the process of killing innocent people who never did them any direct harm. These are mass homicide perpetrators including school shooters. It turns out they and suicide terrorists have a lot in common.

Criminologist Adam Lankford has done a lot of important work in this area. Psychologically speaking, suicide terrorists and mass homicide perpetrators are very similar.[7] First, to be clear, suicide terrorists aren't martyrs heroically sacrificing their lives for others—they actually are suicidal in the most basic understanding of that term. They want to die because they are angry, depressed, despondent, and hate their lives, just like the typical mass homicide perpetrator. That's part of what makes them so dangerous; the typical self-preservation instinct has been switched off.

Mass homicide perpetrators are typified by three basic characteristics. First, they tend to have a long pattern of antisocial behavior and thoughts. They are angry, unpleasant individuals. Second, they tend to have significant mental illness, usually either suicidal depression or psychosis.[8, 9] Not everyone who's chronically mentally ill is a mass shooter, but never let anyone tell you that there's *no* link between mental illness and mass homicide; that's an outright fable. Indeed, certain types of mental illness such as psychosis elevate violent crime risk by three to five times,[10] no matter all the gibberish well-meaning activists try to tell us. Third, they tend to nurse grievances and ruminate on them to a greater degree than most of us; the term "injustice collectors" is sometimes used. They tend to see others as being at fault for failures in their own lives. Eventually they come to view their own life as effectively over but want to enact revenge on those they feel are responsible, whether specific individuals or society at large. Their motivation is to inflict as much suffering as possible as a prelude to their own death. This is as evil as an act can be.

Suicide terrorists are largely in the same situation, the main difference being that, before committing a horrific act of violence, their rage has been subverted toward a specific ideological goal. Though not all mass homicide perpetrators are ideological (in fact, most are not), many are drawn to hateful ideologies, whether racism, sexism, or fundamentalist beliefs that may lead to terrorism. We talk a lot about fundamentalist recruitment (whether for fundamentalist Islam, far-right white nationalist groups, or, for that matter, far-left groups as well), but such recruitment is typically not successful in attracting the interest of well-functioning individuals. Rather, capitalizing on rage, terrorist groups can direct angry, suicidal individuals toward terrible acts of violence.

So, if we're asking the question, "Why did these 9/11 attackers think killing civilians would help the Middle East?" we are fundamentally mistaking their motivation. They might have used the language of righteous struggle and Islam, but the truth is that they were angry individuals who just wanted to hurt people whom they perceived somehow contributed to their own anguish. Breaking stuff was the entire point; solving world problems was not.

What about terrorist leaders such as Osama bin Laden? What makes them who they are? Work in this area is hampered by several issues. First, and perhaps most obvious, terrorist leaders rarely make themselves available for psychological assessment. Second, the political and social context of terrorism varies from one organization to another, making findings difficult to generalize. Third, delineating the line between justifiable resistance and "terrorism" can be difficult, and the label of terrorism can be political itself, as a kind of propaganda or to justify resource expenditures or commitment for law enforcement, military supplies, or increased government control over personal freedoms.

The case of bin Laden is an interesting one and perhaps illustrative. Born into a privileged Saudi Arabian family, bin Laden was given a strict upbringing that brought him into contact with fundamentalist Islamist thinkers. This school of thought involved extricating the Muslim world from Western influence and, hopefully, creating a pan-Islamic state governed by Islamist principles. When the Soviet Union invaded Afghanistan in 1979, bin Laden became involved, providing logistical support and recruitment for the anti-Soviet resistance fighters. Ultimately, the Soviet Union withdrew from Afghanistan in 1989, its efforts to subdue the country unsuccessful. The war wasn't a ringing success for the Afghans, however, ushering in an age of brutal, repressive Taliban government. Bin Laden fell out of favor in his homeland of Saudi Arabia, given his fiery anti-Western rhetoric. Though he was correct in foreseeing the Iraqi aggression against Kuwait and potentially Saudi Arabia in 1990, he was appalled that the Saudis invited help from the United States, effectively ushering in the very Western infidel influence that bin Laden hated.

The thing that stands out is that the initial goal might be vaguely reasonable: to free the Muslim world of outside influences that may be exploiting it. Sure, most of us probably wouldn't want the fundamentalist regime bin Laden envisioned, but we might relate to the desire to free our homelands from outsider control. But both the tantalizing taste of success in Afghanistan as well as the frustration of being ignored in his own homeland may have pushed bin Laden into progressively more extreme tactics, lashing out against military targets and civilians alike.

Then again, lots of people become frustrated with the politics of their countries or even the outside influence of other powerful nations. Some peacefully protest, others just try to get by quietly. Some might even form rebellions that target only military or political targets that are arguably "fair game." What differentiates those like bin Laden who turn to brutal violence, including toward civilian targets? With bin Laden, we can see a few clues, both in the rigidity of his worldview, but also its grandiosity. He saw himself and his followers as ushering in a global jihad that would become a powerful world force. In other words, he was a bit of a narcissist.

Given that terrorism almost never achieves its goals, one would have to be a narcissist in order to think one would be successful.[11]

At present, it has been difficult to establish a definitive "profile" of terrorist leaders.[12] Terrorist leaders tend to be young, unmarried males (though there are female exceptions) from higher socioeconomic and educational classes (as with bin Laden) than one might expect. However, beyond this, identifying clear patterns of either mental illness or personality traits that differentiate terrorist leaders from the general populace has not been terribly fruitful. Nonetheless, some evidence suggests that individuals drawn to terrorist organizations are often motivated by the perceived excitement as well as nurtured grievances and an opportunity to give vent to them.[13] Recruitment for such organizations often targets the young, when passions and ideological commitment can run high and critical thinking can run low.[14]

Other scholars have pointed to an interaction between narcissistic personality traits and humiliation.[15] A combination of narcissistic and paranoid (a tendency to see malevolence in the motives of others) personality traits has been proposed as common among terrorist leaders.[16] Couple these traits with a sense of humiliation—that their grandiose worldview has been threatened by apparently corrupted influences—and such individuals may feel justified in lashing out, with the ends justifying the means. Such individuals are not true psychopaths in the sense we may see with career criminals, but their personality types nonetheless give them a resolve and resiliency that deflects moral qualms back onto their victims. Again, this proposal appears to fit nicely with the developmental path and worldview of a figure like bin Laden.

In essence, terrorist leaders have a grandiose vision of the world, one for which they feel is justification for the violence they commit. This in turn provides them with considerable moral and personal resilience in the face of adversity and justification for their own brutal actions. As a consequence, they persist in a dangerous and destructive pattern of action, one that is fundamentally irrational, given how seldom terrorism succeeds in achieving its goals. Like bin Laden, they almost inevitably do more damage than good to the very communities they sought to uplift.

SCREWING UP 9/11

Arguing for generosity for terrorists is an odd position, but if we're trying to be a smidge generous to al Qaeda, we might say that, even if its general world goals are in tatters, at the very least it provoked the United States in a series of disastrous decisions of its own. Other than simply breaking the Middle East more than it already was, these decisions did little to advance either the United States' or al Qaeda's worldview and produced considerable misery. But 9/11 presents an important historical case study in poor reactions to catastrophe by both the general public and decision makers. So, what went wrong?

It's probably hard to even remember now, but after 9/11 the United States enjoyed considerable worldwide support. We were the victims of brutal terrorism, the people who died in the attacks, innocent civilians. The headline of a major newspaper in France, a country not known for its effusive praise of Americans, declared, "We Are All Americans."[17] Like Austria after the death of Archduke Franz Ferdinand in 1914, the United States enjoyed widespread sympathy. And like Austria, the United States would squander that sympathy with irrational decisions and useless wars.

In the first months and even years after the attack, Americans coalesced like no other time in my (as I write this) fifty years. American flags flew everywhere, even on many cars. President Bush's approval rating shot up overnight. People spontaneously thanked soldiers for their service. Everyone was on board, and dissenting voices were largely muted.

Exceptions to this were largely considered wingnuts. Most famous perhaps was University of Colorado professor Ward Churchill who wrote an essay comparing the victims of 9/11 to "Little Eichmanns" and suggested that the United States deserved to be attacked due to its various interventions in foreign countries. Widely shunned, Churchill was ultimately investigated and fired for academic misconduct. In a subsequent trial, a jury sided with Churchill that he'd been unfairly fired, but later court decisions went against him. Churchill's essay is repulsive, though it's certain to me that his firing was politically motivated and a violation of academic freedom. Nonetheless, the vehemence of the reaction against him was a demonstration of the unity in the country at that time. If he had released his essay in the last few years, I suspect it would garner widespread acclaim from an increasingly nihilistic progressive left. Churchill was, to his chagrin, simply before his time.

Soon after 9/11, in October 2001, the United States launched air attacks on and ultimately occupied Afghanistan, a central Asian country, which had harbored al Qaeda. In this case the United States probably had a reasonable casus belli (or justification for war). Destroying al Qaeda in retaliation for 9/11 wasn't unreasonable. Had the United States limited itself to this goal, had clear and strategic outcomes for the war, and a plan to disengage once those goals were achieved, the world might be much different today.

Instead, the United States took its eyes off Afghanistan, underinvesting in its mission there, and in 2003 invaded Iraq, a country that had played no role whatsoever in 9/11. It's worth asking now: What the hell happened? How did we make such a terrible mistake? This war, the Iraq War, squandered the goodwill the United States had garnered, cost considerable resources and lives, and left Iraq with sectarian violence and a shaky regime, hardly the shining lighthouse of democracy President Bush's team had envisioned. The United States also set a course on restricting individual liberties and setting up the nucleus of a surveillance state, the impacts of which we still live with today. How did all that flag waving go so wrong?

For social groups, there appear to be dangers both in having too little social cohesion, but also in having too much. As I write this, the United States (and much of the West) is experiencing the former. Increasingly we fracture into partisan tribes that loathe each other and view each other as enemies. This is not helpful at all for the health of our society. But the years following 9/11 saw the reverse: dissent and questioning of government was forbidden, even shameful. We trusted our president and our leaders, and this was a crucial mistake. Because, as it turned out, they were full of shit.

Discussing a society's reaction to an event like 9/11 is complex, and there are numerous moving parts that are important to consider. So, for instance, the massive social cohesion that occurred after 9/11 was far different from the vast polarization that occurred after COVID-19, despite these events presenting serious threats to the United States (and larger world). So why did US society react so differently, becoming cohesive after one and polarized after the other?

There are many reasons for this, including the political dimensions undergirding society at the time, preexisting social cohesion (Democrats and Republicans didn't tend to view each other as fundamentally evil in 2001, unlike 2020), the quality and charisma of our political leaders, and the nature of the threat in question. When presented with external threats, social groups have a tendency to cohere more closely, but if society already has fractured into multiple competing social groups, as had happened by 2020, this is far less likely to occur. Leadership matters, as well, and whatever his other flaws (and he had many), George W. Bush was able to rally a grieving nation with his "aww, shucks" charm in a way that Donald Trump with his explosive partisanship could not.

If George W. Bush had the charm to unite the country, he unfortunately did not have the strategic skill to make good use of it. The initial invasion of Afghanistan was successful, though incomplete; al Qaeda and its Taliban supporters having gone to ground (it would take a decade and a new presidential administration to finally hunt down and kill al Qaeda leader Osama bin Laden). But in 2003, the Bush administration shifted to Iraq, a Middle Eastern nation that had been a thorn in the United States' side for years, but had no involvement in 9/11. This was one catastrophic mistake to arise from 9/11.

Iraq had been ruled by military strongman Saddam Hussein. Like many dictators, Hussein not only suppressed and murdered his own people, but also set his eyes on regional conquest. He dragged Iraq into a long and ultimately stalemated war with neighboring Iran. Once that ended, he infamously invaded wealthy Kuwait, sparking the Gulf War, which was essentially between Iraq and the world. George H. W. Bush (George W. Bush's father) led a coalition of countries to kick Hussein out of Kuwait but stopped short of overthrowing Hussein himself. This set up an unresolved conflict between the United States and Hussein during the next decade with sporadic airstrikes and veiled threats that Hussein might have weapons of mass destruction (chemical, biological, or nuclear weapons). Hussein also murdered his own people, particularly using poison gas against the restive Shi'ite Muslim population (Hussein and the ruling elite were mainly rival Sunni Muslims). So, sure, "It couldn't happen to a better guy."

But Hussein surely had nothing to do with 9/11. He was a secular ruler, not a religious fanatic, who was not on good terms with al Qaeda. The average person in the United States undoubtedly had little informational basis for understanding the differences between al Qaeda and Iraq, Sunnis and Shi'ites, or much of anything else happening in the Middle East, other than it seemed like one big mess. What's less clear is what the US government leaders might have known. Surely, someone in charge knew there was a big gulf between Saddam Hussein and Osama bin Laden?

What is clear is that the Bush administration used the momentum of 9/11 to start a war with Iraq to finally oust Hussein. They implied potential links between Hussein and al Qaeda, and frightened people with the possibility that Hussein might one day use nuclear weapons against the United States. Perhaps the most infamous quote, attributed to the otherwise talented Condoleezza Rice, "But we don't want the smoking gun to be a mushroom cloud,"[18] best sums up how fear was used to convince the US populace of the need for the Iraq war. To be fair, Hussein had failed to cooperate with nuclear inspectors from the United Nations and often hinted he might have such weapons. Likely he calculated fear of weapons of mass destruction would serve as a deterrent against any further invasion of his country. If so, he was devastatingly wrong.

But the decision to take the United States to war in Iraq benefitted from several things. First, widespread ignorance (I don't use the term pejoratively; it's just the reality) among the general public about the actual situation in the Middle East, compounded with past aggression by Saddam Hussein, increased the believability of him as a bad actor in 9/11. Second, widespread fear of terrorism: during times of fear and panic, people often look to a stronger authority for protection, but in doing so, risk sacrificing personal freedoms for that security. And third, the psychological process of groupthink, wherein social incentives reward agreement with the majority and punish transgressions from the majority consensus. Thus, any critique of the impending Iraq War could be framed as unpatriotic or failing to support the troops: in effect, selfishness. The shame and threat of loss of social status that could come with critiques thus ensured most people would stay in line with the consensus, even if they had misgivings.

Groupthink is a well-known and researched phenomenon.[19] Put simply, it refers to a tendency for groups of people to seek conformity and consensus and, in doing so, reduce critical thinking, doubt, and alternate views and solutions. Some of this occurs naturally, but groups can also enforce it by applying incentives for conformity and punishments (often in the form of shame or exclusion) for challenging the consensus. Groupthink can result in artificially high confidence in group decision making and, as a consequence, decision making that is catastrophic. There are ways to reduce groupthink, such as having junior members of a group speak before leaders (junior members otherwise tend to parrot leaders to seek approval), appointing someone whose job is specifically to play "devil's advocate," starting discussions in small groups before moving to large groups, or even rejecting decisions that are unanimous.[20] The perception that a decision is *moral* can increase groupthink (because only the immoral would object).

It's possible to recognize symptoms of groupthink if one is inclined. These involve feelings of group invulnerability (it is right and will prevail) and morality (those who disagree are immoral or evil). Opponents to the group are stereotyped as crude, unintelligent, uninformed, or evil. Arguments against the group's decisions are presented in weak, strawman form. People begin to self-censor their doubts, and some group members may take it upon themselves (or be specifically assigned) to "police" the others.

Scholars have examined specific catastrophes as examples of groupthink. As one example, the 1986 explosion of the US space shuttle *Challenger*, which had been entirely foreseeable and preventable, is thought to be the consequence of groupthink.[21] The shuttle exploded during takeoff due to a flaw in one of the rocket boosters, which rendered it unstable during the unusually cold Florida temperatures on the day of the launch. All crew were killed (likely upon impact with the ocean after the explosion), including Christa McAuliffe, a teacher who had been selected to give a lesson from space (whose students had watched the takeoff and, as a consequence, her death on live TV). Engineers had tried to warn NASA about the flaw in the rocket booster, but NASA was under a self-imposed deadline to make the launch happen. Concerns about the rocket boosters from the lower-ranking engineers were dismissed. Confidence in the reliability of the space shuttle was unrealistic. NASA decision makers had a sense of invulnerability. The result was disaster.

Groupthink can be disastrous in the private sector as well. One classic example is the 1985 decision by Coca-Cola to ditch its "classic" formula and introduce a "new" sweeter taste. The new version was popular in some taste tests, though Coke executives ignored the issue of brand loyalty regarding "classic" Coke. When "New Coke" was released, it was generally received well, though a passionate minority of brand loyalists were very vocal about hating it. The Coca-Cola company appears to have been entirely unprepared for this reaction, perhaps believing in its own invulnerability. Curiously, the social pressures within the company appeared to switch as the company seemed to panic. Despite the fact that New Coke was actually doing rather well, expressing support for New Coke within the company became taboo, and the company switched back to "Classic Coke" after seventy-nine days. The fiasco might have been averted had Coca-Cola introduced New Coke alongside Classic Coke (rather than replacing Classic Coke entirely) or had a plan for dealing with vocal detractors. Some people suspect that Coca-Cola's plan all along had been to gin up controversy to get attention and increase sales for Classic Coke, though most people accept that the incident was a fiasco.[22]

Groupthink appears to have operated both for the planning of the Iraq invasion as well for society at large. President Bush's team thought that the case for the invasion was a "slam dunk" (it turned out that it was not and, not only was Hussein uninvolved with 9/11, but there were no weapons of mass destruction), that American soldiers would be welcomed by Iraqis with open arms (they were not), that a small occupying force could maintain peace in the country (it could not), and that a democracy could be established easily (it was not). The invasion itself went just fine, and the Americans predictably crushed the Iraqi military with ease. But too few troops were initially sent to maintain order in the country. Everything from museums to ammunition dumps were looted. Natural and long-lasting tensions between the Sunni and Shi'ite Muslims in the country, as well as the ethnic Kurds in the north, boiled over. Regional bad actors, particularly Iran, saw an opportunity to stick it to the United States. The United States made the decision to disband the Iraqi Army. As a former foe, perhaps this was understandable but it unfortunately deprived Iraq of its own military, which may have assisted the United States in maintaining control. It also created a massive cadre of unemployed but armed young men resentful of their treatment at the hands of the United States.

The result was a massive and brutal civil war in Iraq, marked by terrorism and torture killings. Much of the violence occurred between different groups of Iraqis, though the US military tried to support a shaky new Iraqi regime. Hussein himself was captured and rather brutally executed by the Iraqis, but by then he was an afterthought. This Iraqi civil war cost the United States thousands of lives and more than a trillion dollars. Exponentially more Iraqis died. The result was a regime in Iraq that remains shaky and only marginally "friendly" toward the United States. The Middle East never transformed itself into the democratic utopia the Bush administration had hoped.

The groupthink didn't occur only within the administration, but also throughout the population at large. News media largely went along with the Bush administration's narrative. Those who were critical were often shamed. Famously, the country music band the Dixie Chicks saw their career deeply hurt when they criticized President Bush.[23] Failing to learn the lessons of cancellation, the Dixie Chicks later dropped "Dixie" from their name during the moral panic following the murder of George Floyd in 2020, but more on that in chapter 7. This kind of societal groupthink can stifle debate and create a kind of "mob mentality." Even if a majority of citizens recognizes something is going wrong, the fear of consequences keeps them from speaking and the mob prevails.

THE PATRIOT ACT

Even if we shrug off the damage done to our military, to the economy, and to other cultures as part of an unnecessary war, the US response did considerable damage to civil liberties. The dubiously named Patriot Act provides an excellent example of propaganda in politics.

Passed in the immediate aftermath of 9/11, the Patriot Act sounds like it's going to help America and maybe fight terrorists. In fact, it greatly expanded the ability of the federal government to surveille and police its own citizens and has had little real impact on fighting terrorism abroad.[24] It allowed unprecedented surveillance of Americans' phone and email records, as well as financial records, often with minimal judicial oversight or accountability.[25] It greatly expanded police powers and increased penalties for crimes involving "terrorism," which, naturally, incentivized the government to massively increase the scope of what constitutes "terrorism," with an increased obsession with "domestic terrorism." It was replaced with the "Freedom Act" in 2015 under the Obama administration, though concerns remain regarding the threats to civil liberties created by these laws.

These laws and their impacts point to two interesting phenomena. First, the powerful propaganda effect of naming. And second, the degree to which people forgo personal freedoms in response to perceived threat.

Both the Patriot and Freedom Acts have a fairly obvious propaganda appeal; after all, who is against patriotism or freedom? Critiques of these laws can be reframed easily as moral shortcomings. *Oh, so you're against patriotism and on the side of the terrorists?* The names that bills or laws take are often meaningless and can mask many real problems within the actual law. Politicians do this all the time with "Won't You Think of the Children?" and "We Love Kittens" bills that in fact conceal grift for special interests, real threats to civil liberties, or simply garden-variety dumb ideas. This pops up a lot when bills and laws focused on criminal justice are named after actual victims of crimes. The bills/laws themselves may be incredibly poorly thought out, sometimes with harsh or draconian approaches to criminal justice, but who wants to oppose a bill or law named after the child victim of a horrible crime?[26]

There is again a subtle use of shame in this tactic. Opponents of the bill have to be willing to endure the predictable slings and arrows of moral assaults to stand their ground. That's often the trap: politicians are rarely brave enough to lose the votes of a populace who often can't see beyond the name of a bill. When a bill is named "Stop Hating on Puppies," it can be tough for a politician to vote against it even if he or she knows the bill is in fact terrible for puppies and pretty much everyone else.

It's not just a politician thing either. Advocacy groups often make use of the same tactic, framing rigid ideology, illiberalism, or just plain bad ideas in the vein of protecting some marginalized group or important moral cause. "Save the Planet" is tough to argue against, even if the idea on offer is terrible or ineffective. Advocacy groups can be quick to label criticism of their views as racist, sexist, fascist, anti-environment, and so forth in order, once again, to use shame to enforce compliance (and indeed, complicity). For example, the acknowledgment that biological sex is real, largely binary (which does not preclude our offering respect and support for the minority who do not fit that binary), deterministic of behavioral and attitudinal differences, important to health outcome, and supported by a wealth of science has increasingly been discouraged even in medical settings. Examples abound, though in one recent case, a medical school professor apologized for using the term "pregnant women," which some students found offensive for allegedly excluding trans men who also can become pregnant.[27] Shame and fear of being called "transphobic" result in increasingly convoluted word games and thought policing, even when biology itself helps to explain why some individuals may feel their gender identity does not match their biological sex.[28]

This is a phenomenon sometimes called *ideological capture*. Put simply, this occurs when institutions or authorities become so afraid of shame that they increasingly repeat ideological, anti-science nonsense so as to avoid shaming. If this sounds reminiscent of the social control that occurred under Communist regimes with their struggle sessions, that's because there are indeed similarities. Threaten people's livelihoods and social reputations and, in effect, they'll begin to say almost anything and apologize for any thought crime, even if they know it's not the truth. More on this in chapter 7.

The other fascinating aspect of the Patriot Act is the degree to which Americans were open to enduring an unprecedented reduction in their legal rights so as to reduce the threat of terrorism. As noted, generally communities come together and adhere into groupthink when presented with external threats. But people also become quick to put more power in the hands of paternalistic authorities, who we hope will act to defend us. It's not unlike behaving as children, retreating behind mother's skirts when frightened. Except that, unlike mother, government doesn't always truly have our best interests at heart.

Using the fear of external others as a lever to pressure the populace to accept reductions in personal freedoms has been a tactic of authoritarian governments across time. Those perceived threats may be internal (often Jews, immigrants, people of other ethnicities, Republicans or Democrats, Labor or Tory, etc.) or external (the Russians, the terrorists, the capitalists, etc.). People have something of a natural tendency to respond to external threats (real or imagined) by handing greater control to authorities. We want to be told what to do to keep us safe. Often we accomplish the exact opposite.

Really, this is the ultimate lesson we need to remember: fear and crisis often lead us to make decisions that are not in our best interest, and those who seek power will take advantage of this. By repeating this pattern, we often make a crisis worse, as occurred after 9/11. In that case, we continue to live with the consequences two decades later at the time of this writing.

It seems that in the proper management of a crisis there is something of a balance. We don't want to descend into chaos and partisanship as occurred after COVID-19. Neither do we want to allow ourselves to be subsumed under groupthink as occurred after 9/11. We need to become alert to the propaganda tactics that governments and advocacy/pressure groups alike use to manipulate our emotions. We need to become resilient to shame, lest we buy into "The Emperor's New Clothes." We need to figure out how to work together while maintaining our ability to be constructively critical of bad ideas or policies. In other words, we need to remember the founding principles of our nation, including free speech and due process (for American readers at least), which we so often forget during times of catastrophe.

The last two decades haven't offered much optimism in our ability to rise above this pattern. Even our shining moments, whether World War II or the civil rights movement, are replete with some of the ugliness of our human reactions to crisis. Yet I remain optimistic that we can learn from our past failings and continue to advance. Bringing light to our failings and remembering them during future times of crisis can often help.

6

SCHOOLS ABLAZE

Back in 2019 Warner Brothers released *Joker* starring Joaquin Phoenix as a mentally ill and socially isolated young man who turns to violence and anarchy when society fails to offer him support. Beautifully written and acted but also stunningly graphic, the movie was met with a cascade of pearl-clutching reviews in which mostly progressive movie reviewers (is there any other kind these days?), worried about *what message* would the movie send. After all, here you have a white man, involuntarily celibate, who doesn't get what he wants from society and turns to violence. Is that really the story we should be telling? Don't we have enough white, entitled mass killers?

Much of the fear focused on the concept of "incels," or involuntary celibates, typically applied to young men who couldn't get dates and, as a consequence, became resentful toward women. Many movie reviewers appeared beside themselves worrying that the movie would set off an army of incels, shooting up theaters nationwide. Some movie reviewers almost seemed to *want* violence, providing them with some kind of morally sanctimonious told-you-so moment. In a sneering review for *Time*, Stephanie Zacharek refers to Arthur Fleck as "the patron saint of incels."[1] *Slate*'s Sam Adams likewise argues that "the movie plays right into advance fears that it could act as a kind of incel manifesto, offering not just comfort or understanding to disaffected young men angry at the world, but a playbook for striking back at it." Adams also adds, with un-self-conscious drama, "it feels like a risk to feel too much for him, not knowing who might be sitting next to you in the theater using his resentments to justify their own."[2] David Ehrlich referred to it as "potentially toxic" and "profoundly dangerous," though leaving it to the reader to decipher the implications.[3] *Vulture*'s David Edelstein referred to *Joker* as "an anthem for incels" and implies links between superhero movies and mass shootings such as the 2012 Aurora, Colorado, shooting.[4] Common to these reviews is a kind of elite contemptuousness of the dystopian tone of the movie, its sympathy for a mentally ill white man and sneering disregard for the disaffected young men it might represent. The reviews express a fear of violence inspired by the movie with the sense that the links are all-so-clear *if only people would listen*. Despite these attempts to dissuade people from seeing such a dangerous film (or, indeed, perhaps because of them in part), the movie became a roaring success. And how many violent acts were directly inspired by the *Joker* film?

Exactly zero.

What happened? Why did so many movie reviewers (mostly progressives in this case) assert with such confidence that the movie was so dangerous? Why did they take positions of moral clarity and even sanctimoniousness in order to assert their concerns? And how were they so wrong about the outcome?

We have a weird relationship with media. We love it, including all the sexy and violent parts we pretend not to like. But media also pushes boundaries and challenges conventions. We particularly get nervous when our kids get close to it. Thus, media can be an easy scapegoat for whatever seems to be wrong with the world. This is nothing new. In Plato's dialogues, older Athenians sound a lot like the grumpy old people of today, complaining about how youth are disrespectful, unlike how the old people were in their day. This they attributed to the new dramatic plays making the rounds, plays that 2,500 years later we force adolescents to read in high school. The Athenians weren't kidding around: they executed Socrates in large part for causing delinquency among youth (as I sometimes joke, Socrates was basically the violent video games of his day). The twentieth century was rife with media-based moral panics, everything from the radio to pornography, from Dungeons and Dragons to Harry Potter. Pretty much every genre of music came under scrutiny. (I still remember the 1980s congressional hearings where old politicians were convinced that artists ranging from AC/DC to Cyndi Lauper and Prince were causing satanism, violence, suicide, and teen sex.*)

We can look back on these moral panics and laugh. What idiots were afraid of the radio or comic books? However, we seem incapable of learning from this history. Since the video game panic, parents, politicians, activists, and some scholars have focused on new media such as social media and smartphones as the source of mental illness and suicide (hint: they're not). Why do we keep doing this?

Let's take a look at one particular mass homicide to examine the various ways our cognition breaks down during such an event. In February 2018, a nineteen-year-old male (I'll refrain from using names) walked into a high school in Parkland, Florida, and began shooting. By the time he was done, seventeen students and staff were dead and seventeen others wounded. The shooter somehow managed to escape the scene but was arrested an hour later. The shooter had a long history of emotional and behavioral problems and had been a student at the school in the past before being sent to alternative placement. He had a history of both bizarre and threatening behavior. Unfortunately, neither the mental health system nor law enforcement managed to get him into long-term residential mental health care, which might have prevented the tragedy.

During the shooting, law enforcement response proved to be confused. School officials were unsure about who could authorize a lockdown when the shooting started. A sheriff's deputy assigned to the school during the shooting remained outside the buildings, rather than moving inside to confront the shooter. When other police arrived, they too formed an outside perimeter rather than moving inside the building. They also held back some paramedics from entering the building initially.

The shooting, as shootings often do, began another cycle of the typical polarized debate over gun control, with progressives leveraging the shooting toward a gun control agenda and conservatives attempting to block it. As part of the blocking strategy, some Republican politicians, including President Trump, suggested that violent video games may be a potential cause. Indeed, the president's comments led to hearings in Washington, DC, where I gave testimony on this issue.

---

* Forty years later, some scholars have begun to worry teens aren't having *enough* sex and blame that on media too, I kid you not.

This shooting includes several serious errors committed either by society or individuals, which exacerbated this catastrophe. First, a clearly disturbed individual was deprived of long-term residential mental health care, despite multiple individuals identifying him as a potential threat. Second, individual police officers became confused during the shooting, failing to take action that may have saved lives. Third, society became distracted by a moral panic in trying to understand the causes of the shooting.

HOW PEOPLE BEHAVE DURING A CATASTROPHE

Let's start by examining the behavior of some of the police officers in the Parkland shooting. I approach this with some apprehension as these officers have endured public shaming and approbation. Many readers may feel this is appropriate, but I don't wish to contribute to it. As such, my comments should be interpreted merely as an attempt to understand the cognitive processes that underlie mistakes, not as moral grandstanding or a desire to add to the dogpile.

Many of us imagine ourselves as heroes awaiting the right moment for our superheroism to have its chance. We are one burning building or drowning child away from *doing the right thing*. Indeed, the allure is so tempting that some people manufacture crises themselves. Perhaps the most famous example is that of firefighter arsonists: firefighters who set fires themselves then heroically rush in to put them out. Most such firefighter arsonists come from difficult backgrounds, underperform academically and in their work life, have mental health problems, and view firefighting as a way to be a hero and escape boredom. One of the most famous cases was that of John Orr, a firefighter who set multiple fires, mainly in Los Angeles during the 1980s, including one in a store that killed four people. He was eventually caught by matching his prints to a print left behind at the scene of one of the fires. He had also written a novel—about a firefighter who set fires! He was convicted and sentenced to life in prison.[5]

In the case of the Parkland shootings, most of the attention focused on Sheriff's Deputy Scot Peterson, the assigned school resource officer. As noted earlier, Peterson remained outside the school building during the shooting rather than moving inside to confront the killer. Peterson stated to investigators that he initially believed that the sound of shooting was a firecracker and, once aware that the shooting was gunfire, believed it to be coming from outside. However, the official investigation report[6] disputed this account, suggesting Peterson had at least some idea that the shots were coming from inside a school building, as evidenced by his own actions in approaching (but not entering) the building and his statements to other individuals. He also failed to call in a "code red" or school lockdown response to the shooting. Accounts of Peterson's movements indicate a highly stressed individual (who wouldn't be?) and someone clearly shocked. As other police arrived, an officer queried him about what was happening. While pacing back and forth he answered, "I don't know. I don't know. . . . Oh my God, I can't believe this." These are probably key words. Why did Peterson melt down, failing to enter the building and engage the shooter, as is current law enforcement protocol and training?

Peterson claimed that, in fact, his training had taught him to remain outside the area of a shooting and contain the area until SWAT arrived. Since the 1999 Columbine killings, this has not been standard law enforcement training. According to the investigation report, Peterson had been well-trained in modern active shooter protocols including single-officer confrontation with a shooter. Peterson had been a police officer since the late 1980s; is it possible some earlier, outdated containment training rushed to mind, crowding out newer updated training on engagement during a moment of crisis? It's possible.

However, the official investigation report did acknowledge one shortcoming in his experience. Reading between the lines a bit, the report implied that being a school resource officer (SRO) is a relatively cushy gig compared to being a police officer on other beats. Despite all the hand-wringing about school violence, American schools are actually remarkably safe, and violence on school grounds is rare and declined significantly from 1992 through at least 2017.[7] That means SROs don't have to deal much with homicides, domestic violence, serious assaults, etcetera, to the degree that many other officers do. As such, they don't have the ability to maintain their tactical skills other than in artificial training exercises. Training and experience are critical to keeping individuals in high-stress situations from freezing. Having been an SRO for twenty-eight years, Peterson may simply have been unequipped to deal with a high-stress, potentially fatal scenario.

Training and experience can each help with decision making during crisis situations. During a crisis, we may be presented with an unfamiliar situation, one we'd assumed (as Peterson's "I can't believe this" quote suggests) was so rare it wouldn't happen to us, with unclear goals and a panoply of decisions, all which seem bad. With good training, the best decisions can become somewhat rote, informing us of what we should do without our needing to think our way through them. Some people are excellent at thinking of novel solutions during a crisis, but far more people become overwhelmed and uncertain or panic. This can result in indecision, the "deer in the headlights" effect. With good training, even if the situation seems unreal, we know what the next step is and can undertake it without needing to think of it ourselves.

Experience can reduce our emotional response to a crisis situation, something that is called desensitization. Desensitization involves decreased emotional responses to a repeated situation. Desensitization often gets a bad rep, particularly in the violent media debate, as people imagine hordes of zombified youth shambling through a pitiless world. But in reality, desensitization isn't necessarily bad and can be good for some individuals. In general, we want first responders to be desensitized because emotions such as fear or sadness can get in the way of good decision making. If I accidently cut off my arm, I don't want the emergency medical technicians who respond to become emotionally overwhelmed at the sight, running around in circles. I'm probably doing that myself (assuming I'm still conscious from the blood loss). I need someone who coolly responds, knows what to do, even reassures me that I'll be OK, and provides the best assistance. That comes only with repetition of stressful incidents.

School shootings are, thankfully, exceedingly rare (we tend to overestimate their frequency due to the news media attention they get—the availability heuristic, as you may recall). This means that few school resource officers get any kind of experience in that particular scenario. Training can help. But many officers on patrol see other forms of violence or have to respond to other crisis situations. Though not the same as a school shooting, this can engage emotional desensitization, which can reduce the risk of panic or confusion during a new crisis. The official report on the Parkland shooting suggests that being deprived of that level of experience, Peterson, in effect, didn't benefit from the opportunities to reduce his emotional response to a crisis situation and, as a consequence, behaved like most people would: with confusion, panic, and indecisiveness.

My intent is not to pick on Peterson (plenty of people are already doing that), but rather to point out that his behavior is less a sign of moral weakness and more simply the kind of normal response the average person might have in a moment of crisis. Of course, for law enforcement officers, we expect more. They should be trained (as the official investigation says he was) to deal with crisis situations and have the experience (which the investigation implies he did not have) to remain cool under pressure. Naturally, I do not know what is in Scot Peterson's head, so I will refrain from making any judgments. Yet I suspect the official report is correct in noting that the experience of an SRO likely wasn't sufficient to prepare Peterson for the emergency. That's not to say every long-term SRO would respond the same way—a combination of personal/ psychological factors, training, and experience will result in divergent outcomes for different officers. But making sure SROs get relevant experience with crisis situations may help more SROs deal with emergency situations that involve life or death decisions.

THE MORAL PANIC OVER MEDIA

Now, let's turn to the issue of why we always seem to blame video games/ media for these shootings despite clear evidence that video games, movies, and other media play no role in school shootings or other mass homicides. In truth, complaining about the corrupting effects of media (as well as complaining about the new generation of youth) is a familiar tradition that can be traced back to at least the ancient Greeks. The idea that external forces are somehow corrupting the youth appears to be a historically common fear of parents everywhere.

During more recent decades, we have seen a steady slew of moral panics. Many of them are smaller in scope than the entertainment industry.

For example, for a few years there was a moral panic involving the belief that scary clowns were stalking schools. Clown sightings seemed to be everywhere for a brief while, but these mostly proved to be hoaxes and no actual wave of stalking clowns actually emerged.[8] Soon after there was the panic over the "Momo Challenge," a spooky character that allegedly encouraged teens to commit suicide. Nonetheless, evidence that any teens committed suicide due to the challenge proved to be thin.[9] There are also plenty of moral panics that focus on the basic premise that youth today have discovered some extreme ways to misbehave that previous generations have not. These may involve things like the "Knockout Game" in which youth punch strangers and get points if they knock them out with one punch or "Rainbow Sex Parties." These bacchanalian festivals involved teen girls wearing different shades of lipstick and giving boys a rainbow by each performing oral sex on the boys. Publicized on the *Oprah Winfrey Show*, there turned out to be scant evidence the phenomenon was real.[10] Oddly enough, in recent years as concerns have focused on social isolation due to the use of video games, smartphones, and social media, the tone in some circles has switched to complaining that teens aren't having *enough* sex. The kids can't win.

Not all moral panics necessarily focus on the youth, but we can see it's a common occurrence. During the late nineteenth through the twentieth century, we saw moral panics range from everything from novels to television violence to the role-playing game Dungeons and Dragons. One of my favorites from the 1940s is an article in the prestigious *Journal of Pediatrics* about the dangers of radio.[11] More recently, people have worried that smartphones and social media are leading to teen suicide (they're not[12]). Some of these panics—such as those about movies during the early twentieth century, comic books in the 1950s, rock music in the 1980s, video games in the 1990s (and several times since)—have made it into congressional hearings.

Probably the most famous series of hearings about media effects were those in Congress during the 1980s for music lyrics. These hearings were pushed by an anti-media pressure group the Parents Music Resource Center (PMRC). Started in 1985 and led by Tipper Gore (the wife of then-Senator and later Vice President Al Gore), the PMRC focused on the sex, occult, violence, and strong language that became increasingly common in 1980s rock, pop, and rap. Apparently, Tipper Gore was partly inspired by Tom Petty's video for "Don't Come around Here No More," a whimsical take on the *Alice in Wonderland* stories. Admittedly, the video ends with Alice being turned into a cake and the other characters eating her. Supposedly this scared Gore's daughter and led to charges that the video promoted cannibalism.[13] The PMRC also compiled a list of the "filthy fifteen" worst songs due to their inclusion of sex, occult themes, or violence. They targeted bands such as Motley Crüe and Black Sabbath (OK, fair enough), but also Prince and Cyndi Lauper, not exactly historical supervillains of the music industry. Lauper, for instance, was tagged for her song "She Bop," which jokingly refers to masturbation (watch the video). Apparently the PMRC thought the song would lead teens to masturbate (as if they needed Lauper's help with that). Somehow they got Congress to take note of all this rubbish and hold hearings (being married to a senator likely helped).

The hearings, much of which still can be found online, are, in retrospect, funny to watch. Most classic is the testimony of Dee Snider, the lead singer of Twisted Sister, odd looking even when not dressed in drag, who eloquently points out that Congress and PMRC had misinterpreted the lyrics of many songs and the government's efforts amounted to unnecessary censorship. Nonetheless, fearful of government regulation, the music industry agreed to put the "explicit lyrics" sticker on records, which continues to this day. Naturally, when you tell people something is dangerous or forbidden, they typically want it more. Probably nothing has sold records more successfully than having that sticker affixed to them, something the PMRC probably should have considered.

Over generations, a lot of energy has been uselessly spent trying to "save the children" from the latest bugaboo. But why the heck do we do this? There's also the question of the cost of being distracted by the wrong thing, but I'll return to this later.

Why moral panics over media and technology occur is a difficult question to answer. One thing that seems apparent is that they are generational and age related. Meaning, to put it bluntly, it's mainly the older generations who are the "audience" for the panics. That's one mechanism by which moral panics die (probably, if I'm speaking frankly, more powerful than presenting good research data to people). They quite literally die—

the generation of people worried about *X* eventually dies off, and the panic dies with it. Without the audience, the politicians, news media, and scholars who profit from promoting the panic (and they do), move on to other topics, typically without acknowledging how totally wrong they all were.

We can see this with those old PMRC hearings. Nobody today really worries that Twisted Sister (let alone Prince and Cyndi Lauper) is promoting violence, sex, or anything else. Then again, if you go to a concert for one of these acts—if they're still alive and touring (RIP Prince)—the average age of a fan these days is about 104. Fans of this 1980s music now *are* the old people. So we don't worry about that music, but we worry about whatever is new.

One possibility is that these moral struggles are something of a stand-in for our concerns about our own mortality. We grow up at a certain time (the 1980s for me) and, culturally at least, many of us get kind of locked into that developmental period: 1980s music, Dungeons and Dragons, and *Star Wars* always will be the epitome of popular culture for us. But as we age, that stuff slips away, the actors and musicians die, and the younger generations have barely heard of some of it (Seinfeld who?). Things change, popular culture changes, even larger social narratives change (such as the woke effort to dismantle and "decolonialize" American history and culture, but I'll return to that later), and this can lead people to realize that nothing we hold dear and, indeed, nothing about ourselves will remain once we are gone. Our own legacy is threatened, and we react, as humans do, with fear and anger. The predictability of this cycle across generations and our apparent inability to learn from it suggests that this is some kind of hard-wired reaction to rapid social change. Experiencing being the target of moral panic as a teen at one phase of life doesn't seem to protect us from indulging in moral panic once we become parents and grandparents.

Related, it's also possible that there are aspects of struggle over power in these battles. Status in societies (not just human, but other ape societies and other social mammals as well) tends to be held by middling-year adults, though the youth are often aggressively trying to push their way in. Ultimately, elderly adults can no longer compete for status and, for the most part, tend to lose it almost entirely.* As such, struggles over popular culture and technology can be a kind of stand-in for status battles between generations.

Lastly, there is simply the issue that as we age, our efficiency at learning via imitation appears to decrease, which can make new technology threatening. As one example, there is the story of Imo, a female Japanese macaque or snow monkey. This story has taken on somewhat mythic proportions as good origin stories in science often do, so I'll try to represent it as faithfully as I can. Briefly, Japanese snow monkeys live on a small island off the coast of Japan and are famous for soaking in the hot springs there. In the 1960s, researchers started bringing them food, notably sweet potatoes. Most monkeys ate the potatoes off the ground, dirt and all, but Imo, an enterprising young female, figured out how to wash the potatoes in a local stream to get the dirt off. This was a unique behavior she figured out for herself. And when other monkeys saw her do it, they began imitating her. This is evidence for cultural transmission of information in other primates, which is, itself, pretty cool. But more importantly, the monkeys that imitated her were mostly either close relatives or similar-aged or younger monkeys. Older monkeys unrelated to her tended not to imitate her.[14]

Naturally, generalizing from potato-washing monkeys to older adults griping about *kids today with their music and their hair* is speculative. But it provides one potential clue suggesting that older adults have more difficulty adjusting to changes in culture, making us more hostile to these changes, which can seem intrusive and threatening. After all, in our day, we ate potatoes dirty and that worked just fine for us!

Unfortunately, these tendencies to exaggerate the harmfulness of new media can also play into the complexities of politics. After the Parkland shooting, many Republican politicians began pointing at video games as a potential causal factor in the shooting. President Trump himself got into the picture, blaming games. Trump called representatives of the video game industry to the White House where they pointed out that youth violence had declined by more than 80 percent even as action video games soared in popularity. With that, he seemed to lose interest, thankfully.

---

* There are exceptions of elders retaining general status in some societies, although my impression is that these narratives tend to be exaggerated as part of a "noble savage" mythology.

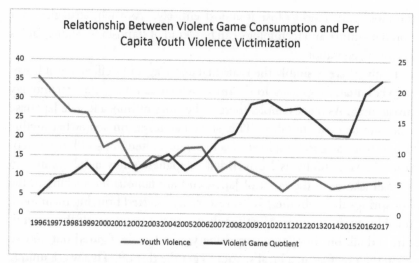

Youth violence data from childstats.gov; violent games data generated from sales figures for top five bestselling games according to IMDB adjusted for ESRB content rating. Graph created by the author.

Nonetheless, the matter led to hearings that summer for the School Safety Commission led by Education Secretary Betsy Devos. I was among the scholars called to testify and I assured the commission that the evidence clearly exonerated video games from any role in causing mass homicides. Fortunately the commission listened, and its report did not conclude that video games or other media were an important causal factor.[15]

But why did so many Republicans raise this issue in the first place? In part, it's likely because a fair percentage of their voting constituents are just the sort of older adults who don't like video games. Meaning, politicians tend to play to an audience. They stop once the audience is dead. But also, the issue of video games distracts people from gun control, and Republicans are generally Second Amendment supporters. The more politicians can distract people with video games, the less they are focused on gun control. It's cynical and perhaps pandering, but it's often the way that politics works. It's simply quite difficult for the voting public to keep its attention on more than one issue at a time (or any issue for very long). So if video game debates help kick the can down the road for a bit, so much the better.

In fairness to Republicans, caterwauling about the dangers of video games has been a historically bipartisan issue. Indeed, back in 2005, when introducing anti-game legislation into Congress (it didn't pass, thankfully), Hillary Clinton compared the effects of video games on child aggression to smoking and lung cancer.[16] Goofy statements, like referring to games as "digital poison," had been around for decades. But by 2018, the United States had become deeply polarized, such that anytime one party took a position on something, the other side reflexively took the opposing position.

Thus, when Trump declared video games to be one source of mass homicides, a fascinating thing happened: half the country suddenly realized it wasn't true! Trump's comments got significant pushback, particularly in the liberal press and from liberal and progressive politicians. They were right to push back but, I'd argue, for the wrong reasons. They weren't making a decision based on the data, after all, there had been good reasons to be suspicious of claims linking video games to violence all along (the typically more cautious Supreme Court noted this in the Brown v. EMA court case in 2011). As such, this was clear myside bias, as we've discussed earlier. People weren't skeptical of Trump's claims because they'd become well-informed of the extant data; they were skeptical of claims linking games to homicide because they came from Trump. Nonetheless, as a researcher in this area, one should not look a gift horse in the mouth. People have come to the right conclusion, and even if it's for the wrong reasons, I'll take it!

WHAT'S UP WITH MENTAL HEALTH?

Thus far, in most of the book, I've examined situations in which people's judgments about a crisis were clouded by various types of biases or emotion. As a consequence, making an active decision turned crisis to catastrophe. People's willingness to engage in moral panics about video games constitutes one such example. By becoming distracted by video games, we spend less time focusing on issues that might reduce homicide rates, such as reasonable efforts at gun control.

However, not all errors result from taking action based on the wrong conclusion, but also from wallowing in inaction despite coming to the correct conclusion. Violent crime is a complicated problem and no one cause leads to violence. That doesn't mean *everything* leads to violence, and, as we've seen, the evidence is now clear that violence in media plays no important role in violent crime. By contrast, the easy availability of firearms may make it easier to convert assaults into homicides. For instance, according to United Nations data, the Unites States isn't a particularly violent country—in fact, its per-capita assault rate is lower than the United Kingdom, Belgium, France, Australia, and New Zealand and on par with many other European countries.[17] However, its homicide rate is astronomically high. This suggests that guns may be converting some assaults into homicides in the United States. Supporters of gun rights point out, correctly, that this isn't an easy one-to-one relationship. Some countries such as Switzerland have relatively high gun ownership but low gun violence. And, as some of my own work suggests, when all nations are compared, gun ownership is a poor predictor of homicide, with homicide particularly prevalent among poorer, economically unequal nations.[18] Be that as it may, the culture wars around the Second Amendment in the United States are so entrenched that it's difficult to be optimistic about the two sides coming together and compromising on reasonable gun control efforts.

By contrast, most people are aware that mental illness—or at least some forms of mental illness—are contributing factors to violent crime. Granted, some well-meaning advocates for the mentally ill have tried to convince us otherwise. They argue that the chronically mentally ill—typically meaning those with schizophrenia, bipolar disorder, or other disorders involving psychotic breaks with reality—are more likely to be victims of violent crime than non-ill populations (true) but are no more likely to be violent (false). In fact, evidence consistently documents that the presence of a psychotic illness increases violence risk in an individual somewhere between three to five times the non-ill population.[19] Unfortunately, this is one of those examples in which more educated individuals may actually be less informed. This is because left-wing advocacy statements (like those attempting to downplay mental illness as a predictor of crime) may tend to permeate through academic spaces, whereas people's gut instinct is, in this case, largely correct.

This is not to stigmatize the mentally ill, however, which is why I say that these advocacy efforts, if technically bullshit, are at least well intentioned. Most people, even with chronic psychosis, don't engage in serious crimes. It's just a matter of elevated risk in comparison to the general non-ill population. And this observation doesn't mean that these folks are bad people. Often they are unable to control their actions or are responding to delusions or hallucinations that lead them to perceive that they are in danger and are defending themselves.

Returning to the issue of mass homicide perpetrators, the presence of serious mental illness, either psychosis or suicidal depression, appears to be nearly universal in this population of individuals. One solution is to improve our mental health system, offering better, more consistent care to individuals teetering on the edge of serious illness. Now, some readers will rightly point out that predicting who will and who won't commit a mass homicide is tricky business, but that's rather irrelevant here. If we offer comprehensive, government-sponsored mental health care to *everyone* with serious mental illness, we'd catch at least *some* of those otherwise destined to commit acts of mass violence. Everyone gets treated, regardless of violence risk. My observation is that most people acknowledge the links between chronic mental illness and crime (other than a few well-intentioned advocates), and the idea of offering comprehensive mental health services is popular. Why then don't we do it?

Here is where our inertia sets in. The issue of mental health is raised by both of our political parties in the United States. The idea of tackling it doesn't seem to create the endless culture war battles that gun control does, nor is it useless in the way that worrying about video games is. Yet, although we seem to agree on abstracts, converting that into an actionable plan simply hasn't happened.

Part of the reason is that many things sound good in the abstract but look terrible when put on paper. *Why don't we just emit fewer greenhouse gases* sounds like a capital idea until we realize that a substantial reduction in our quality of life would be necessary, at present, to achieve this. The same basic situation is likely in play here. Offering government-sponsored mental health care sounds great until we realize that someone has to pay for all this, and that means higher taxes.

I touched on this in my other recent book, *How Madness Shaped History*. Basically, prior to the 1960s, states did sponsor asylums—long-term mental health care facilities for the chronically mentally ill. These often weren't great places. There were issues regarding due process and improper care. But they were also expensive. When pharmaceutical drugs started to become available in the mid-twentieth century, states were only too happy to shed funding for these expensive and unpopular asylums. The result was the deinstitutionalization movement of the late twentieth century, a classic example of how good intentions (returning mentally ill citizens to their private lives) can pave the road to hell (widespread poverty and the increasing crime associated with it).

The reality is, we probably need to bring asylums back. Granted, they should look different from the early-twentieth-century asylums. They need to have clear procedures for due process and judicial oversight so that people aren't unfairly committed. And they need to be based on the best standards of care and regularly supervised so that they maintain humane conditions. These two criteria mean that a new, modern asylum system would be *more* expensive than the old one. But I suspect it would be successful in alleviating some percentage of both poverty and crime.

The trick is getting people to move on it. This means that public officials would have to do the hard work of convincing the public that asylums would be worth the tax investment and would avoid the horrible conditions that gave them a bad name. This is probably doable with effort, but then there's the rub: what's in it for any public policy official to invest in this?

Everybody kind of thinks mental health is important but, for lack of a better way to put it, it doesn't seem to be a "sexy" issue. Oddly enough, the fact that there's kind of a tacit underlying agreement about the importance of mental health may actually work against it in some ways. The controversies about video games and gun control make them appealing to news media. Mental health just doesn't seem to arouse most people's passions. For a policymaker on the rise, investing in promoting mental health may seem like a career dead end. It would be a slog of work, requiring years if not decades to put together, and probably result in relatively few ostensible rewards. It might be rather like the folks in charge of sewers—it's an important job and cities need them to run, but nobody's excited about it. The difference being that there are already regulations in place requiring adequate sewage, whereas creating a well-regulated, state-sponsored mental health system from the ground up would require work.

So, we see time and again that emotional passions are often the detriment to good decision making. But not being passionate at all can also lead to inertia and inaction. The trick is finding the balance between the inertia of disinterest and the destructiveness of excessive passion. That band is often narrower than we might hope. In the next chapter, I turn to just such an example: how the United States has so often failed to find the balance in its consideration of race relations, seesawing between inaction and irrationality.

7

A RACIAL RECKONING?

On August 9, 2014, Michael Brown and a friend entered a small market in Ferguson, Missouri. Brown, who was a black man, stole several packages of cigarillos and confronted the store clerk, shoving him aside. This was caught on security cameras. As Brown and his friend moved away from the store down the center of the road, they were confronted by Officer Darren Wilson, who is white, responding to the reports of the theft and the description of the suspects. Wilson aggressively confronted the unarmed Brown. Fearing for his life, Brown ran away and was shot in the back. In a last effort to save himself, Brown put his hands up in a clear sign of surrender, but Wilson killed him anyway. A clear incident of racist violence by police against black Americans. Except that isn't what happened at all.

In fact, the Department of Justice (DOJ) report on the shooting, ordered by then President Barack Obama and Attorney General Eric Holder (both black), found that this version of the events was inconsistent with the forensic evidence or credible witness accounts. What in fact happened is that Brown blocked Wilson from exiting his police vehicle, punched Wilson, and tried to grab Wilson's firearm. Wilson and Brown struggled for control of the weapon, and Brown was shot in the hand. Brown did then run away for a distance but was not shot in the back. For some reason, Brown turned around and charged at Wilson. Fearing he was in danger from Brown, Wilson fired his weapon until Brown fell to the ground, dead. The DOJ concluded that the autopsy and other forensic evidence as well as those of credible witnesses all largely supported Wilson's version of events. Put simply, the death of Michael Brown was the result of a justified shooting given his aggressive behavior toward Wilson.[1]

Why then do so many people still believe the mythical version of the Michael Brown story? The slogan "Hands up, don't shoot!" used at many rallies against police violence is inspired by the fictional version of the Brown shooting. Songs have been written about him and art commissioned in his honor. Civil unrest ranging from peaceful protests to riots struck Ferguson, Missouri, and other cities for at least a year. These gave rise to the theory of the "Ferguson effect," meaning that delegitimizing police through protests and riots leads to spikes in violent crime. The death of Michael Brown gave impetus to the black lives matter movement.* It's worth noting that, even if the shooting of Michael Brown was justified, a simultaneous DOJ report of policing in Ferguson, Missouri, revealed that many criminal justice policies placed particular burden on low-income black communities, so the Ferguson police were hardly exonerated.[2] Yet this appears to have been driven by the department's hyperfocus on revenue generation (via fines, tickets, etc.) than on overt racism. Nonetheless, these fell heaviest on black communities, sowing the kind of distrust that can lead to mythmaking in the Brown case.

Issues of race, policing, and crime are nuanced and complicated and the data is murky. However, the raw emotion surrounding this issue, given the longstanding history of racism particularly against black Americans in the United States, can cloud a careful data-based examination of the current evidence. Yet, failing to remain focused on data can lead to more harm than good. In this chapter I'll examine several related issues. First, what is the reality of policing and race: Is there a genocidal wave of police violence toward black Americans, is the United States a racial utopia, or is the story more complicated than either of these poles? What exactly is "systemic racism" and does the evidence support that this is a real thing? Are some ethnic groups overrepresented in committing crime, and how can we understand this? What role does news media play in our understandings and misunderstandings of race and policing?

---

* To help distinguish the larger movement and slogan from the organization, I capitalize the organization but not the larger movement. No disrespect is intended either way. One can, for instance, agree with the movement but criticize the organization, which some have critiqued for misusing funds and for lack of financial transparency.

And perhaps most importantly, is it possible to move these discussions into a constructive data-based approach rather than the polarized place of moral grandstanding and inaction that it currently occupies?

IS THE US EXPERIENCING A "PANDEMIC OF RACISM"?

Since 2014, the United States (and perhaps other countries as well) began experiencing a weird and unexpected slip into pessimism. On the right, this seemed to take the vision of a lost utopia, perhaps best illustrated by the 2016 slogan of the Trump campaign for presidency, "Make America Great Again." This inherently pessimistic view of America opened up opportunities for the left to ask the obvious question of when America had stopped being great, thus seizing the mantle of optimistic patriotism. Instead, the left continued its own slide into hysterical nihilism, increasingly viewing the United States as a permanently historically tainted country of racism and oppression that only could be fixed via "radical change" or some quasi-Marxist gobbledygook that would certainly be a disaster if these folks got hold of the reins of power. The 2020 murder of George Floyd, a black man suffocated by police in Minneapolis, catalyzed this movement on the left. At once, the left seemed to coalesce around the notion that the United States, despite much evidence to the contrary, was and had always been an apartheid state. The American Psychological Association, never shy of trying to shove its way into prominence during a crisis, declared a "pandemic of racism," rather clumsily borrowing the key term of the COVID-19 crisis.[3] But what does "pandemic of racism" even mean (other than a rather naked attempt to grab headlines), and does the evidence support such a notion?

Of course, the United States has a shameful history of slavery and oppression of minority groups that only ended with the civil rights movement of the 1960s. Of course, on the other hand, slavery was ubiquitous and brutal across almost all societies in history (including in Africa, Asia, and among the indigenous people of the Americas). The United States and other Western nations were hardly unique, aside from the West setting a historical precedent of voluntarily eliminating slavery (though it took a civil war in the United States). Slavery, in fact, remains common in many areas of the world today, though it is technically illegal under international law. One advocacy organization estimates that there are more slaves in the world today than at any other point in human history, perhaps forty million people.[4] China appears to be engaged in a largely genocidal campaign against the Uyghur minority in its northwest provinces, including slave labor camps, an issue that gets only tepid news media attention.[5] We need not argue the United States is a racial utopia—some disparities remain and, as we've seen before, racial tensions have increased since 2014. But it's important to maintain perspective too: most indices suggest that outcomes for racial minorities, including black Americans, have drastically improved since the 1960s, and racial and ethnic tensions are much more critical in many areas of the world. Understanding these nuances can help us address real issues that remain. But how did this conversation become so irrational?

This, of course, is a complicated question involving the evolution of social narratives, the partisan nature of politics, the worsening of culture war. But much of this operates in a culture of shame. On one hand, shame about the darker aspects of our nation's history may lead some people to downplay them. Particularly on the right, people may downplay the impact of slavery and historical racism in the United States and how these may still have negative impacts on black Americans today (at least those descended from former slaves—more on this in a bit), even if explicit racism has largely (but not totally) been expunged from society. On the left, people may not acknowledge uncomfortable truths, such as that young black men are overrepresented as perpetrators of violent crimes, which may help us to understand why they are also overrepresented as victims of police violence.[6] Shame can also be a powerful motivator: to avoid it we not only say things we know not to be true if that seems to be what the group wants, but we also avoid saying things we know to be true if the group does not want to hear it. This was the insightful theme of "The Emperor's New Clothes" parable, which also generally has been supported by sound psychological research on conformity.

Shame, as an emotion that guides one toward social conformity, appears to have evolutionary roots in social primates related to loss of status. The typical behavior posturing of shame, shrinking posture and averted gaze, can be witnessed in primates as well as humans. It is thought that shame helps motivate the individual toward behaviors that restore status. Though this is evolutionarily adaptive, for the current context, this increases conformity.[7] People, thus, tend to feel shame when they have violated some community norm such as cheating on a test, engaging in infidelity, or holding a viewpoint considered beyond the pale for one's culture. Failing to acknowledge shame can lead to worsening sanctions. For instance, anthropologist Daniel Fessler reports that, among the people of Bengkulu Indonesia, failing to demonstrate acknowledgment of shame results in one being labeled "thick eared" and possibly killed! Thus, acquiescing to shame, whether deserved or not, is itself evolutionarily adaptive.

Historically, given the power of shame, many punishments such as placing someone in the stocks, or public dunking in tanks of water, the local pond, or river were designed to humiliate as much as cause pain. The modern "cancel culture" on the internet is a similar tool unleashed on a broader scale and often needing relatively little provocation. Consider the case of Emmanuel Cafferty, a Mexican American gas and electric worker fired from his job for supposedly flashing a white supremacist hand sign. Cafferty was driving in his work vehicle when another driver took a picture of him making what looked like an OK sign with his fingers, which some people believe to be a white supremacist signal (Cafferty maintained he was cracking his fingers, which unluckily happened to look like this sign).* Because we now live in what can only be called a tattletale culture, the other driver put this photo on Twitter and Cafferty lost his job. Soon the other driver admitted he might have gotten the situation wrong, but Cafferty's employer nonetheless fired him and has stood inexplicably by that decision. As of this writing, Cafferty is suing the company.[8]

Stories such as Cafferty's serve not only to punish the infracting individual, but also frighten the public in general that transgression will result in loss of status and employment and result in shame. "Cancellations" are nothing new and certainly not limited to the political left, but they've seemed to grow in frequency in recent years and truly accelerated in the moral puritanism that followed the murder of George Floyd at the hands of police officers in 2020. As with much of this tale, 2014 appears

---

* There are whole levels of absurdity both with white supremacists trying to co-opt the entirely inoffensive OK sign, and culture warriors on the left actually reinforcing this rather than denying it to them.

to have been a key year for acceleration of this trend. For instance, that year, the world became briefly transfixed by a teen girl who happened to smile (a largely reflexive action) while taking a photograph of herself at Auschwitz.[9] With all the actual horrors existing in the world, how did this bit of goofiness become international controversy?

All of this is to say that, for an issue as complicated as race relations in the United States, shame can get in the way of honest and nuanced discussions. Put simply, it can distort facts, result in self-censorship, and lead people into policies or worldviews that may make things much worse rather than better, all in the name of protecting ourselves from shame. This isn't just true for white Americans, for whom the shame of being labeled racist is among the worst possible humiliations, but also for black Americans, who, if they deviate from the accepted narrative of oppression, may be subjected to racist slurs from progressives ostensibly fighting against racism![10]

The reality is that the data do not find that the United States is a genocidal police state or even that race is a strong predictor of police behavior. Nor does there appear to be a "systemic racism" that benefits white Americans. White Americans are not, in fact, the ethnic group doing the best either in terms of police interactions or economic success in the modern United States. This does not mean that all is a utopia, and we are free of all racism. But there is a wide gap between an apartheid state and Whoville, and it is important to have a clear understanding of the actual data.

If we look to police violence in the United States, we find a morass of evidence that can be difficult to fully comprehend unless looked at from every angle. According to the *Washington Post*, which has been tracking police shootings since 2015, approximately one thousand individuals are shot by police in the United States each year, mostly armed, male, and between twenty and forty years old.[11] According to the *Washington Post*'s calculations, black Americans are shot by police at roughly twice the rate of white Americans (37 per million compared to 15 per million), with Hispanics in the middle (28 per million). Note that between 2015 and 2021, far more white Americans (2,962) were killed than black Americans (1,552) or Hispanic Americans (1,081). However, given the relative sizes of the underlying populations of white, black, and Hispanic

Americans, the per capita rate for black Americans is twice that of white Americans. Evidence for systemic racism in policing?

Nobody doubts that some police officers are racist, of course. But whether that is a widespread, indeed, systemic problem that explains this discrepancy is less clear. For instance, men are overwhelmingly represented as the targets of police shooting (95%), but we don't think police are sexist toward men. Men get shot by police more often because men are much more likely to get involved in the kinds of aggressive crime that are likely to provoke a shooting than are women. What everyone seems nervous to say out loud but is also undeniably true is that black and Hispanic men also tend to be overrepresented in the commission of violent crime compared to white men, once again, the sorts of activities likely to provoke a police shooting. According to Bureau of Justice statistics, black individuals are greatly overrepresented as perpetrators of violent crime (36% of such crimes versus 13% of the population) whereas white individuals are underrepresented (46% of violent crimes versus 60% of the population). Native Americans, though only a small percentage of the population (0.7%), were also overrepresented as perpetrators (1.9%). Hispanics were more evenly represented as perpetrators regardless of their race (i.e., black or white Hispanics; 18% of perpetrators versus 18% of the population).[12] And, by contrast, Asian Americans are vastly *underrepresented* as perpetrators (1.3% of perpetrators versus 5.7% of the population). I've created the figure on page 120 from the Bureau of Justice Statistics data to show these racial and ethnic representations regarding violent crime perpetration.

To be clear, it is not my intent to say certain racial groups are *inherently* prone to violent crime. Far from it. Multiple cultural and social issues undoubtedly contribute to this phenomenon, and it is critical we understand these dispassionately so as to reduce this violence. Further, the vast majority of people from these ethnic and racial groups are not involved in violent crime, so we're discussing a few outliers here. However, these numbers largely track those of police shootings, so it is important to understand these phenomena as parallel processes. This doesn't mean every police shooting is justified (though shootings of unarmed individuals are quite rare). But just as the overrepresentation of males among the targets of police shootings reflects something about men, these racial and ethnic discrepancies do seem to indicate real sources of stress in some

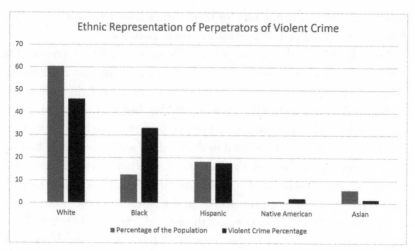

Graph created by the author using data from the Bureau of Statistics (2021).

communities. In the 2020 left-media climate a feeling arose that all police shootings were unjustified and due to racism. All police shootings are certainly tragic, but data suggesting racism is the key element is lacking. After all, the best outcome data for both police shootings and involvement in violent crime isn't for whites but for Asian Americans, but I'll return to that in a moment.

The good news (if we can think of anything about people being killed as "good news") about this is that shootings of unarmed individuals are comparatively rare. Of the 6,569 fatal shooting incidents between 2015 and 2021 in the *Washington Post* database, 421 (6.4%) involved unarmed individuals. Of these 421, 137 (32.5%) were black, 175 (41.5%) were white, 79 (18.8%) were Hispanic, whereas the rest weren't tracked for specific race/ethnicity (i.e., Asian, Native American, etc., were lumped together as "other"). In the figure on page 121, we see much the same pattern as with perpetrators of violent crimes.

Note, once again, more white individuals are actually shot than black individuals, but shootings of white Americans rarely get news attention, whereas shootings of black individuals often get international news attention. This creates a distorting effect, causing people to believe that the racial discrepancies are much clearer than they actually are, particularly if it becomes taboo to mention the violent crime data. Black Americans are

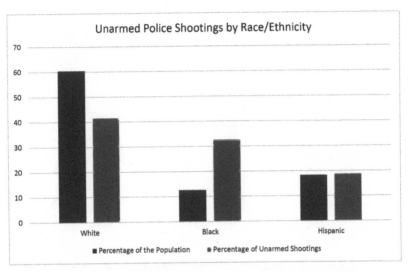

Graph created by the author using data from the Washington Post *(2021).*

overrepresented among unarmed victims of police shootings, but it's possible that this may be prompted in part by officers' awareness of racial disparities in *perpetration* of crime. This is still tragic when a particular shooting victim is unarmed (and as such, unfairly stereotyped), but we have to be honest about the full range of data if we are to reduce these incidents.

Fortunately, shootings of unarmed black individuals are rare. As of this writing, the United States is a country of 331 million (in fact, the third largest in the world), which includes roughly 41.4 million black Americans. According to the *Washington Post* data, fewer than twenty unarmed black Americans are unjustly shot by police in any given year. To be sure, the correct number should be zero (as it should be for white Americans, Hispanics, etc.). But that's hardly the genocide some have suggested. And the trend in these numbers generally has been decreasing. They are much lower than police shooting figures from earlier decades. Indeed, police shootings of black individuals have plummeted dramatically since the civil rights era.[13] The *Washington Post* data, which include only the years 2015 through 2021, shows a declining trend even during these years (however, 2021 data was available only through late September; nonetheless, it would require a dramatic uptick for the numbers to change much).

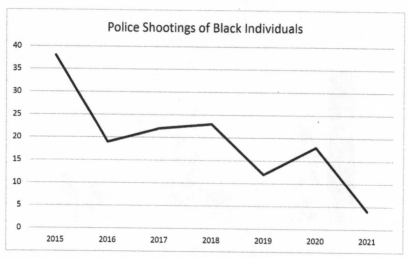

Graph created by the author using data from the Washington Post *(2021).*

So, generally, on the issue of police shootings of unarmed black individuals, there has been dramatic progress since the civil rights era, such that they are now exceedingly rare. Black individuals are still proportionally shot more often than white or Asian individuals, though racial and ethnic disparities in *perpetrating* crime are more likely contributing to this than racism in the more traditional sense (though awareness by police of those numbers may certainly result in the unfair, panicked targeting of some law-abiding citizens).

We can agree that there is a problem, though that problem is likely far smaller than many people think it is. Data about people's perceptions of police shootings suggest that people vastly overestimate the number of shootings of unarmed black people in the United States. A recent report of the Skeptic Research Center found that although actual police shootings of unarmed black individuals are less than a few dozen in even the worst recent year (2015), most people estimate that the number is more than one hundred, with many believing the number is more than one thousand or even ten thousand! No wonder some people think there's a genocide in progress in the United States! That's particularly true among progressives. Among the very liberal, 31.43 percent thought there were more than one thousand unarmed shootings of black Americans each year in the United States, with a further 22.15 percent believing the number was ten thousand or more![14]

But even if the numbers are far lower than we've been led to believe by news media, surely any discrepancy in race is bad. Absolutely true! However, the empirical evidence isn't even certain that race is the central variable. Here's a tricky situation. I'll get to economics in just a bit, but class or socioeconomic status and race are somewhat correlated. Or, put simply, there are more poor black Americans than there are poor white (or Asian) Americans. Most black Americans aren't poor, but proportionally they are overrepresented in lower socioeconomic strata. If we are concerned that *race* is the key variable, we'd expect a poor black American to be treated worse than a similarly poor white American. However, if *class* is the key variable, we'd expect to see poor white and poor black individuals treated similarly by police. Keeping in mind there are other confounding variables (black Americans, on average, are younger than white Americans), this is something that can be examined empirically.

Here the data are nuanced and not all studies agree. Some studies suggest that, accounting for class, black Americans nonetheless receive more fatal aggression from police.[15] However, other studies suggest that controlling for class completely eliminates any predictive value of race.[16] Still others suggest that context matters, with black individuals more often shot in urban areas, but white individuals more often shot in rural areas.[17] The study that is, to my mind, the best in this area, suggests that police may be slightly more aggressive in targeting black individuals for issues such as traffic stops and searches and other nonfatal interactions. Though such negative interactions may be quite rare compared to the backdrop of all police/civilian interactions that occur each year, we tend to remember negative interactions and these may nonetheless explain the perception many black Americans have of being unfairly treated by police. However, with class controlled, this study found no evidence of race being a predictor for fatal interactions with police.[18]

Some of my own research supports this. I, and some colleagues in Florida and Texas, have looked at the issue of race and policing from a few different angles. In one study we examined reports of excessive police aggression among all the municipal police departments in California. We wished to see what social variables might predict which police forces

experienced more such complaints. We found that racial demographics were, in fact, a poor predictor of police aggression. Black majority
communities didn't report more force than did white communities,
and reports of excessive police force were actually *lower* among Latino
communities. What did tend to predict excessive police force was the
amount of mental illness present in the community. This fits with other
data to suggest that mentally ill individuals are more likely to be shot by
police, as they may have difficulty complying with police instructions.[19]
According to some data, mentally ill individuals are sixteen times more
likely to be shot by officers than others in their community.[20] Our data
seems to fit with other studies suggesting race is not a factor in serious
acts of police violence.

Lest those on the right get too excited, this appears to be an issue that
cuts both ways. If class issues (mental health in this case) are a better
explanation for police violence than is racism, that also appears to be the
case for perpetration of violence as well. In another study we conducted,
we examined relationships between violent crime and social factors as well
as race in four high-crime American cities (Houston, Baltimore, Jackson,
Mississippi, and Wilmington, Delaware). Within these cities, in bivariate
analyses, higher proportions of black citizens were associated with higher
violent crime, consistent with other data. However, when we controlled
for class-based issues such as unemployment, low household income,
single-parent households, and even the proportion of sexually transmitted
diseases, these class factors predicted violent crime, but race itself did not.
Thus, to be very clear, black individuals are not inherently more prone to
violent crime but tend to more often experience the social class issues associated with violent crime. Nonetheless, contrary to what some appear to
believe, evidence suggests that police treat low-income white individuals
and low-income black individuals more or less the same.[21]

Failure to understand the nature of police violence can lead to bad
policy. This appears to occur in a repetitive cycle when news media
highlight unjust shootings of black individuals (but fail to highlight
unjust shootings of white individuals). Although the Michael Brown
shooting was ultimately found to be justified, it nonetheless touched off
widespread protests and riots against police that delegitimized policing.

This can cause what is sometimes referred to as the "Ferguson effect," named after Ferguson, Missouri, where the Brown shooting took place. The essence of this theory is that delegitimizing police causes police to pull back from patrols in fear of being the next bad guy highlighted by national news media and also may lead to citizens cooperating with police less. This ultimately leads to increased violent crime, mostly hurting the lower income, minority communities that protestors ostensibly protested to support in the first place. Following the riots and protests after the Michael Brown shooting, homicide rates spiked in many cities, particularly in lower income neighborhoods. However, the United States was also experiencing an opioid epidemic crisis at the same time, so it was unclear which might have contributed to the rise in homicides. Ultimately, data suggested that both had an effect. However, this highlights that policies or protests that broadly delegitimize policing (rather than focusing on specific reforms) can have a paradoxical effect of resulting in more deaths of black individuals due to homicide.[22] This is an example of how well-intentioned moral advocacy, when not carefully informed by the nuances of data and reacting to a single high-profile event, can actually cause more harm.

Thus, the evidence seems to suggest that class issues and mental health are big drivers of both violent crime and police force. To the extent there are racial disparities, they appear to be driven by these elements, more so than active racism on the part of police officers. This is not to say that there are no racist police officers, of course—our tendency to judge others based on differences appears so hardwired that it's difficult to stamp out entirely (though I'd suggest this is as true for progressive protesters as it is police officers). However, we also must have a sense of the fuller issue as this can help direct policies. For instance, those that target class issues may lift up all individuals who are struggling. If some racial minorities are disproportionally disadvantaged, they may still be aided in greater numbers but without leaving out poorer whites who may otherwise feel resentment. However, if racism isn't the key issue for police violence, perhaps it is for the economic issues that lead to the overrepresentation of some ethnic groups among low-income communities.

SYSTEMIC RACISM IN ECONOMICS

There are basically two ways to look at how racism influenced economics in the United States. The first is that, due to a history of slavery and Jim Crow in the United States, even if racism was vastly reduced since the 1960s, the legal playing field largely made equal, and some programs such as affirmative action specifically target minority advancement, it can simply take generations for wealth gaps to disappear and there's no "magic bullet" to change that. The second is the argument of "systemic racism," namely that whether intentional or not, there are still thumbs on the scales in favor of white Americans as compared to nonwhites and, as such, the United States remains a white supremacist state. Overall, the evidence supports the first view and falsifies the second. Once again, this is important to understand if we are not to enact policies that are harmful.

Ethnic disparities in wealth and income definitely exist in the United States, and there's little question that a history of slavery, Jim Crow, and past racist policies such as redlining (effectively segregating housing by race) contributed to disparities that continue to exist today. But there's an important distinction to be made: Are we still experiencing the sequelae of past racism, even if anti-black racism today is but a shadow of what it once was? Or are we today still in an effectively anti-black apartheid regime, where spoken or unspoken rules continue to put the thumb on the scale against black people? Knowing the difference helps us know what policies may help—or for that matter, actually hurt. In other words, we need to be sure, otherwise any decision we make may worsen rather than improve issues.

It's important to point out that not all disparities are due to racism or sexism. Otherwise, the criminal justice system is sexist against men (men are vastly overrepresented in prison), as is academia (men are generally falling behind women in educational success). The mental health system would be prejudiced against whites (whites are overrepresented both as victims of suicide and opioid overdoses). Some disparities are due to systemic injustices, some simply are not; even reflecting real differences among groups (for instance, although there are fewer women in STEM careers or among Fortune 500 CEOs, part of the issue may simply be that women are less interested in these careers than men). Of course, things can be complicated. For instance, I suspect few people would agree that centuries of explicit racism in the United States have no impact on today's disparities particularly influencing African Americans (I use this term deliberately here as we'll see in a bit). But as Wilfred Reilly has noted in his book *Taboo*, it's also important to recognize the impact of things such as fatherlessness, poorer academic outcomes, and even the comparative younger age of black versus white Americans.[23] Economist Glenn Lowry (a black man) makes much the same point—it is important to acknowledge historical impacts such as racism in the United States, but also cultural issues within communities, such as fatherlessness (which is more prevalent in, though hardly unique to, black families), that can maintain disparities.[24] Thus, as with the data on policing, we can look at disparate datasets together. For instance, according to the Pew Research Center, the average net worth of white families is approximately $144,000 in 2014 dollars, whereas for black families it is approximately $11,000.[25] Poverty rates among blacks (26%) and Latinos (24%) are much higher than among whites (10%) and Asians (12%). This is a real problem, and we should be concerned about this. However, as Lowry points out, black children are more likely to be raised in single-parent households (usually mothers, 57%) than are most other ethnicities (the numbers for whites and Asians are 18% and 12% respectively). So single-parent households both hold less wealth and can also contribute to disadvantages that affect later educational attainment.

The issue is people tend to ping-pong back and forth between two extremes—either there is systemic racism that explains these disparities, or this is an inherent "black" problem and therefore the rest of us can remain indifferent. Both of these are poor conclusions that only exacerbate the problem. To be clear, as with policing, these are class issues far more than race issues, and just as these data should not enforce beliefs in systemic racism, nor should they be used to support racist hereditarian views of disadvantage that promote inaction.

Unfortunately, racial or ethnic disparities can be difficult to undo, even in systems that are by and large democratic, just, and equitable. For instance, England has experienced significant waves of racial apartheid states due to successive invasions thousands of years ago (literally). The Anglo-Saxons largely replaced Celtic Britons in the fifth and sixth centuries ACE, creating a racially oppressive state.[26] In turn, the Anglo-Saxons were conquered by the Normans and themselves reduced to second-class status. Fascinatingly, some scholarship suggests that the disparities created by this 1066 ACE invasion of Anglo-Saxon England persist to the present day, as families with Norman last names such as D'Arcy or Mandeville still hold greater wealth than families with traditional Anglo-Saxon names such as Baker or Allwright—after almost a thousand years!

South Africa is another illustrative example. Long an apartheid state, South Africa's system of explicit racial segregation and oppression ended only in the early 1990s. Because, unlike in the United States, South Africa is by majority black, power largely transferred to the African National Congress, a party that had opposed apartheid (its most famous leader Nelson Mandela remains a powerful symbol of peaceful resistance). Although black South Africans now occupy a greater proportion of power than ever before, significant racial disparities remain among black and white South Africans.[27] Put simply, pervasive social issues simply aren't fixed easily in short time frames or even across several generations. That doesn't mean this is due to bad faith. No one thinks South Africa, the United States, or anywhere else on the planet is a racial utopia, but we must also remain alert to multiple explanations for disparities, not all of which imply an active apartheid state.

Nonetheless, many on the left speak of the United States as being white supremacist or "anti-black." But here's the most interesting data of all: if the United States is white supremacist, it's really bad at it, as some of the best economic outcomes are not experienced by whites (who are actually in the middle of the pack), but by East Asians, South Asians, Jewish, and black immigrants from Africa and the Caribbean (hence my previous distinction between African Americans descended from slaves and more recent waves of black immigrants unrelated to US slavery).

It is pretty well known that, according to US census data,[28] families with Asian ancestry have the highest household income, followed by white Americans, Hispanics, and black Americans. This, in fairness, obscures a considerable amount of variation within those groups (indeed some reports suggest income inequality among subethnicities of Asian Americans is considerable). In the figure on page 129, I've taken a smat-

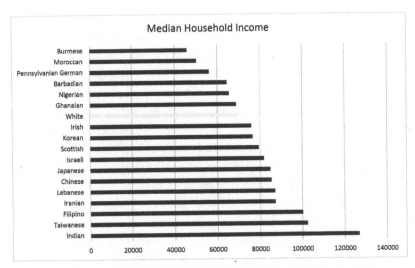

Graph created by the author using data from the US Census Bureau (2021).

tering of census data[29] from varying ethnic groups living in the United States to compare them to the mean white American household income (including my own ethnic subgroups of Scottish and Irish). This is, of course, a partial list designed to illustrate a point.

As can be seen, many South and East Asian groups outperform median white Americans, as do people from some Middle Eastern cultures such as Lebanon and Iran (and, of course, Israel despite the potential of anti-Semitism). People from some African or Caribbean groups such as Ghanese, Nigerians, or Barbadians are very close to the median white income. These numbers are particularly interesting, hinting that the income and other issues facing black Americans are less due to anti-blackness (which should also impact these other groups) than to specific issues relevant to the black American community. Obviously, the historical legacy of slavery and Jim Crow (which is different in concept from an ongoing systemic racism) are part of this, as are issues such as fatherlessness and comparatively high crime. It's a complicated issue that, if we're being honest, gives everyone something to be embarrassed about, which is why it's so difficult to discuss rationally. But until we do, the problems will remain.

It's also interesting to note, within these ethnicities, how subgroups differ. Even among white Americans, for instance, my fellow Scots and Irish are doing a bit better than the median, whereas Pennsylvania Germans are doing relatively poorly. This is an excellent example of how not all disparities are due to injustice, racism, etcetera. Presumably the United States isn't out to get Pennsylvania Germans; rather, issues related specifically to that culture contribute to income disparities. Similarly, though many Asian groups are doing well, others such as the Burmese are not doing as well economically. Nonetheless, it's absurd to suggest that the United States is warmly welcoming Indians and Chinese but not Burmese. Something more complicated is going on. Once again, economic data can't be divorced from other data, whether on crime and fatherlessness on one hand or political and "elite" disengagement from poorer communities on the other.

The good news is that average household incomes are going up across the board. The bad news is, even with overall increases, disparities among groups remain because no group is remaining stagnant. Figuring out how to fix these disparities will take both time and finesse, the latter in short supply in modern polemical and ad hominem debates.

I'm not going to claim to have the magic wand that, if only given unfettered power, I could fix everything to the acclaim of everyone. But I remain optimistic it can be done with sound, data-based policy, the requirement that we become more honest about inconvenient and ugly data on both sides of these equations and focus primarily on social and educational policies that can help disadvantaged children of any race escape the cycle of school disengagement, poverty, fatherlessness, and crime.

So, we're not experiencing a genocide or an apartheid state. The United States is not riven by systemic racism, but it is riven by racial disharmony. Disparities do exist, but their nature is complex and multi-faceted. We can't erase the ugly history of slavery and Jim Crow, nor even in an egalitarian present is it easy to just wave away their legacies. Moving forward is possible, but this would require a dispassionate and honest appraisal of messy data, shielded from the polemics and confirmation bias of polarized electoral politics. That sounds tough, but I'm convinced we can do it. So, what's stopping us?

THE AVAILABILITY CASCADE OF
THE POLITICAL AND SOCIAL LEFT

The political right have a lot to answer for with their elite-favoring policies and race baiting and xenophobia, most glaring under the administration of Donald Trump. But I think it's important first to understand
the implosion of all sense of reason and proportionality on the left that
occurred beginning around 2014 and most notable after the murder of
George Floyd in 2020. Specifically, I believe that this failure on the left
directly cost the lives of many black Americans in the aftermath of the
2020 protests and riots but more on this in a bit.

In September 2021, photographs emerged of Border Patrol agents on
horseback trying to contain Haitian immigrants who'd managed to get to
the southern US border in Texas. An estimated fifteen thousand immigrants had arrived at the border, fleeing dire environmental, economic,
and political conditions in their native Haiti. The Biden administration
would send most back either to Haiti or to Mexico. We can debate the
merits of this policy and the understandable tension between compassion and immigration control, but that wasn't what attracted the most
furor. As vastly outnumbered Border Patrol agents tried to keep order,
photographs emerged of them whipping Haitian immigrants in scenes
Congresswoman Maxine Waters claimed were worse than the slavery
era. President Joe Biden, responsible for the policy of turning most of
these desperate immigrants away, declared of the Border Patrol agents,
"These people will pay."[30]

Except that wasn't what happened at all. In fact, the Border Patrol
agents were holding reins for controlling their horses, not whips. There
is, as of this writing, no evidence that anyone was whipped, and even
the photographer who took those photographs acknowledged this. Why
were so many people willing to rush to judgment, perhaps forever alter-
ing the lives of those Border Patrol agents, without due process or waiting for a sober assessment of the facts?

George Floyd was killed in May 2020 when officer Derek Chauvin
kneeled on his neck, causing or at very least significantly contributing
to his suffocation. Floyd was no saint, having been involved in prior

crimes, including a brutal home invasion, and more recently for trying to use counterfeit money. But he also had been involved in charity work and appeared to generally care for his community. My impression is that he was one of these unfortunate souls lost in our system, who might have benefited from a comprehensive approach to substance abuse and mental health. He certainly did not deserve to die over a $20 bill, even if, as is often the case with police brutality cases, he had mental challenges that made it difficult for him to safely comply with police requests. Officer Chauvin was convicted of the murder in 2021, and as of this writing, three other officers present at the scene also face charges.

Floyd's death set off a firestorm of both peaceful protests and violent riots during the summer of 2020, the same summer riven by the COVID-19 outbreak, which is probably no coincidence. But this outpouring broke the dam on many radical ideas that had been percolating in left-wing circles for a decade or so. Suddenly words like "systemic racism," "white supremacy," and "anti-racism" became popularized, as did the view that the modern United States was akin to a genocidal apartheid state. Many people likely were stunned by this sudden change in the culture. What had happened? Was the country they knew so vastly different than they had thought? Only slowly has it come out that the data don't really support this left narrative, as I've explained a bit earlier. If so—if the data don't support this worldview of an irredeemably racist United States—how did it achieve such prominence so quickly?

In fairness, the groundwork had been laid decades earlier, through academic approaches such as critical race theory[31] (CRT). Briefly, this theory posits that race issues occupy a central position at most social exchanges, people can be separated by race into oppressor and oppressed groups, cultural, economic, and political systems are developed to maintain these power systems, and liberal virtues such as free speech, scientific objectivity, and due process merely maintain this status quo. This theory was developed within law schools but has slowly spread throughout academia and even into K–12 pedagogy.

Much of the groundwork for its influence was laid by worthwhile social projects. For instance, explicit racism has dropped precipitously in the United States, and despite the race-baiting of President Trump, that has continued in recent years as well.[32] This, of course, is excellent news.

That doesn't mean racism doesn't exist at all nor that we shouldn't be vigilant for incidents of real, explicit racism, but it's also news to celebrate. As part of this positive trend, being labeled a racist (or other terms implying prejudice such as homophobe, transphobe, or sexist) has taken on enormous social stigma, such that individuals will try to avoid these labels at great cost. Again, this isn't necessarily a bad thing, so long as these labels are used when people engage in clear examples of prejudicial behavior.

Yet, when terms become stigmatized, they are also easy to weaponize and simply using the terms, whether deserved or not, can stop any reasonable debate. If one questions the effectiveness of affirmative action, for instance, one can be labeled a racist, quickly shutting down any discussion. If we incentivize the weaponization of such terms by silencing ourselves (and such terms are quickly used against dissenting minorities as well as those in the majority), that further incentivizes their future use. It can result in a cycle of fear that leads to "The Emperor's New Clothes" effect: everyone knows that something about the predominating worldview (and, for all their complaints about power, progressive worldviews are enormously powerful) is wrong, yet most people are afraid to speak up against it. This is further enforced by what is called *standpoint epistemology* wherein it is assumed that only people from marginalized groups have the personal experience to speak to racism, transphobia, and so forth. Of course, people from historically marginalized communities should be listened to and their viewpoints respected. But they are not immune to the various self-serving biases that affect us all and their perspectives still need to be exposed to the harsh realities of data. Nonetheless, this use of shame coupled with standpoint epistemology (which, again, does not protect dissenting members of those marginalized communities from attack[33]) is incredibly effective at silencing dissenters, particularly among those within left-leaning communities such as academia, news media, K–12 education, and human resources departments.

Consider the case of Paul Rossi (mentioned briefly in chapter 3). Rossi was a teacher at the private Grace Church School. He became concerned that his school's antiracism policies were indoctrinating kids in ideas rooted in CRT. Rossi was concerned that this ideology was, itself, racist: shaming people for their race, setting up conflicts between students based in race, and using coercion to stifle disagreement by students, whether white or non-white. Rossi believed that these approaches, however ostensibly couched in the language of virtue, could do harm to students (and there are good psychological reasons to agree). For openly critiquing these policies, Rossi was removed from teaching and kicked off campus. The school disparaged him for his comments, claiming they contained "glaring omissions and inaccuracies."[34] However, before he left the school, he recorded a conversation with his headmaster in which the headmaster (who had publicly condemned Rossi), *agreed* with him, saying, "the fact is that I'm agreeing with you that there has been a demonization that we need to get our hands around, in the way in which people are doing this understanding . . . We're demonizing ki—. . . . We're demonizing white people, for being born. . . . We are using language that makes them feel less than, for nothing that they are personally responsible for."[35] This is a clear example of how during moments of intense social pressure people may say one thing publicly, but their true thoughts are revealed to be something entirely different in what they think is a private conversation.

Here's how this comes together. In an essay in *Quillette* Matthew Blackwell discussed how an availability cascade occurs.[36] It begins with the availability heuristic I've discussed previously in this book. Basically, people tend to overestimate the frequency of an occurrence if they can easily recall examples of it, and shocking incidents tend to be easy to recall. This happens with mass homicides, for instance, which people tend to assume are far more frequent than they actually are. On the issue of police killings of unarmed black Americans—even if such incidents are remarkably rare, happening perhaps one or two dozen times a year in a country of 330 million, which, according to the *Washington Post* data, is about the actual frequency—that's enough for news media to highlight such a story every few weeks. In other words, if news media decide that the topic of police shootings of black Americans is "trendy" (for lack of a better word), they can highlight such killings, while ignoring police killings of white individuals or those of other ethnicities (Latino, Asian, etc.). As a consequence of being exposed to this news media, people come to think police killings of unarmed black individuals are much more common than they actually are, while thinking that police killings of unarmed white individuals are much rarer than they are. Hence, such a large proportion of the US population, particularly progressives already primed not to trust the police, believe thousands of unarmed black Americans are killed by police each year, when the actual number is magnitudes smaller.

News media do this sort of thing all the time. "If it bleeds, it leads" is an old cliché, but news media really do get hung up on "trendy" social narratives and tend to exaggerate them. Like any media, they have an audience to pander to. I remember some years ago getting a call from a reporter in St. Louis about what she considered an epidemic of the "Knockout Game" in the city. The idea (mostly a myth) of the Knockout Game is that youth try to knock out a stranger with just one punch and "get points" or some such (note how often adults think teens engage in primitive point-accruing rituals) for succeeding. Of course, it's an unfortunate reality of humanity that youth commit assaults, sometimes against strangers, and have been doing so since the dawn of humanity. The reporter was calling because a stranger attack had just occurred in St. Louis and people were worried there was an "epidemic" on their hands. I asked them when the last stranger attack had occurred, and it was about a year previous. So, news media were inclined to see an epidemic based on two incidents occurring nearly a year apart!

Unfortunately, this is kind of what news media do because panic sells. Once a social narrative has emerged that something is *very bad, very upsetting*, news media tend to search desperately for news stories to fit the narrative and ignore cases or evidence that conflict with it. Again, this is because they know what sells and, like all of us, need to put food in their bellies.

The only question is whether news media *cause* these false beliefs or pander to an audience that already believes them. The answer, though complex, seems to lean toward the latter. In one recent study, I examined whether the decline in race relations during the past few years was related to actual incidents of fatal police shootings of unarmed black individuals or news media coverage of those same police shootings. The outcome: race relations were not related to the actual incidence of police shootings, which are rare and declining. However, race relations are correlated with news media coverage of police shootings. In other words, whatever is happening in race relations and in news media coverage, it is not connected to the actual phenomenon of police shootings. However, the data suggested that, although the two phenomena were operating in tandem, it wasn't clear that news media were *causing* the decline in race relations.[37] Instead, they may have been catering to audience feelings that already existed. That's an important distinction to my mind—albeit an unfortunate one that lacks an obvious fix if news media aren't the proximal cause of our declining race relations. I hope to further analyze long-term trends in follow-up research.

So, if the issue is that people are being misled by the availability heuristic, why not just make the actual data on police shootings (and other issues related to economics and so forth) clear? Such data don't suggest that there's nothing at all wrong with our current state of race issues, of course, but do suggest that things are much better than many people believe. Panicking people with the belief that they're likely to be shot by police every time they leave home is clearly not in their best interests, given the data suggest that this isn't at all true. So why don't people speak up more?

This brings us to the shaming nature of a moral availability cascade. Wrong beliefs fostered by the availability heuristic are one part of it. But then those wrong beliefs are socially reinforced by shaming anyone who disagrees with them. Thus, if you don't believe the United States is inherently, structurally racist or anti-black, it's easy to be referred to as a racist for disagreeing. Given the shame associated with that label, it's easier to pretend to go along than to raise doubts, even if the doubts are obvious and shared by most. Shame and fear breed conformity, pure and simple. This can be exacerbated when advocacy groups use names like Black Lives Matter. The naming is clever—the sentiment behind it is obvious. However, the result is that the organization itself might be advocating policies that are actually harmful to black individuals but criticizing it is difficult because doing so may appear to criticize the innocuous and uncontroversial sentiment it selected as a name (this kind of naming is a version of motte-and-bailey arguments, wherein something controversial or problematic shields itself with an adjacent concept that is unassailable). Will Smith inadvertently highlighted this when he recently said, "anybody who tries to debate Black Lives Matter looks ridiculous."[38] He's right, although he himself appears to be conflating the sentiment for the organization, though the two are not the same thing. Smith, like many others, has fallen into this motte-and-bailey trap.*

The problem is that this conformity can lead to catastrophically bad policy or social decisions. Hence 2020 saw various "defund the police" or "abolish the police" efforts. Some of these were quite literal, whereas other advocates suggested these terms weren't meant literally (however, arguing that your slogan doesn't mean what any reasonable person would think it means simply indicates you have a bad slogan). This was part of a general disrepute of the police, with ACAB (i.e., "all cops are bastards") graffiti scrawled at many protest/riot sites, violent clashes between antifa groups and the police, and even a movement to remove police from television, including the puppy cop in *PAW Patrol*.[39] This type of anti-cop sentiment can result both in reduced patrols, particularly in high-risk neighborhoods (lest they be involved in the next career-ending incident caught on camera), and reduced citizen cooperation with police due to lack of trust.

The year 2020 saw a massive spike in homicides, particularly in urban environments such as Minneapolis, Chicago, and New York City. Undoubtedly, both the COVID-19 pandemic and the protests and riots after George Floyd's murder played a role in this. However, as with 2015, the timing of the homicide spike appears to have been specific to the outburst of protests and riots in 2020.[40] I wish to be clear: people have the constitutional right to peacefully protest and I fully support this right for those protesting the death of George Floyd (COVID-19 risks notwithstanding). But to the extent that the protests/riots delegitimized policing and that the beliefs of the protestors may have been ill-informed, the black lives matter movement may reasonably be criticized for having led to the deaths of many more black individuals than were saved due to reduced police presence. But raising this concern is perilous because, as Will Smith demonstrated, people are stuck on slogans and afraid to dig into the sticky nuances of data, lest they appear ridiculous.

---

* Ironically, Smith has since had his own major controversy, slapping Chris Rock for making a joke about his wife at the Oscars. Perhaps no longer the best person to tell us what's ridiculous.

THE AVAILABILITY CASCADE OF
THE POLITICAL AND SOCIAL RIGHT

I've spent a lot of time critiquing the left on this issue and, particularly given the spike in homicides after 2020, I think this is warranted. But let's not pretend the political right are innocent. After all, they elected an explicitly xenophobic and racist president in 2016, and we're staring down the nadir of his possible reelection in 2024 (as I write this, Joe Biden has generally proven himself something of a dud as president, so it's not a trivial worry).

Much of the right's hysteria about race mirrors the kind of bad information and availability cascades on the left. For instance, it's a fact that young black men are overrepresented as perpetrators of violent crime. However, this is not because they are *black* but because they are more likely to live in circumstances of considerable social stress. I touched on this earlier with a study examining this issue in several high-crime cities in the United States, specifically Houston, Wilmington, Delaware, Jackson, Mississippi, and Baltimore. As is the case for national data, young black men were overrepresented as perpetrators of violent crime. However, when we adjusted for other social factors related to poverty, community stress, or environmental conditions (crowding, pollution, etc.), race was no longer a predictor of violent crime. In other words, if we're going to make the argument that a young white man from a difficult background is just as likely to be shot by police as a young black man from a difficult background, it is also the case that that young white man is as likely to commit a violent crime as a young black man. In other words, race does not make people violent, difficult social circumstances do.[41]

Similarly, many on the right tend to assume that immigrants, particularly illegal immigrants from Latin American countries, are particularly prone to violence (this was reflected in President Trump's comments about illegal immigrants being criminals and rapists). In fact, evidence suggests that illegal immigrants are far less likely to commit violent crimes than are US citizens.[42] But the conservative news bubble works the same as the progressive news bubble, with choice anecdotes and comments from political leaders reinforcing people's a priori biases and neuroses.

When we look at declining race relations, it may be tempting to think this mainly has to do with progressives assuming there is more racism than there actually is, and undoubtedly that's part of it. But it may also relate to overblown fears of immigrants, Muslims, and ethnic minorities among at least some people on the right. The irony is evident from recent voting patterns suggesting that ethnic minorities are shifting slowly toward the conservative side. This could be a windfall for the Republican Party if only it could jettison its pandering of extreme xenophobes on their fringe and consider popular economic strategies beneficial to all Americans while remaining true to conservative social values. That the Republicans have proven unable to do so, thus far mired in a cult of Trumpism, is yet another example of catastrophic decision making.

FINAL THOUGHTS

The past decade has seen a stunning decline in race relations, which had been reasonably good during the previous decade. There is no evidence that social conditions have worsened for racial minorities during this time period, whether we look at policing, economics, or other indicators. However, rhetoric about race has ratcheted up to feverish levels on both the left and right. Figuring out how to fix what problems do exist, assure people they needn't worry when a concern is unfounded in the data, and focus on community and unity rather than division—the old racism of the right or the neo-racism of the "anti-racist" left—will take calm rationality and an ability to consider data dispassionately. Until we recover the ability to do so and remember our commitment to free speech, open debate, and respect for all, we will continue to hurtle toward social catastrophe.

8

JUMPING THE SHARK

In October 2021, protestors from a group called Insulate Britain glued themselves to major roads in London (yes, I'm still wondering exactly how gluing oneself to a road works, too), blocking traffic. Motorists were understandably furious, particularly as reports suggest the protestors may have blocked an ambulance and definitely blocked one woman anxious to visit her elderly mother who'd just been taken to the hospital.[1] What does Insulate Britain want? Pretty much what it says on the tin: it wants the government to provide up-to-date insulation for housing and make all UK homes energy efficient to combat climate change.[2] Details about what taxes would pay for this aside, that's not an inherently unreasonable goal. But its tactics of annoying the general public and the optics of preventing people from accessing health care (or attending to other emergencies) is almost certainly catastrophic in relation to public support for its cause. What was it thinking?

Hey, it's getting attention, for one thing. Even I'm writing about it. People can mistake attention for progress (watch how People for the Ethical Treatment of Animals [PETA] has floundered for decades). Adopting bad strategies or bad methods can actually hinder support for or progress toward otherwise worthwhile goals. And sometimes this can have truly catastrophic consequences. In this chapter, I'll take a look at the issue of climate change and why it's been so hard to come to a consensus about what to do about it.

If you've been living in an isolated shack these last few decades (thanks for venturing out to get this book), climate change (previously "global warming"—note how it got rebranded) refers to concerns that pollutants produced by humans, whether through industry, travel, or agriculture (cows fart a lot of methane as it turns out, and just like all aspects of climate change, there are really dumb internet debates about just how dire cow farts are for the planet) are contributing to an overall heating of the planet that is, well, bad in a lot of ways. This used to be called "global warming" until some winters proved to be extremely cold, confusing the rubes without PhDs, so now we talk about "climate change."[3]

I'm gonna start by stating an obvious thing: I know less than nothing about climate change science. I'd like to think I'm a pretty smart guy (though finding some who disagree probably wouldn't be too hard), but geophysics just isn't my gig. Like most people, I have to make a decision to trust (or not trust) the eggheads with doctorates in this stuff, hope they're not too far down the rabbit hole of institutional capture (when institutions begin saying false things to make their members or audience happy), and let a bit of common sense guide the way. Then again, common sense is neither common, objective, or even tethered to reality, so we'll see. But, to get it out of the way, my general sense is that whatever the truth may be about climate change, pumping pollutants into the atmosphere *can't* be a good thing and looking for ways to reduce that without cratering our standard of living is a reasonable goal.

So, why listen to me? This chapter is less about the science of climate change itself and more about the way people are trying to affect change and whether that's working; we're looking at human behavior, persuasion, and thinking. So why are people so *angry* and *nasty* with each other over climate change? Are we really on the cusp of annihilation, or should we fire up the vintage '70s Buick and let it run in the driveway for no good reason?

A BRIEF AND ADMITTEDLY '80S NOSTALGIC HISTORY OF ENVIRONMENTALISM

Environmental catastrophizing is nothing new, of course. I remember as a precious lad becoming aware of a wider world beyond GI Joe action figures,* Space Invaders, and sledding in winter† that included stuff like holes in the ozone layer and acid rain. Ah, the good old days when a dip in the pond could melt flesh. These were real issues, though nobody talks much about them anymore.

Ozone is a molecule consisting of three oxygen atoms. It's rare at ground level although lightning can produce it, and it's ozone that gives the air its characteristic smell during or after a thunderstorm.[4] Don't suck it in too eagerly though—ozone is poisonous and destroys lung tissue. In the upper layers of the atmosphere, ozone absorbs UV radiation, acting as a kind of sunscreen for the Earth. Strip it away and everyone gets a really bad sunburn (oh, and cancer). It turned out that the release of chlorofluorocarbons (CFCs), commonly found in cooling devices like air conditioning and refrigerators, was depleting ozone. Good news: a simple switch (albeit expensive for anyone with old air-conditioning units) to different coolants cuts down on CFC emissions and the ozone layer is (mostly) fixed.[5] Voilà, environmentalism at its best.

The story of acid rain is kind of similar. Acid rain is caused by pollutants from cars and factories (sulfur dioxide and nitrogen oxides, specifically). Once up in the atmosphere, they change the pH of rain to acid. This, in turn, changes Bob Ross's happy little trees into decidedly unhappy stumps and kills wildlife in ponds. In the '70s and '80s, the United States and Canada struggled against industry (and sometimes each other) to reduce emissions of these poisonous gases and also to remove acid from lakes and ponds using acid-eating bacteria and alkaline substances. With concerted, determined effort, the problem of acid rain has been reduced greatly in North America.[6] For some middle school science fair project, I remember testing the acidity of ponds in my local area in Rhode Island. I think I won third prize for that. Impossible to do now, as the ponds are mostly fixed (at least on that issue).

So, it's possible to identify an environmental problem and, with concerted effort, fix it and roll back the damage we're doing to the environment. I don't want to be Pollyannaish about either of these—both took decades and faced considerable resistance from industry. But advocates stayed on message, resisted the urge to indulge in culture war, and

---

* They are *not* dolls. Stop it.
† It would be years before I came to my senses and moved to Florida.

developed interventions that didn't require life-altering sacrifices from the general populace (other than the price tag for that new central air unit). Why can't we do this with climate change?

Resistance on climate change from various industries is to be expected. But, unlike the issues of acid rain and ozone holes, with climate change, the issue slipped into dumb internecine culture-war squabbles on both sides, which I'd argue many scholars themselves got caught up in (as did journalists who increasingly saw themselves as advocates). Further, some of the proposed "fixes" would require rather extreme sacrifices from the general populace, from eschewing all air travel to becoming vegans (a hard pass from me—if my avoiding steak is what's required to save the planet, the world is gonna burn*) to effectively dismantling capitalism and enduring what even proponents appear to acknowledge would be significant reductions in standards of living, economic recession, and more authoritarian quasi-Marxist governmental systems.[7] If fighting climate change is going to require people to live like they did in 1920, 1820, or 1720, that's just not going to happen. Climate change activists may counter that will happen anyway once the climate emergency is upon us, and they may be 100 percent right. But human behavior just doesn't work that way, so we're going to need to figure out something else.

WHY DON'T PEOPLE PRIORITIZE CLIMATE CHANGE?

If we're going to figure out solutions to climate change, we have to understand the psychological blocks that make it difficult for people to get on board. Grousing that "people suck" or expecting massive changes in people's behavior isn't going to help. Figuring out policies that work well with human behavior can. It helps to understand that other societies have managed to survive and thrive through periods of calamitous climate change,[8] and apocalyptic language today may be getting in the way of progress. If the ancient Romans could do it, we can too, but we have to understand the psychology behind how people make decisions in order to organize policies that will work.

---

* In my own defense, I have some dietary issues I won't bore you with but that make eating most vegetables and fruits more difficult for me than the average person. Nonetheless, I won't deny enjoying burgers and steaks either.

For some time, psychologists have wondered why people don't do more to combat climate change. In what is perhaps the classic paper on this, psychology professor Robert Gifford at the University of Victoria highlights the main roadblocks to individuals contributing to mitigating climate change.[9] Here are some of the main blocks from his work.

Cognitive limitations. Put simply, climate change is a complex problem, and it can be hard to wrap our minds around it. It's a bit hard to notice in real time (Is Florida really getting hotter? Hard to say, it was always hot . . .); our brains aren't really wired to prioritize long-term problems, and we tend to perceive our own ability to contribute as being fairly limited. If it's really another generation's problem (since we'll be in the ground before it really hits hard), and there's not much we can do as individuals, why do anything?

Worldviews. People may not want to take action on climate change because they hold various worldviews opposed to doing so. Some of these may be quite reasonable (perhaps Dr. Gifford would disagree with me on that score), whereas others perhaps are less so. This may include everything from being in favor of free-market capitalism and suspicious of regulation, to being caught in the current political death spiral and wanting to "own the libs" and being willing to let the world boil to do so (I admit the libs are so annoying sometimes that "owning" them is an understandable goal, but maybe this isn't the hill to die on).

This can be a tricky issue to deal with, since confronting worldviews head-on with anger, sarcasm, and snideness (the general fare of internet discourse) tends to backfire, entrenching people into their positions rather than persuading. The worldview bias issue isn't just an issue for the right—just as people on the right may disbelieve climate change because that's what people on the right do, people on the left may believe in climate change because that's what people on the left do (even though they are no more personally informed). So, the whole thing becomes a partisan mud fight that simply entrenches people more.

Social comparisons. People tend to be motivated by how they perceive themselves in comparison to others. If there's perceived inequity in the system, that tends to produce relatively little buy-in. That's one good reason why wealthy celebrities or politicians showing off their Priuses while jetting around in private helicopters and planes make terrible role models for climate change. It can come across as pretentious and hypocritical. Why should the struggling coal miner with a family of six listen to someone preening around on the red carpet? Local outreach through communities can be much more effective.

Sunk costs. The more we invest in a thing, the less likely we are to want to pull loose from it. This can cause people to invest in things that are bad for the environment but be reluctant to give them up. Car ownership is an excellent example of this, but in general the push toward greater affluence and consumption is also part of it. Convincing people they need to give up their washing machines and go back to clotheslines while living in smaller houses and eschewing most travel by car and plane is simply a hard sell. I've said earlier, changing from a carnivore to a vegetarian diet would be difficult for me.

If the message is, basically, "you need to live a worse life than your parents did and probably by far," it's going to be difficult to change people's behavior. Trying to force it isn't likely to be super successful. Looking for incremental changes that can be effective without provoking resistance can be a lot more productive.

Distrust. Part of the problem is simply that trust in experts and politicians has steadily eroded during the past few decades. Some of this is due to self-inflicted wounds by the scientific community itself. Perhaps the most stunning example was something called Climategate. In 2009, hackers released thousands of emails and files stolen from climate scientists at the University of East Anglia. The emails appeared to suggest that climate scientists were basically rigging the data on climate change, although the scientists complained conservative news media were taking some choice statements out of context. People continue to argue over the significance of the emails, and the scientific community has stood behind the scientists in this case (which is hardly going to convince skeptics, since the whole perception was that scientists were rigging the game).

My own perception is that some of the emails do reveal that scientists are human. Sometimes they're careless about what they say in emails. Is there some hint that there could be an ideological bias among climate scientists? I think there may have been and, frankly, given how common that is to science, I would have been more surprised by its absence. But I think there are some legitimate concerns climate scientists may not be as open to counter-hypothesis data on climate change as would ideally be the case. Some of the emails do suggest a hostility to attempts to publish skeptical data in scientific journals, and that's not good. On the other hand, was there evidence of anything like fraud or deliberately tricking or fooling the public? I don't think so. It's neither the death blow to climate science some folks on the right portrayed it to be nor is it the complete nothingburger some on the left suggested. As usual, everybody entrenched, nobody talked to one another, and neither side did any soul-searching. But even this little peek behind the curtain portraying scientists as human was enough to reduce at least some public confidence in climate science.[10]

Other organizations such as the American Psychological Association have reduced confidence in science by taking factually untrue positions on issues such as video game violence[11] or by appearing to condone therapeutic approaches for men and boys that are likely harmful and many perceive to be something close to sexist.[12] As noted earlier in the book, scholars leaned in heavily on progressive causes such as during the George Floyd protests and riots in 2020, taking positions supporting protests during COVID-19. Such behaviors reinforce public perception of scholars as crusading liberals, not disinterested experts.

Undoubtedly, the social sciences and humanities are in rougher shape than the hard sciences, but with goofy "decolonize science and math" movements spreading, all the sciences are rapidly approaching a credibility crisis. We need to reverse that to move forward with important initiatives that are data based. Some of these, like climate change, may align nicely with progressive goals whereas others may not. But science needs to follow data, not political and social narratives. On that score, we've increasingly lost our way and public distrust is often a self-inflicted wound.

Perceived risk. Changing behavior always comes with perceived risks. If I switch from driving a car to public transport, will I be late for work more often or, for that matter, catch the next plague being spread through crowded places? How much is all this going to cost? If I'm already struggling to support my family, is this going to put me over the edge? If the perceived risks are higher than immediate gains (not just the abstract idea of global temperatures), it's tough to get people to change their behavior.

Limited behavior. People often tend to engage in small, token behaviors toward a moral goal. They'll happily recycle, as this has few costs, but not take more substantive action (recycling, it must be said, is one example of how to utilize small behaviors toward positive outcomes). Or they'll "rebound," assuming positive action in one area gives them license in others. For instance, perhaps an individual eschews air travel but then takes driving trips he or she wouldn't otherwise take. Most often, people aren't really aware of this. They think they're doing good, perhaps better than they actually are.

Fixing these issues will, itself, require complex and sophisticated efforts. Some aspects of human nature simply can't be changed. But it may be possible to work within human limitations to help people identify concrete behavior changes that are keyed toward minimizing personal sacrifice as much as possible while providing concrete incentives to mitigate any unavoidable sacrifices. For instance, it may prove difficult to convince most people to switch from eating juicy steaks to twigs and leaves, but if scientists can develop cost-effective, lab-grown meat or plant-based meat substitutes that actually taste like meat,* that may be a more probable route. Public trust in science must be restored, but this can only occur when scientists adopt more transparent and honest approaches to science and make an active effort to divorce science from the ideological biases that are now common among scholars. This may, for instance, require examining ways to include more conservatives among scientific communities. This also will require people to stop screaming at each other and, on this score, both sides are to blame. People need to glue themselves to roads less and do the harder work of persuading, listening, and dialoguing. Persuasion requires patience, persistence, civility, and humility. Let's see how this might work in regard to climate science.

JUMPING THE SHARK

Let's admit one thing up front: people are drawn to ridiculous and alarming claims, even if those claims aren't true. Get those claims out in front

---

* Having tried some recent burger substitutes, they're getting a bit closer than the ridiculousness of tofu, but they're not quite there yet.

of enough people and, absent any fact checking, some of those people will kind of buy those claims. This may look like a success for an advocacy effort.

A classic example is the well-known fact that the movie *Jaws*, released in 1975, so frightened people about the almost nonexistent threat of shark attacks that human civilization set out to kill sharks, leading to massive worldwide shark depopulation. This talking point connects widespread beliefs in the power of fictional media effects on viewers with a very real problem. Shark populations absolutely declined during the latter half of the twentieth century. Now we understand why: Steven Spielberg's famous monster movie is a major contributor to the problem. In fact, the link has been so well-established that even the author of the novel on which the movie was based, Peter Benchley, later regretted writing the novel.

Except that's not true at all. In fact, there's no evidence that *Jaws* contributed to shark depopulation. And though Peter Benchley did say in some interviews that he felt *Jaws* had indulged some already common misconceptions about sharks, he did not say he believed the novel caused shark depopulation. As we can see in the figure below,[13] shark depopulation

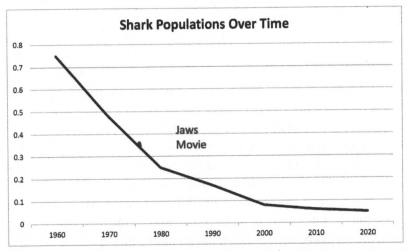

Shark Populations Over Time

Data from Roff, G., Brown, C., Priest, M., & Mumby, P. (2018). Decline of coastal apex shark populations over the past half century. **Communications Biology, 1**, Retrieved from: https://www.nature.com/articles/s42003-018-0233-1

was already well underway by the time the *Jaws* movie was released, and *Jaws* had little effect on the trend.

The data in the graph are for great white sharks, the subject of *Jaws*, though similar patterns are seen for other shark species. The other data we can note is that movies highlighting the dangers of other animals such as alligators have not resulted in similar depopulation. In fact, alligator populations have soared in the United States due to conservation efforts, even as scary movies about alligators continue to do well in theaters (*Crawl* being the most recent as of this writing). So, it if wasn't the *Jaws* movie what done it, what happened?

Simple. Shark depopulation is due to overfishing, and shark and shark fins are considered a delicacy in many countries. We don't need a more complex story about scary movies and gullible audiences. People were terrified of sharks long before *Jaws* came out and with good reason: sometimes sharks do indeed eat people, even if shark attacks are generally rare. The cause is good: conservation of shark populations, but the story here is just wrong. Nonetheless, it's such a good story that people keep on telling it. However, telling falsehoods in support of an advocacy goal can backfire.

Similarly, the cause of climate change is a good one, but how people go about convincing others is often done poorly. This can fall into two particular traps. The first are Armageddon claims. The second is name-calling. Both backfire against advocates, yet advocates continue to do them.

Armageddon it. In 2019, a meeting of the United Nations on climate change declared "Only 11 Years Left to Prevent Irreversible Damage from Climate Change," with General Assembly President María Fernanda Espinosa Garcés declaring, "We are the last generation that can prevent irreparable damage to our planet."[14] These types of claims are easily picked up by politicians and activists, with, for instance, Congresswoman Alexandria Ocasio-Cortez declaring, "The world is gonna end in twelve years if we don't address climate change and your biggest issue is how are we gonna pay for it?"[15] The UN secretary general said also in 2019, "If we don't urgently change our ways of life, we jeopardize life itself." Pretty scary stuff, but do these kinds of warnings work?

Probably not for a few basic reasons. First, these types of vague but cataclysmic warnings have been common in environmental activist circles. Again, to be clear, I'm not doubting climate change is real and having a deleterious effect. But these types of warnings can create a "boy who cried wolf" response. During my lifetime, I've seen these cataclysmic warnings come and go on everything from vanishing fossil fuels leaving us in the dark ages to the ozone hole wiping out life on the planet. In most cases, these were legitimate issues worth considering, but they either were more fixable than the doomsayers tended to assume or weren't necessarily as immediately life-or-death as was implied.

Do people take action only when a vague global problem is put in apocalyptic terms? It may intuitively seem so; however, the evidence suggests that may not be the case. In particular, the language of immediate crisis, or what one scholar calls "dispatches from hell," may actually foster a feeling of helplessness.[16] If the planet is going to burn to a crisp in eleven years, what the hell am I supposed to do about that? I might as well eat my burgers over a coal-fired stove and enjoy my gas-guzzling sports car for whatever time is left. Apocalyptic narratives, perhaps counterintuitively, appear to increase disengagement by the audience, prompting denial (after all, the claims sound outlandish), overwhelming audiences, and fostering helplessness and deferral of responsibility. By contrast, communication scholars suggest positive framing, focusing on changing behaviors as an opportunity, and connecting the abstracts of climate change to immediate improvements in the local environment (such as immediate air quality).[17]

Related to that, people in the general public can develop what I call *warning fatigue*. We're bombarded all the time about warnings of impending catastrophe: climate change, screen time, policing practices, failing economy, inflation, COVID-19, endless wars, violent video games, young adults having too much sex or maybe not enough, cats and dogs living together, Chinese slave labor used to construct the pavers for the Yellow Brick Road, etcetera. Sure, each individual issue is important and should get attention from *someone*. But to the general public, this all becomes overwhelming and difficult to track, particularly if they're told to be immediately concerned with each of these, all the time. And when some turn out to be less of the blatant catastrophe that advocates claimed, that can decrease trust in the next set of warnings. Ultimately, advocates can't expect public demand to instigate every positive change and, besides, such waves of public demand are often irrational and lead to as much harm as good.

You idiot. Persuasion is hard. It requires calm and patience and a mastery of data, as well as willingness to acknowledge when the person we're trying to persuade has a fair point that runs counter to what we're trying to persuade them of. Few people will visibly change their minds during a debate, as "saving face" makes them reluctant to do so. As such, persuasion is often incremental and occurs over time, and we may never actually see the fruits of our labor. Put simply, to persuade, we must persist in doing so without necessarily ever being tangibly rewarded for doing so.

It's much easier to preach to the choir of people who already agree, who respond with accolades, likes, shares, and so forth. This can reinforce group values and individual status within the group but is otherwise civically useless. If anything, the result may be conformity and myside bias. Nonetheless, the immediate gratification reinforces these behaviors, often at the expense of actual persuasion. Thus do polarization and siloing of opinion grow. Think of how often people share flattening, unsophisticated, misleading political memes among members of their ingroup and how little critical thinking of the value of the meme actually occurs, even among people who are very intelligent and educated.

As such, much of the discourse surrounding many important issues, certainly including climate change, degenerates into snarky mudslinging rather than persuasion, simply because the former is more satisfying than the latter, even if it doesn't move us any closer to the end goal. As a totally scientific project, I typed in the search term "Climate change deniers are assholes" just to see what hits I got. Sure enough, that returned plenty of hits within mainstream media sources. The newspaper the *Guardian* led with the headline, "The Four Types of Climate Denier, and Why You Should Ignore Them All."[18] These four types included the shill, the grifter, the egomaniac, and the ideological fool. Note that it seems impossible someone might simply have a wrong but good-faith opinion on the issue. A few news outlets went gaga over clothing maker Patagonia sewing "vote the assholes out" into the tags on their clothes.[19] The *Intercept* starts off one article[20] saying, "It can feel good to make fun of climate deniers. So, let's take a little romp with one," which rather beautifully makes my point for me. Certainly, not every news article takes a deep dive into snark, but those are hard to find. Some journalists, like *Time*'s Jeffrey Kluger, seem oddly obsessed with calling Americans idiots.[21]

Look, I get it. I certainly have my moments when I've given people free, good advice, and they don't take it, resulting in predictably calamitous results (Netflix, I'm looking at you[22]). The problem is, although snark can be—as the *Intercept* at least honestly notes—fun, it rarely convinces anyone. As I've said before, nobody listens to you more after you call them an asshole. In fact, quite the opposite. People tend to dig in and entrench further into their positions, not come around. So, to be clear, if you pass around politicized memes engaging in snark and snobbery toward those who disagree with you on climate change, you are *actively contributing to the problem and slowing down any solution to the problem of climate change*. So stop it.

So what does work? A few things. First, data does kind of convince, but it has to be trustworthy, which is the real failing of the Climategate fiasco. Second, negative emotions like anger or fear don't really work; focusing on the positive and helping people feel good about making small changes tends to work better. Third, keep it calm and be willing to disengage and return to the issue later if the other person appears to be getting upset. Fourth, focus on small steps people can implement easily, at least at first. Telling people that the end of the world is nigh or, for that matter, that everyone has to become vegan or hang their clothes out to dry instead of using machine dryers just isn't going to connect. Fifth, be willing to acknowledge when the other person has a fair point. This is called idiosyncrasy credits. When we acknowledge the contributions of another person, they're more likely to be open to our ideas as well. Acknowledging nuance also generally makes us seem less ideological. Sixth, keep it civil. No name-calling or ad hominems. Seventh, be truthful. Don't engage in logical fallacies, gaslighting, motte-and-bailey arguments, and so forth. Finally, don't piss people off. Stop gluing yourself to roads.

It's easy for me to say all this stuff. I'm the first to acknowledge that I don't always take my own advice (particularly on social media). But if we each make an effort to be a little bit better about how we interact with others and try to persuade rather than preach to a choir, we might each make a small but tangible difference over time.

To this point, I've focused on the catastrophe of climate change and our confused response to it. But people make a lot of other dumb decisions when it comes to weather. So, for the remainder of this chapter, we'll take a broader look at why people do dumb things in horrible weather. It's fun as long as you're not the one who drowns while trying to surf in a hurricane.

I should state my intent is not to pick on or stigmatize any individual. Indeed, the point of this book is that we all have the potential to make disastrous decisions. Sometimes, as the saying goes, "there but for the grace of God go I." Undoubtedly, I've made my own share of dumb-ass decisions in my life and only luck allows me to tell the tales.

Indeed, I'll start with one of my own near misses. Back home in Rhode Island visiting from college in Florida during my early twenties (and, as we'll see, it is often young men and teen boys who are prone to this tomfoolery), some friends and I decided to go to the beach. This was in May, when the beach water in Florida is warm and beautiful, and the beach water in Rhode Island could easily keep your beer cold. For some reason, rather than going to a normal beach, we went to one of these rocky outcroppings where the waves crash against jagged rocks.

My prior assumption was that we were going swimming. I'd brought my suit, after all, as had everyone else. But those rocks sure looked daunting. Did people actually go swimming at that kind of beach? Not people who survive! Those kind of precipices along the shore are notoriously deadly, with dangerous currents and a tendency to bash foolish swimmers against those horrid rocks.

In this case it was probably the water temperature more than wisdom that saved us. The average ocean temperature at a Newport, Rhode Island, beach in May is about 53 degrees Fahrenheit, reaching a balmy 62 degrees by June (only in August does it even reach 71 degrees—bone chilling by Florida standards). Screw that! We didn't go in but, looking back, I'm not sure it was good thinking that carried the day.

The lure of the ocean is magnetic for many of us. Even the hellishly cold (with yearly average temps between 50 and 60 degrees—an invitation to hypothermia) waters of San Francisco Bay inexplicably attract swimmers despite its notoriously deadly currents. Just this year a young gentleman died trying to brave the cold waters. A current pulled him out to sea where he was rescued by a surfer, but he went into cardiac arrest and died after being returned to shore. Unfortunately, he is one of a string of swimmers, both male and female, to die in those waters.[23]

In some cases, such as a fifty-eight-year-old man who died after ignoring warning flags at Daytona Beach in 2021,[24] swimmers blithely ignore red (dangerous current) or purple (jellyfish) flags and go swimming anyway. Who the heck wants to swim with jellyfish? It's like taking a stroll through an angry wasp garden. Yet people do it. Part of it again is that we seem to be drawn to the ocean. Some experts who lament the damage done by extreme weather such as hurricanes criticize humans for building stuff so near the beach, but we always have done so, and such locations probably brought with them many benefits, even though they also bring some dangers. But with these beach trips there may be something of a sunk costs effect. In other words, people blew a day and some money to get to the beach, which can put them in a mindset to ignore all the signs telling them to go home. In the face of some irate and tantruming kids, it may seem worth it to send them into the jellyfish sea so they make up their own minds to go back home again. But when the danger isn't jellyfish, but deadly currents, the outcome can be tragic.

Deadly tides aren't the only weather or climate events we ignore. Every year in the United States a dozen or two people are killed by lightning.[25] Looking across several recent years, common activities at the time of death include working in the yard, golfing, and beach activities. As an example, this year in New Jersey, a seventy-year-old man was killed after being caught in a thunderstorm on a golf course. In 2019, two women were killed after refusing a ride to shelter from a security guard at a cemetery. They were struck by lightning after sheltering under a tree. At least the choice of venue was ironically convenient.*

These events likely occur due to our difficulties in assessing risk, particularly once we're engaged in some activity. In fairness, in many situations, a thunderstorm can brew so fast that a person simply can get tragically caught in the open (just this year I got caught on my bike in a Florida thunderstorm that quickly went from blue skies to downpour, but fortunately didn't get zapped). But often we continue an activity—beach, golf, yardwork—because we don't want to lose out when the risk

---

* If you didn't want morbid humor, you're reading the wrong book.

seems minimal. Of course, by doing so, we can become motivated to downplay risk to tragic outcomes.

This is true not just with weather but things like wildlife. In 2018, an Indian gentleman was killed when, for some ungodly reason, he decided to take a selfie with an injured wild bear. It was the third selfie-related death in India that year, the other two a consequence of elephants who also are not naturally cuddly with humans.[26] Similarly, though most venomous snakebites are truly accidental,[27] perhaps one-third in the United States are due to dummies (usually men, once again) trying to catch or play with snakes. In a classic example, during a social gathering with alcohol in 2007, one young gentleman sought to impress his ex-girlfriend by demonstrating how friendly his (newly acquired from the wild) pet rattlesnake was by putting its head in his mouth.[28] You can see the ingredients here for male stupidity: a woman to impress and some choice beverages to evaporate any hesitation. The rattlesnake, not well-rehearsed with his lines in that script, bit the young man's tongue, causing life-threatening swelling of the tongue, face, and throat. Fortunately, his life was saved by medical professionals.

Sure, putting a rattlesnake in one's mouth is dumb. But we (particularly men) have a propensity for this sort of thing. Where does it come from?

The propensity for male risk-taking appears to be evolutionary in nature. Simply put, for men, it tends to work out more often than it doesn't. We just tend to highlight the cases when it spectacularly fails for men, shaking our heads and asking, "Why are men so stupid?"

Basically, in our hunter-gatherer past, men and women took on separate roles, with women engaged in less dangerous (though often back breaking) gathering work and males as hunters. Risk taking is inherent to hunting, since the animals don't just passively lie down on the plate. Thus, males who were able to engage in reasonable levels of risk taking tended to be more successful at hunting. This success increased their status and desirability to women as potential partners. By contrast, risk-taking is counterproductive for women as gatherers, not to mention primary caretakers of young. It doesn't award them any status and dying during a dumb risk is a death sentence for any young children as well (the general gist being that though fathers are important, they are less critical than are mothers).

In essence, as often as women cluck their tongues and shake their heads at men's behavior, they often reinforce it via sexual selection. The inverse is often true as well. Many women who've come through college gender studies courses will lament the rigid gender roles that keep men from explicitly discussing their feelings or crying openly. But as much as people say this (cuz it's the politically correct thing to say!) evidence is pretty clear that men who cry are judged negatively and lose status.[29] So as much as the gender studies classes tend to interpret this through a maze of jargon and complex theories, this effect appears to be straightforward evolutionary sex selection. Even women gender studies majors don't have sex with men who cry a lot.

If male risk taking is evolutionarily selected, of course it still exists on a continuum, with some males more likely to take bad risks than others. The reality is that the snake swallowing routine may kind of work but maybe don't try it with a rattler. Men who take too many risks are weeded out of the gene pool through natural selection. Men who don't take enough risks are weeded out of the gene pool through sex selection (i.e., women see them as undesirable partners). This isn't a "blame" thing ("Oh, so you're saying *women* are responsible for men's bad behavior? Typical chauvinist!"); it's just how nature works. Hell, as a dude who was never exactly the poster boy of traditional masculinity, I wish it weren't so!*

Women aren't immune to risk taking, of course. In many cases, such as the joggers at the cemetery, our failures often result from simply miscalculating the risk in the first place. Storms surge up suddenly, the benefits of living seaside tempt us to downplay the risks of flooding or hurricanes, we don't realize how far lightning can jump from the outskirts of a storm, and so on. Given that we live in a bigger world than our ancestors ever did, we also may be reluctant to accept help when offered, such as with the joggers at the cemetery who turned down a ride from a security guard. Our sense of not wanting to inconvenience others who owe us nothing may cause us to take risks upon ourselves we needn't have done. All of this, alas, seems simply to be part of human nature.

---

* Though I had the good fortune of finding a beautiful woman who was immune to this effect.

9

FIRE!

Back in 2003, the '80s rock band Great White played a show at the Station club in Rhode Island. As the band took the stage, their manager lit several stage fireworks, a common feature of their show. However, in this case, the fireworks ignited the foam coating around the stage used to control and dampen sound. As the flames began to spread the band's singer said, "Wow . . . that's not good," and an egress began.

The band easily escaped out a side door near the stage, but inside disaster quickly ensued. Two exit doors had been chained shut and a bouncer turned people away from a third near the stage, causing a crush at the one remaining door. The flames quickly spread along the foam across the Station's ceiling. Patrons trampled each other or became overcome by smoke and flames, packed like sardines at the one functioning exit. One hundred people died in the end. The Station's owners as well as the band's tour manager each faced prison time.* It was one of the worst nightclub fires in US history.[1]

In the midst of it, Great White guitarist Ty Longely did the unthinkable: having safely exited the burning building, he then *went back inside*, reportedly to retrieve his guitar.[2] Unfortunately, he did not return from inside the building. What would possess someone to return to a burning building to retrieve a replaceable material object? Unfortunately, it's a

---

* One owner ultimately received community service, whereas the other owner and tour manager both did stints in prison.

common enough response that people must be reminded not to do it. When a loved one or mementos or valuables are threatened, it can be tempting to take the risk, but it often does more harm than good to one-self and even to others trapped inside.

In this chapter I'll take a look at our dread of fire and how we so often respond so badly to it.

BURNING HORSES

Our species' domestication of fire—discovering the means to reliably produce and contain it—is certainly one of the most notable advances in our social history. Fire allowed us to eat and digest a wider range of foods, often sterilizing it of bacteria in the process. Fire allowed us to heat our shelters, allowing our conquest of colder lands beyond our natural ability to survive in. And fire assisted our development of tools and crafts.

In our early world, fire was also likely relatively rare, and the threats fire posed in the natural environment, mainly through forest fires, required the simple tactic of running away as fast as one could manage. Meaning, we never seemed to evolve a natural fear of fire to quite the same degree we have to, say, snakes or darkness.* Indeed, we are, if any-thing, *attracted* to fire, with our continued love for bonfires, fireworks, and movie explosions. This evolved attraction to fire is likely what assisted our domestication of fire in the first place.

We can see it in children, who are often fascinated by fire. That's one reason we have to teach fire safety to young kids; they often don't have the kind of instinctive fear to stop them from playing with matches in a house full of flammable things. One of the things we hope to do in fire safety courses is to teach kids to be at least a little afraid of fire: keep being naughty with matches and you'll go up in a puff of smoke and Satan will drag you straight to Hell! Alright, maybe not quite that far. Unfortunately, it's not clear how well these things work—training programs often do a good job training people to get the correct answers on quizzes without actually doing much to change motivation, attitudes, or behaviors.

---

* Note, I'm not implying humans evolved *no* fear of fire, rather that our approach to fire is more complex. No doubt we still ran from forest fires like other animals.

In 2002 a fire, possibly arson, at the Woodbine Racetrack broke out in barns that were not equipped with sprinklers. Staff on hand managed to free many of the animals, but in the ensuing chaos, the stable doors were left open, and many horses ran back to their stables where they perished.[3] I'm no horse expert, and this sounds like one of those old wives' tales that must be false, but there are too many news accounts of this type to dismiss it and expert recommendations also note this phenomenon.[4] The gist of the explanation is that a horse's stall is its home where it is fed and where it feels safe. In the confusion of a crisis, with not only the fire but also a bunch of panicked humans running around screaming, "Fire!" and grabbing at the animal, it can become frightened and confused and will try to retreat to where it feels safe.

Before we say, "Dumb animals!" let's observe that humans don't always instinctively do well in a fire. For instance, in a 2020 fire in Seattle, one little girl panicked and hid in a toy chest during a home fire. Fortunately, firefighters found and rescued her.[5] Unfortunately, such behaviors are common among young children. In approximately one-third of the situations in which young children died in fires, they set the fires themselves, typically by playing with matches or lighters then retreating to bedrooms or closets where they felt safe.[6] As we saw in the introduction to this chapter, adults don't always know what to do, either, underestimating risk or engaging in behaviors that seem entirely counterintuitive and not that different from the horses running back into burning stables.

In some cases, competing instincts can prove to be our downfall. In one unfortunate incident in Milwaukee, two young children, a brother and sister, died when they became trapped in a townhouse fire. According to news reports, neighbors held blankets for the kids to jump into from second story windows. Too frightened to jump, the children remained inside. One was found hiding in a closet.[7] We're generally programmed to avoid heights and certainly to avoid jumping from them. Blankets aside, even a two-story fall can cause injuries that, evolutionarily speaking, could have been catastrophic. Sure, miles away from the situation, we can understand it's a better option than remaining in a burning building, but for kids panicking amid an unfamiliar crisis, those height-avoiding instincts may have been difficult to overcome.

We see again that panic is often the culprit. That's true not only for children. Returning to the topic of burning horses, one woman, upon realizing her barn was burning, ran to the barn to try to free her horses. She found the barn door jammed and was reduced to running around in circles listening to her horses die. In the end, it turned out that although she was intimately familiar with the barn, in her moment of panic, she had tried to open the door from the hinge side.[8] Fright, as it often does, prevented her from realizing her error. This is a common theme we see with terror, from the French airliner crash to the barn owner: people persist in repeating the same faulty behavior instead of stopping, thinking, and trying something new. This perseverance continues as people think that the behavior just *has* to produce the desired outcome even though it clearly is not.

FIRE SAFETY TRAINING

We have established that relying on our instincts either to prevent or respond to a fire is garbage. As we've seen, that's particularly true for young children, but also for elderly people who may be experiencing cognitive declines that also put them at risk for bad outcomes (e.g., leaving the stove on unchecked). Nonetheless, no age group is great when it comes to natural abilities regarding fire. That's why fire safety programs have been developed. So, do they work?

Broadly speaking, fire safety training has two goals: to impart knowledge that may help the prevention of fires in the first place and to routinize responses to fire to maximize good outcomes. Or, put more bluntly, to stop people from doing dumb things that start fires (e.g., deep-frying a turkey inside the house) and to make fire response behaviors so automatic that they don't require the kind of cognition that often vanishes in a panic-filled moment. Hence the old "stop, drop, and roll" saying that helps people remember what to do if they catch fire rather than merely running around screaming, which appears to be the instinctive response.

The good news is that fire safety training does indeed seem to work! Granted, some kids are still going to play with matches, but the programs seem to instill knowledge about fire prevention and promote fire safety behaviors. Such programs seem to work well for young kids, one of the most at-risk groups,[9] but they also work for adults, too, and tend to promote preventative measures such as stocking smoke detectors, fire extinguishers, and fire blankets.[10] I spend so much time imparting bad news about human psychology that it's nice to find something that actually works.

How has all this worked? Well, we can look at trends in fire data. Keep in mind, these trends are undoubtedly due to multiple factors. Safer building materials, widespread use of smoke detectors and even sprinklers in some homes, decreases in smoking, and so on all contribute to positive trends. According to the US Fire Administration,[11] about twelve thousand people died in the United States each year from fires in the 1970s. In more recent years (2008–2017), the numbers have hovered between 2,800 to 3,400, even though the US population has grown. That's a remarkable decline! The last couple years have seen a slight uptick in deaths, but nowhere near twelve thousand, and the number of fires has declined overall.

Once again, we can't say that fire safety training programs are solely responsible for this. But if it ain't broke, don't fix it. We're on the right track to helping people survive residential fires better than they ever have. This has created the kind of problem we want: firefighters have many fewer fires to fight. As a consequence, they often act as backup paramedics at medical emergencies, which is why we now see the big trucks often responding to non-fire events.[12]

So residential fires down, that's good news. But what about forest fires? Here we have a very different problem and, fortunately for this book but regrettably for those who live near wooded areas, our response to it has too often been nonsense.

WHAT WOULD YOGI SAY?

In September 2020, a young couple were celebrating the impending birth of their child with a "gender reveal party." These celebrations have become trendy in recent years, making a big fuss when ultrasounds have revealed whether the couple's forthcoming varmint is a boy or a girl.

As tends to happen, people often try to stage more and more elaborate celebrations, some of which have involved fireworks and pyrotechnics.

In this case, a smoke generator appears to have malfunctioned, creating a fire that burned twenty-two thousand acres in California, destroying several homes and businesses, and leading to the death of one firefighter and injuries to several others. The couple who held the party have since been charged with involuntary manslaughter in the death of the firefighter.[13] This hasn't been the only gender reveal party to end in fiery disaster.

Gender reveal parties are an easy target for criticism as there's something self-indulgently obnoxious about them to begin with, an obnoxiousness that expands exponentially as we move from a small gathering over coffee to fireworks spelling "boy" in the sky. And a segment of the woke left don't like them because they essentialize a biological gender binary (then again, the woke left often comes across as being defined by not liking stuff, and the biology of gender is a debate for another day). The truth is, there's nothing magical about gender reveal parties that set forest fires. Pretentiousness may be cringe inducing, but it's not inherently combustible. Human-caused wildfires are due to two main things: people behaving badly around things that burn like, you know, wood and well-intentioned but data-deficient policy decisions that make forests more easily burnable.

In the United States, humans, not things like lightning strikes, are responsible for the vast majority of wildfires. According to one study, 84 percent of wildfires are caused by humans, tripling the length of fire seasons.[14] Accidental fires are caused by a number of factors, particularly debris burning, although July 4 is the single most prime fire-starting day due to the combination of dry, hot weather and celebratory fireworks. Some are largely beyond anyone's control, such as if a car catches fire and the fire spreads to nearby wilderness.

In many accidental fires, people simply underestimate the risks of fire and start fires despite regulations prohibiting them or fail to observe fire safety protocols such as keeping the fires away from flammable brush or properly extinguishing fires. A 2002 fire in Utah was started at a Boy Scouts' camp, according to the state of Utah, when some boys were left largely unsupervised to start a fire. Without adult supervision overnight, the boys started a fire against state regulations and failed to implement proper fire safety. When the boys left the area, they left the fire smoldering, and it eventually grew into a fire that burned 14,400 acres and cost $13.3 million to put out. The Boy Scouts of America eventually paid about half that to replace trees in the area.[15]

Why do people do it? Well, as we've said before, starting fires is fun, and not starting fires is not fun. When faced with a decision between a fun but unwise choice or a wise but unfun choice, people often lean toward the former. It becomes easy to convince ourselves that the risks and consequences are minimal. As we see, that isn't always the case.

But some fires are also started purposefully.

In 2002, Leonard Gregg, a contract firefighter (meaning he only gets paid when there are fires), used matches to light up some dry grass in Arizona. He needed the work he would get fighting the fire. Unfortunately, it got out of hand and eventually merged with a second fire that had been set accidently by a woman who'd gotten lost and started a signal fire. The fire would eventually burn 460,000 acres, destroy 491 structures, and cost $43 million to put out. Gregg was arrested and imprisoned for nine years.[16]

Most firefighters are brave individuals doing hard and dangerous work to keep us safe. But it turns out, a tiny number actually set the fires they themselves try to put out. The problem is common enough that a federal investigation looked into this in the early 2000s[17] and the National Volunteer Fire Council (NVFC) released a similar report in 2011.[18] There aren't good official statistics on firefighter arson, but the NVFC estimated that about one hundred firefighters are arrested each year for arson (out of about a million volunteer and professional firefighters). There is no clear "profile" of firefighter arsonists. Although the "average" such arsonist is young and male, often working with others, and more likely to be volunteer or contract, those arrested have included women firefighters, older firefighters, ranking officers, and so forth. They tend to come from difficult backgrounds and have instability in their social lives. They are often intelligent but underperform academically. Of course, that describes a lot of people who never do anything wrong so, again, avoiding the temptation to overapply a "profile" is critical.

Why do some firefighters set fires? Motives are myriad. Some want to be heroes, whereas others are just bored and crave the excitement of fighting fires. Others, such as Leonard Gregg, have financial motives, and still others may do it for revenge or vandalism. Interestingly, the motives can sometimes extend to firefighters' friends and family. In 2014, Sadie Johnson reportedly set a brush fire using a flaming firework because her firefighter friends were bored and needed work. The resulting fire raged for weeks, burning fifty thousand acres and costing $8 million to put out. Apparently in the midst of it, she posted "Like my fire?" on social media. Reported to have had drug and alcohol issues, she was eventually sentenced to eighteen months in prison.[19] Pro tip: if your firefighter friends are bored, buy them the latest video game instead.

There is also the phenomenon of pyromania, an obsessive condition in which individuals feel compelled to set fires, often deriving pleasure (sometimes sexual, though that is quite rare, occurring in perhaps 1 to 2% of cases) or relief from the experience. Most fires set by pyromaniacs are small, though they can escalate. Individuals with pyromania are typically male, of below-average intelligence, and suffer from other impulse control disorders. The urge to set fires builds into a kind of tension that can be released only with an actual fire, with the frequency of fire setting about every five to eight weeks.[20]

One example of this phenomenon is Peter Dinsdale, a confessed serial arsonist in the United Kingdom. Born into a difficult life (his mother was a prostitute) and with neurological issues including epilepsy and partial paralysis on his right side, Dinsdale struggled academically and socially. He became known as "daft Peter" due to his cognitive limitations. He began setting fires around age twelve, with some of these fires resulting in deaths of persons within the dwellings. Most of these were random and Dinsdale later claimed not to have intended to cause death in most of these situations, but a few were targeted against people whom he felt had bullied or teased him. One man he burned to death for clipping his ear.[21]

In 1979 he set a fire at the home of Edith Hastie, who was inside with her four sons. He claimed that her eldest son (age fifteen) had coerced him into sexual acts then blackmailed him and that the family had ridiculed him for his attraction to one of the family's daughters. Three of the boys died in the fire, including the primary intended target. Dinsdale was convicted of multiple counts of manslaughter due to his diminished mental capacity and sent to a psychiatric hospital.

Dinsdale also confessed to one arson that was later ruled an accident, suggesting he sometimes confessed to crimes he did not commit. Given his reduced mental status and physical disabilities, a new appeal in the United Kingdom alleges he falsely confessed to the arsons.[22]

The issue of wildfires doesn't boil down entirely to the bad decisions of individuals, however. Many of our public policies, even those designed to help the environment, have contributed to the problem. Let's have a look.

EVERY TWIG IS PRECIOUS

As the old cliché goes, the road to hell is paved with good intentions. We've already seen this in previous chapters, whether environmentalists' unwavering suspicion of nuclear energy or the dawning recognition that the black lives matter movement of 2020 may have unintentionally led to the *loss* of black lives through burgeoning crime waves caused by delegitimization of policing as a whole. It's not too hard to figure out why.

Let's imagine you decide to commit yourself to a worthy moral cause. Let's say you've joined the Resurrect the Dodo movement. Poor dodo birds were rendered extinct by human action, now we can right that wrong by bringing them back using new ultra-scientific DNA methods. You pour your heart into the effort, perhaps helped along by a few grifters who want your donations, giving thousands of dollars to pro-dodo advocacy groups, marching in protests with little dodo hats on your heads screaming, "Hey Odo, bring back the dodo!" to police officers who have no earthly idea what you're talking about, and boring even your most patient relatives at family holidays with your lectures on how the dodo was a victim of European colonization, capitalism, GMOs, little green men from Mars, or whatever the trendy bad guy is at the moment. Then, voilà! the government passes the Dodo Rights Act of 2045, and scientists start bringing the birds back by the dozens. Then two things happen.

First, you've put so much of your identity into this that once you've actually achieved your goal, there's a "now what?" moment. Advocacy efforts very often get paralyzed when they're successful, often feeling pressured to move goalposts toward more and more extreme outcomes.

Soon you're marching for the rights of dodos to vote, marry, drive, serve in the military, or whatever, so long as you can still be outraged by the injustice of it all. How *dare* The Man tell us that all is right with the dodo when *not once* has the United Kingdom had a dodo prime minister! The dodos don't even *want* any of this stuff because, you know, they're birds, but that doesn't stop you. Grinding yourself into outraged action is the point, actually, not achieving any particular goal and declaring success. A great example of this is the strange effort to get people to use the term Latinx, despite consistent evidence that people of Latino or Hispanic descent don't much care for the term at all.[23]

Second, what if your effort turns out to actually do more harm than good? Maybe what nobody realized is that dodo birds only eat other endangered animals. So they multiply and set out about the world (catching flights on Delta, since you advocated for their rights to free airline seats, given that they are flightless birds or, excuse me, birds whom capitalism has assigned flightless) eating koalas and pandas, sea otters and elephants (hey, you advocated for their right to bear arms). Pretty soon it's clear the return of the dodo is an ecological disaster. But more to the point, *you helped to make that happen.* That's a difficult reality for most people to face and, as such, they tend to dig in deeper and ignore reality, because facing that a morally pure motivation backfired into disaster is a difficult pill for people to swallow.

This example is silly, of course, but it highlights actual struggles that advocates and advocacy groups face. Consider for example, March of Dimes, a worthy organization that was created to fight polio. Did March of Dimes go away once polio was eradicated from most of the world? For that matter, what advocacy organization wants people to mail them a dime anymore? No, they just shifted their mission to other childhood diseases. There's nothing wrong with that, and in fairness March of Dimes doesn't try to pretend polio is still widespread, unlike some advocacy groups for social causes. But nonprofit status aside, many of these organizations become perpetual advocacy machines or, in some cases, perpetual outrage machines. They rarely declare victory and close shop, because there is still money to be made.

Alright, back to wildfires. No single issue is responsible for the increased problem of wildfires, particularly in the West and Southwest.

Climate change, for instance, can play a role. But so has decades of environmental policy designed to protect forests. As environmental historian Stephen Beda has noted, environmentalists have worked hard to protect forests, not just from fires, but also from logging.[24] The result of this protectionism, though understandable, has been the accumulation of dry tinder on forest floors. Bereft of natural or controlled burns that get rid of this tinder without the fires spreading out of control, many forests are now powder kegs ready to ignite into massive conflagrations. Both an overfocus on fire suppression rather than the use of controlled burns and avoidance of any and all timber removal (championed by environmentalists fighting logging companies) have made matters worse. This is not to say environmentalists were wrong, for instance, in limiting logging to save forests in the Pacific Northwest, but rather that in going too extreme, we've moved from policies that are helpful in supporting natural ecosystems to some that put them, ironically, in danger.

To recognize that a well-intentioned (and in many respects very important) set of efforts may have actually caused unexpected harm can be difficult to accept. That's particularly true in the hyper-partisan environment of climate change debates, in which any capitulation can be seen as humiliating weakness. Thus, despite strong scientific identification of the problems, changes to policy have been slow.

A lot of cognitive processes contribute to this: confirmation bias, cognitive dissonance, motivated reasoning, and the need to save face and avoid humiliation. However, once committed to a course of action, particularly if there is reputational, moral, and emotional investment in that course of action, people are often difficult to dissuade from it, even as it becomes disastrous. A classic example of this is the self-esteem movement, the notion that increasing self-esteem, whether in schools, businesses, among police officers, or elsewhere, would boost a host of positive outcomes. This created a massive industry for interventions, school programs, seminars, books (think *Chicken Soup for the Soul*), not to mention newspaper articles highlighting these efforts. The millennials were largely educated in a school system obsessed with self-esteem. Schools stopped using red pens for fear students would be traumatized, competitive sports no longer had winners and losers, and everyone got a trophy for just arriving. Ultimately, it turns out all this stuff doesn't work.[25] People, if anything, fail to develop resiliency and experience *more* anxiety in the long term when they perpetually are shielded from every stress. But now that it's in the public consciousness and a whole industry is built around it, it has become an unkillable monster.

Unfortunately, as we can see from wildfire suppression efforts, even issues related to environmentalism can be like the self-esteem movement. Once we become rooted in a good idea, particularly one that makes us feel like good people, it can be difficult to change course even when that idea leads us toward disaster.

10

BARBARIANS
AT THE GATE

B ack in high school I remember learning that the Western Roman
Empire fell, in large part, because it had absorbed a large number
of Germans who were more loyal to their tribes than to the empire itself.
Thus weakened with irresolute barbarians, some of them becoming
soldiers within the legions, the empire was later helpless when other
German tribes such as the Vandals and Franks invaded the lands that
would, in the future, become France (thus starting a German tradition
that continues to the present day). Other German tribes such as the Sax-
ons invaded Britain, and the Goths would ravage the south, eventually
sacking Rome itself in 410 ACE.

The message seems clear: beware immigrants (particularly if German). The actual truth of the fall of the Roman Empire is more complex
than boiling it down to Germans didn't like eating pasta. Rome had actually been a reasonably successful multiethnic state for centuries (barring
the occasional genocide or diaspora). It tended to welcome immigrants
and its policy toward immigration was pretty straightforward: immigrant
groups would be disarmed, broken up into smaller units, and dispersed,
where they would be acculturated into Roman culture rather than maintaining loyalties to their tribal identities.[1] The multiculturalists of today
probably wouldn't like this policy, but it's actually a good one: welcome
immigrants but break their ties to their previous identities, encouraging
acculturation within their new identity.

Rome's problems with the Germans, the Goths specifically in this case, stem from a *failure* of its policy, not simply because it allowed the Goths to immigrate. In the fourth century ACE the Goths were desperate, fleeing the scary Huns. The Roman Emperor Valens allowed them to settle within the empire, but then things broke down. There may simply have been too many Goths for the local authorities to manage, but the Goths' weapons weren't taken away nor were their tribes broken up and scattered. To make matters worse, corruption set in among local authorities, and food and supplies were withheld from the Goths or sold at exorbitant prices, rather understandably pissing them off. Long story short: the Goths revolted, killed Valens in battle, and got to stay in the empire, basically becoming an autonomous group of rebels who ultimately helped break the empire apart.

So immigration was basically good until it was bad, or, more accurately, the failure to adjust policy for changing circumstances while maintaining that policy as clear, strategic, and humane was ultimately bad. Like anytime else in history, immigration was tainted by mutual suspicion and hostility between different ethnic groups (no, racism isn't an invention of recent history). The very word *barbarian* originated with the Greeks to describe their perception that other peoples sounded like they were babbling incoherently (their speech sounding like incomprehensible "bar, bar"). It was not a compliment.

The other thing we have to remember is that migration of human groups has historically been violent, whether in Europe, Asia, Africa, or the Americas. Throughout the history of human migration, later groups slaughtered, disposed of, or aggressively absorbed earlier groups. Some evidence, though controversial, suggests this may have occurred even with the Neanderthals, who were wiped out as modern humans spread out of Africa, partly due to absorption, partly due to resource competition, and partly due to mass homicides, at least it is conjectured.[2] What does this mean for modern immigration debates, whether in the United States or other countries? We're in for a bumpy road, and when tempers flare and moralizing is high, a lot of bad decisions. Let's have a look!

THAT GUY *LOOKS* SUSPICIOUS

Explicit prejudice toward and possibly even hatred of others is a taboo attitude in the modern, industrialized world and rightly so. Via prejudice we inflict horrors small and large on others, and whatever its origin, we should strive to rise above it. Understanding the origins of prejudice can help us. It turns out that prejudice is pretty much universal to the human experience and even as we transcend it in some respects (race, faith, sexuality, etc.), we appear eager simply to shift it to other areas (class, political viewpoint, heterodox beliefs, etc.). Where did this inexorable instinct to dislike those who are different come from?

Like most widespread behaviors, it likely evolved. To be blunt, loathsome as such attitudes are today in the modern world, they may have been adaptive in our historical past. Indeed, explicit racism and other prejudices only really became morally unacceptable toward the end of the twentieth century and, arguably, they remain common in much of the world today where active ethnic warfare or genocide (think of how the Chinese government treats its Uyghur minority) remain the rule rather than the exception. But why would prejudice toward our fellow humans be adaptive?

The simple answer stems from another instinct: our capacity for brutal violence toward one another. Like our nearest ape relative, the chimpanzee, humans have an enormous capacity for within-species violence. Violence is used to secure resources, to establish dominance, to eliminate competition, and in the case of sexualized violence, to force women into sex. Historically, homicide rates among humans were astronomical, much higher than during the present.[3] Archaeological evidence suggests that premodern hunter-gatherer societies weren't the peaceful, matriarchal, "everyone holding hands and singing 'Kumbaya'" groups they are sometimes portrayed as; brutal violence and murder were common.[4] The reality of widespread and ever-present risks of interpersonal violence only diminished as societies formed into more structured units with effective policing.[5] Although violence *within* cultural groups certainly occurred, cultural groups afford their members mutual protection and support. By contrast, violence *between* cultural groups could be fierce and without restraint, as such relationships likely were built on competition more than cooperation (though, certainly, some groups likely traded, intermarried, etc.). If you were more likely to be attacked by strangers than members of your own cultural group, then it paid to be suspicious of others who were visibly different from yourself; that is to say, different ethnicities or cultures.

To be clear, by saying that our brains evolved to have prejudices because they were adaptive in our evolutionary past is not the same as saying they are good or something we should not work to change in our present. I am merely explaining their origin. Perhaps also understanding their innate nature (though certainly family or cultural environments can exacerbate them) may give us some sense of patience in understanding why they persist. Indeed, even as we challenge others about their prejudices, most of us likely continue to hold some prejudices of our own, though perhaps they now focus on class or politics rather than race, religion, sex/gender, or sexuality.

Our intrinsic tendency toward prejudice can be primed even for really dumb things. In a classic psychology experiment, a group of boys at summer camp were divided into two groups, the Eagles and the Rattlers. At first, the two groups were unaware of each other. Then they were brought together for a series of competitions. When the two groups competed, they began to display both verbal and physical prejudice and bullying toward each other. When asked to describe the other group, the boys described the other group in very negative terms.[6]

Let's remember, these boys were *randomly assigned* to their groups. There was nothing really different between them at all. But in a sense of competition, they bonded to their own group and developed prejudice toward the other group. Bringing the groups together for neutral, non-competitive time together actually made the prejudice worse (this is an important point for diversity programs—those that focus on resentments or simply bring people together often backfire). Only when the two groups were forced to work together to remove rocks from a water tank (so they could drink!) did their prejudice subside.

This experiment, called the Robber's Cave experiment, is far from perfect, but it provides insights into how prejudice develops (perceived competition) and can be eliminated (via the need to work together toward a common goal). We can see this reflected in the language of immigration debates: immigrants are coming to steal jobs, warp our culture, commit crimes, and so forth. These concerns are certainly prejudiced but also kind of expected. Understanding that can help us to know how to address them and set effective and reasonable immigration policies.

THE COSTS AND BENEFITS OF IMMIGRATION

Let's start by acknowledging that immigration, like any complex social issue, requires complex solutions and rational, data-based consideration. Any solution that sounds simple—whether "build a wall!" or "open borders"—almost certainly leads to disaster. However, rational, data-based solutions are often thwarted by our less-rational inclination to see things through competitive lenses. As we've seen in the United States, immigration (whether blacks, Asians, Mexicans—or Irish, Italians, or Germans) historically has been met with hostility and racism. Contrary to the conceits of the modern left, this isn't an American thing, but rather the typical response as cultures come into contact worldwide. Racism and ethnocentrism are universal human realities, and no group is immune. But it certainly does muddy discussions about what level of immigration is good for the United States. Yet, that's not the only level of competition, as polarizing debates between left and right can result in immigrants becoming like ping-pong balls for competing political worldviews.

I'm no political scientist with an expertise in immigration, so I'm not going to get into a lot of policy specifics. My curiosity is in regard to how mistaken ideas take hold and continue to be repeated despite evidence to the contrary. As such, I'd like to examine several in particular. For instance, from the left, I'll look at the belief that immigration has little economic impact for working-class workers and any objection to immigration is due to racism rather than economic anxiety. And from the right, I'll consider the belief that recent immigrants, or illegal immigrants specifically, are particularly prone to crime.

First, does immigration—particularly illegal immigration of low-skill, low-pay workers—impact the economic vulnerability of working-class citizens? From the left, we are told over and over that it is racism, not economic anxiety, that drives opposition to immigration.[7] Now, to be fair, these are not mutually exclusive issues and, of course, one can drive the other. People worried about their jobs can become hostile toward those perceived as taking them and this can, of course, bubble over into open racism. This is a comforting message for the left, as it waves away any concerns about pro-immigration policies, including those that lean toward open borders, and also paints their opponents with the big *R* of racism. But is it true?

Evidence suggests that illegal immigration does, indeed, drive down wages and employment, particularly among less-educated workers, namely those most likely to compete for the same jobs. In particular, evidence suggests that illegal immigration may decrease both wages and employment for low-skilled black citizens, a group otherwise considered vulnerable for economic strain.[8] In this case, illegal immigration tends to *benefit* more elite elements of society, who can pay less for services and obtain cheaper goods, while placing strain on lower-income citizens. The economist George Borjas has studied this issue for decades and notes that illegal immigration benefits some, bringing wealth to businesses, and harms others, particularly low-income workers, which include whites, but is particularly hard on black and Latino citizens.[9] This may be a particularly difficult message for the left to assimilate, since it tends to portray itself as champion of all minority communities. Acknowledging significant strife *between* minority communities (even between Latinos) may not fit its political narrative. So, folks on the left claiming illegal immigration is some kind of economic nothingburger are ignoring concerns of many of their own constituents. Never exactly a wise idea.

But wait, you say, didn't I read that some economics studies found that racism, not economic anxiety, predicted things like voting for Trump? Well, yes and no. There have been several studies that have made such claims, but their flaws are considerable. One such study examined the 2016 election and factors associated with voting for Trump, claiming that racism and sexism, but not economic anxiety, predicted pro-Trump voting.[10] However, the way it measured racism isn't what most people think of as racism. What it measured was people's agreement with the current *progressive* worldview on race. When most people think of racism, they think that people are answering questions such as "I think people of other races are inferior to my own" or "this country should be for white people only." Those are obviously racist opinions. Instead, the authors questioned whether "White people in the U.S. have certain advantages because of the color of their skin" and "Racial problems in the U.S. are rare, isolated situations." That's not racism at all, but specific agreement with *one particular view* of race in the United States that is endorsed by progressives but less likely to be endorsed by conservatives. What they found was not that Trump voters were motivated by racism, but rather that Trump voters tended to be conservatives, something that was hardly a shocker.

Remember, academics tend to be liberals and progressives. As such, this kind of deck-stacking against conservatives is regrettably common in social science. As Keith Stanovich, psychologist and professor emeritus at University of Toronto, has pointed out, progressive psychologists regularly use surveys like this to put the thumb on the scale to make conservatives look dumb, racist, sexist, etcetera.[11] Essentially, not agreeing with progressive worldviews is *bad* according to these studies, but this gets mistranslated as unintelligent or bigoted, not simply a disagreement on sociopolitical narrative.

Debates about immigration are riddled with biases and mistakes like these. In this case ad hominem attacks against conservatives were, in effect, disguised as research. But misinformation and outright myths are common to both sides of the debate. As misinformation often does, these mistakes make it harder to implement good, evidence-based policy. Let's look at a couple common misunderstandings on both sides of the debate.

WHAT THE RIGHT GETS WRONG ABOUT IMMIGRATION

Immigrants increase crime. In July 2015, thirty-two-year-old Kate Steinle was shot in the back while walking on a pier in San Francisco with her father and friend. She died several hours later in the hospital. The shooter, Jose Garcia Zarate, was an illegal immigrant who'd been deported from the United States and returned multiple times and had multiple felony convictions, mainly for drugs. Despite his legal history, he enjoyed protection under San Francisco's "sanctuary city" law, which prevented local law enforcement from cooperating with immigration authorities. Garcia Zarate claimed he had just found the stolen firearm wrapped in cloth under a bench and it had accidently gone off when he'd unwrapped it. Garcia Zarate claimed the bullet had been fired at the ground, ricocheted, and then hit Steinle in a freak accident. Ballistics evidence supported the possibility of a ricochet and a jury found Garcia Zarate not guilty. As of 2020, he still faced federal firearms charges, though his mental health issues raised the possibility that he was not competent to stand trial.[12]

This case is gripping as it touches on several controversial issues. First, the Garcia Zarate case fits neatly into concerns about immigrants, particularly illegal immigrants, committing violent crimes while on US soil. Second, it raises questions about "sanctuary cities," which defy federal requests for cooperation in immigration cases. Sanctuary cities are a classic left/right divide, with those on the left far more supportive of them than those on the right. However, the Garcia Zarate case is also an anecdote, and as we've already seen, anecdotes are generally poor sources of evidence. Although the Garcia Zarate case undoubtedly seemed to support conservatives' fears of illegal immigration in particular, what does the overall evidence say about illegal immigration and violent crime?

The good news, at least on this score, is that immigrants, including illegal immigrants, are actually *less likely* to commit violent crimes than are US citizens.[13] Although much of the data relies on Texas specifically, given that Texas is rigorous about documenting immigration status in legal cases, this appears to be a robust finding.[14] If this is the case, why do beliefs about immigration and crime persist? One possibility is that people are mistaking higher crime rates among US-born Latinos with higher crime among recent immigrants. More likely, though, I suspect the issue is the typical "fear of others," largely evolutionarily derived. Worrying about newcomers' violence was likely adaptive in times past as newcomers often were violent. Our prejudice toward immigrants today is likely a leftover pattern of our evolutionary past.

Immigrants will fundamentally change our culture. This fear is sometimes called the "great replacement" and basically goes like this: we've got a perfect, European-majority country that is going to be gradually ruined by an influx of immigrants. This is nothing unique to the United States (and similar ethnic purity concerns occur worldwide). But of course demographics are slowly changing in the United States as it becomes less "white" (depending on how we define that term). Granted, both the left and right contribute to this narrative, with pundits panicking about it on the right, and pundits on the left (often affluent whites themselves) gleefully rubbing it in the faces of those on the right then wondering why the right is so cranky. But is there much to worry about here?

The demographic change is certainly real, though that's been true throughout the course of US history. Most original Americans in 1776 were English Protestants, with some mix of other European nationalities. During the course of the nineteenth and early twentieth century, waves of Irish, Italians, Germans, and other groups drastically altered that demographic profile. Generally speaking, immigrant groups do bring along some aspects of their culture (hence we have St. Patrick's Day, lots of Italian restaurants, and the Germans gave us coronary artery disease). Initially these waves were met with all the hostility and ethnocentrism that are now focused particularly on Latino immigrants (and other groups such as Asians, Caribbeans, and Africans to an arguably lesser extent). What basically happened to these non-English European groups is, even as they contributed elements of their culture to the United States, they mainly acculturated to US culture, becoming gradually more "American" over subsequent generations until distinctions between English, Irish, or German Americans were largely superfluous (and, indeed, most of us are mutts due to intermarriage).

This gradually led to the development of the category of "white," which now included groups that were perceived with considerable venom not a few generations before. "White" and "European" are largely synonymous but imply that such individuals, despite minor differences, now occupy a similar cultural space. But this is the essence of the "melting pot" idea, usually championed on the right and sometimes oddly repudiated as a "microaggression" on the left (never underestimate people's ability to torpedo an effective argument in support of their own policy goals).

What is basically happening with more recent immigrant groups from Asia, Africa, the Caribbean, as well as Latin America is largely the same thing. These groups do bring distinctive food, holidays (like Cinco de

Mayo), culture, and so forth, which they share with the United States (and why the whole concept of cultural appropriation is largely rubbish), but they also are acculturating to the United States. Among Latinos, research clearly notes that Hispanic/Latino identity declines markedly by the third or fourth generation.[15] Third-generation Latinos tend to speak Spanish far less, engage in fewer Hispanic cultural celebrations, identify as "American" more than as "Hispanic," lose connection to their family's country of origin, and intermarry with non-Latinos at high rates. Put bluntly, over several generations, Latinos basically become "white," although we honestly need a better term than that. Perhaps it's better to say that Latinos, like all other immigrant groups, tend to become generically American after several generations. And that's not necessarily a bad thing.

Critics of immigration worried about the Great Replacement can take comfort in this. Immigrants come to the United States because they want to be American and even first-generation immigrants take great pride in becoming citizens. American culture is strong and powerful enough that people who come here become American far more than they change American culture. And the changes they do bring—good food, music, celebrations, and so on—generally are a positive gain for our culture. So, yes, the ethnic composition of the United States is changing over time as it always has, but this is a sign of our success, not a failure of our culture. Along with concerns about crime, critics of immigration can let this go as a major talking point.

WHAT THE LEFT GETS WRONG ABOUT IMMIGRATION

If we accept that many critiques coming from the right regarding immigration are misinformed, we also likely must accept that many defenses of immigration from the left are similarly misinformed. As we've seen, there is evidence that illegal immigration could impact low-wage earners, and the case that resistance to immigration is primarily driven by racism was stacked by surveys that naturally favored progressive beliefs. But what else may the left have gotten wrong about immigration?

A permanent majority of Democratic voters waits just beyond the horizon. This myth is pretty much the mirror image of the Great Replacement myth. Put basically, this belief holds that as the proportion of non-white voters grows, Democrats will eventually benefit from permanent majorities because non-white voters historically have voted for the Democrats. This permanent majority has been "just around the corner" for several decades now. In defense of the Democrats, the Republicans likely have bought into this, too, by using ethnicity during redistricting to gain advantages for their candidates. The main problem is that this is a pretty lazy formulation based on race that results in bad policies for both parties. Republicans may figure non-whites are disinterested in them, doubling down on the interests of whites and ignoring non-whites. At its worst, this can result in outright racism such as that espoused by former President Trump comparing Mexican immigrants to rapists.

It's not great for the Democrats either, however, as they increasingly become a party of mainly elites who appear ready to string along non-white voters with the expectation such voters owe them their votes. President Biden's comment, "You ain't black" if you didn't vote for him is one such example. This also can lead Democrats to turn entirely on the white working class as a "basket of deplorables" in the words of Hillary Clinton. In other words, viewing ethnicity as a kind of voting destiny leads to irrational conclusions by both parties. The disadvantage here, however, belongs to Democrats, as they continue to rely on a future fictional majority that's never coming.

As we've seen in recent elections, particularly in 2020 and 2021, though non-white voters do tend to lean toward Democrats, those numbers are slipping away from the Democrats. For instance, according to a 2021 *Wall Street Journal* poll, Latino voters, once a mainstay of Democrats, are now about equally split between the parties.[16] In 2016, Trump won about 28 percent of the Latino vote but raised that total to 32 percent in 2020. According to the *Wall Street Journal*, if the 2024 presidential election were held today between Biden and Trump, Latinos would be split about equally between them. And let's remember, Trump is the fellow who referred to Mexican immigrants as criminals and rapists! Similar if less dramatic patterns are seen for Asian and black voters as well.

This trend easily could reverse itself, but nonetheless it's interesting to examine it. Why are non-whites turning away from the Democrats?

As mentioned, it's probably because Democrats employed stereotypes of what non-white voters want. For instance, in the name of racial equity, progressive Democrats have moved to eliminate standardized testing, gifted programs, and charter schools. However, doing so greatly disadvantages Asian students in particular, and the implication that black or Latino students can't compete may not be as popular with those communities as progressives think. Similarly, issues of open borders and illegal immigration may not be the clear policy winners with Latinos that Democrats perceive. These issues are complicated, but my understanding of the data is that Latinos are motivated by immigration to the extent that there is perceived racism, discrimination, or brutality in the system, but they are less supportive of open borders.[17] Further, Latinos may be just as motivated by economic issues as anyone else, prioritizing these over immigration debates. Latinos also tend to be socially conservative, which may put many of them at odds with Democrats' increasing lean toward further left progressivism. Similar issues at play in other non-white communities may be weakening Democrats' hold on these ethnic groups. Now, there's still plenty of opportunity for Republicans to blow it and send more non-whites back to the Democrats. But I suspect Democrats have made a fatal assumption that non-whites would be on board with an increasingly progressive agenda to a greater degree than is actually true. Further, we tend to talk about ethnic communities as if they act as a block, but that's not accurate. Certainly, individuals influence each other and community values can be important. Yet voters are ultimately individuals and expecting them to stay in lockstep as loyal political lackeys is a dangerous assumption for any political party.

The United States is operating a vast network of concentration camps. During the Trump administration, Congresswoman Alexandria Ocasio-Cortez popularized using the term "concentration camp" to describe detention facilities housing illegal immigrants caught crossing the border. Though she would later walk back comparisons to Nazi death camps, she otherwise held firm to this comparison.[18] Concentration camps don't only refer to the Nazi death camps but can include any system in which people are forcibly detained due to their ethnicity, faith, or so forth in order to maximize control over that population. Not all are as brutal as the Nazi death camps, though by nature they are coercive and authoritarian. The example of internment camps for Japanese citizens and immigrants during World War II is one such shameful example of the use of concentration camps during US history. But is the term apt to refer to detainment facilities?

Let me note that concerns about inhumane conditions or due process are absolutely valid and don't necessarily require us to believe that detainment facilities are concentration camps. After all, regular prisons, long-term mental health facilities, and juvenile detention facilities all receive complaints about their conditions as well as lack of due process, yet no one thinks they are concentration camps. I am not necessarily defending conditions in the facilities.

The interesting thing about the concentration camp narrative is that it emerged on the left during the presidency of Donald Trump (whom they loathed) but didn't gain nearly as much traction under the Democratic presidencies of either Barack Obama or Joe Biden, despite that the facilities weren't all that different.* To be fair, at times Trump appeared gleeful about using policies such as family separation as a deterrent to illegal immigration. Nonetheless, use of concentration camp language appears to be selective, though it may also pander to progressive narratives comparing the modern United States to fascist, authoritarian states.

The use of detention facilities for illegal immigrants is not a "US thing" but in fact quite common throughout the world wherever migrants attempt to cross borders.[19] Conditions vary, and concerns about humane conditions are common. Most countries have laws that restrict immigration and systems that attempt to return migrants who cross borders illegally if they do not meet the criteria for asylum. The whole debate is emotionally fraught, and getting good information that isn't run through with moralization and advocacy is quite difficult.

However legitimate many of the issues are regarding the conditions and legal rights of detainees in these facilities, they are not concentration camps for several quite simple reasons. First, unlike most historical examples of concentration camps, authorities aren't going into communities, rounding them up, and putting them into detention facilities. Rather, in the case of immigration, individuals are coming *toward* the

---

* Some advocates are consistent, to be fair, but the issue seems to get traction in the press only when a Republican is president.

camps: crossing borders illegally despite knowing that detention may be a consequence. It would be historically unprecedented for targeted groups to willingly move in the direction of concentration camps if the goal of such camps were the same as historical examples. Second and related, people aren't being selected for the camps due to their ethnicity, faith, and so forth, but simply because they crossed the border illegally. Third, the ultimate goal of the facilities, however poorly achieved in practice, is not to concentrate individuals at all but rather to return them to their countries of origin.

None of this is to say I disbelieve individuals are sometimes stripped of their due process rights and forced to live in inhumane conditions. These are very valid concerns. Yet engaging in a misleading "concentration camp" narrative inevitably cues up backlash and a silly high-profile debate over language rather than getting at the core of the issue. Like it or not, nations probably *do* need illegal immigrant detention facilities, but these should be humanely run, with clear legal guidance and assistance for those detained. As with many issues today, much of the public-facing debate on immigration can come across as lacking seriousness: high in emotion and moralization on both sides with little by way of clear, data-based solutions.

CONCLUDING THOUGHTS

Much of modern politics seems akin to people atop floats in parades tossing cheap candy to the crowds. We get excited when it happens, but ultimately when the float passes by and we look at the candy we got, we realize we never really wanted it in the first place. Much of presidential politics can seem like this, with candidates promising big things and sometimes attempting to deliver with the sweep of executive orders. But appealing to one segment of the voting public's emotional wish lists makes for bad policy.

This issue has bedeviled the Biden administration as of this writing. Biden had signaled a more inviting and humane process at the US borders, but not surprisingly this resulted in a surge of illegal immigration that has overwhelmed facilities and border patrol agents, thereby exacerbating the very problematic systems Biden had promised to fix. There was also the previously mentioned account in which Biden managed to undermine his own Border Patrol agents. Responding to a picture of a border patrol agent reining in his horse near Haitian immigrants at the border, Biden promised the agents on scene "will pay" for their actions. It turns out people misinterpreted the photo as the agent using his reins to whip the immigrants, which did not in fact happen. Biden (and other politicians) responded in knee-jerk fashion before all the facts were in.[20] Unfortunately, this sort of behavior is increasingly common among politicians on both sides of the aisle.

Immigration is a complex issue, one that requires level heads and data-driven analyses. Opinions on the issue range from closing down most immigration, all the way to advocating a massive expansion of the US population, perhaps to as many as a billion people.[21] There are many complicated issues to balance: How does immigration affect not only the economy, but specific groups of workers and wages? Should we prioritize high-skill or low-skill immigration, or should family unification be a priority? To what degree should we allow asylum, and should we define this as only individuals specifically targeted by their governments or other groups in their countries (such as criminal gangs), or should this include anyone leaving high-crime countries? How do we ensure humane conditions at detention facilities without inadvertently incentivizing greater migration that those same facilities can't handle?

We're not looking at a sack-of-Rome type scenario. There's no horde of Goths about to descend on Washington, DC. But the issue of immigration, particularly illegal immigration on the southern border, has descended into chaos, finger pointing, and memes. It's an unhealthy situation, and unfortunately the United States has lacked the leadership in recent administrations to tackle this thorny issue. Illegal immigration to the United States, in short, remains a catastrophe.

11

THE END OF REASON

On January 6, 2021, Three King's Day, the US Congress gathered in a joint session at the US Capitol to certify the results of the 2020 presidential election, which resulted in a win for Joe Biden. Usually a pro forma process of counting electoral votes, this session was tense due to efforts by the Republican Party to delegitimize the process and fail to certify the votes. This effort itself was a historic intrusion into a fair election process but was motivated by widespread conspiracy theories on the right that the election had been fraudulent and Republican nominee Donald Trump's victory stolen from him.

Earlier in the day, Trump had held a rally where he inflamed his supporters with claims of a stolen election and imparted on them to march to the Capitol and make their voices heard to support Republican legislators challenging the vote. Though he didn't specifically call upon them to riot, his language was aggressive and many in the crowd began to talk about storming the Capitol. Even as Trump was finishing speaking, many of his supporters had moved on to the Capitol. That same day, several pipe bombs were found near the Capitol but fortunately removed safely. The crowd outside the Capitol grew large and angry. It became clear that the Capitol police presence was seriously outmanned and underprepared.

Inside, to his credit, Republican leader Mitch McConnell spoke against overruling the election results, noting it would forever damage the reputation of the US republic. Outside, the protests grew violent.

Protestors pushed up against the thin lines of police, spraying them with chemicals and hitting them with batons. One officer was dragged away from his group and beaten with, among other things, the pole from an American flag. Another was nearly crushed between a doorway and the throngs of protestors pushing in. Protestors—well, I think we can call them rioters now—smashed through windows and climbed over fences, invading the Capitol. Outnumbered, Capitol police tried to defend the building as best they could. Most officers acted dutifully and bravely, though six were subsequently disciplined for inappropriate conduct such as showing support for the rioters.[1]

The rioters now roamed freely in the Capitol. Some engaged in largely purposeless behaviors, taking selfies or propping their feet on congresspeople's desks. Some, such as the infamous QAnon Shaman who charged into the Capitol bare chested with face paint and a horned helmet, simply seemed odd. Others, however, sought out the congresspeople themselves as a violent mob. Rioter Ashli Babbitt was shot by Capitol police as she attempted to climb through a barricaded door near where congresspeople were hiding. Behind her, a mob were trying to break through the door. The shooting was later ruled as justified.

Hours after the breach of the Capitol, the National Guard was finally called. By 6:00 p.m., four hours after the initial assault, the rioters began to lose steam. Police were able to clear out the Capitol. By 8:00 p.m., Congress resumed session and would ultimately, over some continued Republican objection, certify the election of Joe Biden.

Five people died during the riot: Babbitt, who was shot by police; Capitol police officer Brian Sicknick, who was pepper-sprayed and then died of multiple subsequent strokes ruled to have been brought on by the riot violence; and three other rioters, two of whom died of heart attacks and one who died from a drug overdose.[2] Numerous officers and rioters were seriously injured. Four officers involved in defending the Capitol would commit suicide within a year, traumatic brain injuries potentially precipitating some of these deaths. About 725 rioters were ultimately arrested; many in subsequent weeks following the riot. About $1.5 million in damages was done to the Capitol.[3] But the worst damage was done to the reputation of the US republic as the world witnessed this astounding spectacle.

The January 6, 2021, riot is, of course, a catastrophe. But it's one that built on previous authoritarian inclinations in President Trump and an embrace of conspiracy theories among his supporters. But how did this happen? And what can be done to prevent it from happening again? In this chapter we'll look at conspiracy theories and political partisanship. We'll examine the spiraling descent of the United States and other democracies into chaos, the allure of authoritarianism, and what we might do to prevent it getting worse.

CONSPIRACY THEORIES

The January 6, 2021, riot was built upon conspiracy theories that the Democrats had "stolen" the presidential election from Trump through rigged elections. It was a narrative promoted by Trump himself who broke with tradition by failing to accept defeat in the election. Though no serious evidence emerged that the election was "stolen" from Trump (and the Democrats have never struck me as remotely competent to pull off such a conspiracy, even had they wished to), the narrative nonetheless took hold. As of August 2021, nearly two-thirds of Republicans believed that the election had been stolen.[4] At the risk of being obvious, it isn't exactly healthy for democracy if a majority of voters on one side believe an election was rigged (it may not just be one side either—though Democrats can say, in the usual kindergarten sense, "they started it," the rumblings over voter rights could be setting the stage for widespread Democratic disavowals of lost elections, too—we'll see). Democracy is in danger if the voting public believe lost elections equal fraud.

In fairness, between campaign financing, the influence of the wealthy, redistricting, and so on, there's enough *legal* hanky-panky in elections. And each side tends to disfavor election processes that favor the other side. One side complains about redistricting, for instance, until they gain power and use it as a weapon themselves. People complain about the Electoral College when it appears to favor the other side, then go silent when it favors their side. Some of that is just human nature. Trying to gather power for oneself is natural, even if embarrassing, but we either accept the legal processes or work with the legal system to reform them.

The question becomes whether (A) something *illegal* is going on or (B) if what's *legal* is lopsidedly against one party. Currently, Republicans appear to be worrying more about A, whereas Democrats are worrying more about B (though they've had their own conspiracy theories about Russian collusion).

As we can see, the whole system depends on having some level of basic trust. But to have trust, authority figures need to demonstrate trustworthiness. For instance, I'm reading a book on the Secret Service right now that's quite interesting, and in one chapter it details the events of 9/11.[5] For the narrative to make sense, however, one has to have some trust that what we've been told is correct; namely that Islamic terrorists led by Osama bin Laden attacked America. Personally, I know nothing about 9/11 at all other than what I've read in newspapers, have been told by politicians, or saw at the 9/11 Museum in New York, which I've visited. But if you have reason to distrust politicians or the news media, this can lead to questioning whether the narrative itself is true, which opens us up to all manner of cockamamie ideas about what "really" happened.

As with many things, there's likely a balance between skepticism and belief that is healthy, although it's hard to argue where that line is. For instance, we should generally give weight to scientific evidence, but I'll be the first to say that scientists and science organizations (often actually political organizations or professional guilds; there are few real "science" organizations that are ideologically neutral) regularly misbehave. Psychology is going through a full-blown "replication crisis," in which somewhere between 50 and 66 percent of things we used to teach students may now be proving to be false. Even famous experiments such as the Milgram shock studies, the Stanford Prison experiment, or Watson's studies of Little Albert may not be as valid as we once thought. That politicians lie to us regularly is hardly a controversial point to make. But so do news media who routinely repackage the truth in the most sensational and selective ways to generate revenue. We've covered some of these issues in previous chapters. If the authorities are duplicitous, how can we accept prevailing narratives?

On the other hand, if we reject prevailing narratives, why are we accepting the stories of random idiots on the internet? This is the trick. Challenging conventional wisdom can be good, though there's always a risk of it straying into accepting other goofy narratives such as 9/11 conspiracies, anti-vaccine narratives, QAnon (the belief there are widespread networks of pedophiles in government and the entertainment industry), or for that matter, the belief that Trump was some kind of Manchurian candidate for the Russians or that widespread "systemic racism" or "white supremacy" is in action among the most egalitarian nations in human history.

People are often bad, and conspiracies do happen. So how then do we distinguish between actual conspiracies and a false conspiracy theory? And why do people gravitate toward conspiracy theories?

Spotting a conspiracy theory. The best conspiracy theories require remarkable efficiency on the part of a government that most people recognize, in other circumstances, can barely find their asses with two hands, a treasure map, and a flashlight. Thus, we think that somehow the US government could cover up the existence of alien spacecraft in the New Mexico desert for seventy years but couldn't cover up hanky-panky in the Clinton White House. The sad truth is that humans like to yak and brag, they like book deals and money, and the moment you tell them never to speak about a topic, their seams begin to burst with the urgent desire to tell *exactly that secret.* Keeping a lid on this normal response would be an enormous undertaking. Thus, the first sign of a conspiracy theory is that it requires an inordinate amount of efficiency in government, as well as significant buy-in among hundreds or perhaps thousands of individuals to remain silent for decades. Come on, some of these people would gab to their wives, who would later become ex-wives eager to torpedo their spouses' careers and make a few bucks in the process. Look at either the Biden or Trump administrations. Do we really think either of these governments have even the slightest capability of keeping the lid on a faked moon landing?

That's the funny thing about conspiracy theories. They often require us to believe in an inordinate amount of effectiveness and strategy from governments that we otherwise recognize as stumbling around like blind bulls in a china shop. But how do conspiracy theories come into being?

Consider the strange and infamous Pizzagate story. In December 2016, Edgar Welch, a father of two and otherwise average dude, walked into the Comet Ping Pong pizza restaurant in Washington, D.C., with an AR-15 rifle and a mission to free kidnapped children held there. The only unfortunate thing for him was there were no children. He was the rube of an elaborate conspiracy hoax, which suggested that an enormous pedophile ring existed among powerful elites and that local businesses were being used for human trafficking. At the center of this, supposedly, was Hillary Clinton, who'd just lost the 2016 presidential election and who, according to the conspiracy theory, had a predilection for under-aged girls. Fed a steady diet of these goofy theories on the internet and via far-right agitators such as Alex Jones, Welch waved his rifle around in the restaurant, blew the lock off one door, and found a lot of pizza dough. Welch would go on to serve a four-year prison term. Turns out you can't hold people hostage in a pizza joint even if you have good intentions.[6]

The Pizzagate episode is an obvious catastrophe for all involved. It's certainly a catastrophe for Welch, pulled into a conspiracy theory and his life ruined. It's a catastrophe for the pizza joint, now linked in the minds of many with a false child kidnapping ring and subject to harassment. It's also a catastrophe for good sense and our faith in people's ability to realize when something is rubbish. How did something like this happen?

Pizzagate had all the ingredients for a conspiracy theory gone awry. First, you begin with a polarized environment in which people are will-ing to believe the worst of each other. Second, you give it a sense of plausibility; after all, as weird as the idea of a Hillary Clinton–centered pedophile ring is, there are real-life examples involving other big names. Jeffrey Epstein really did run a prostitution ring of underaged girls and apparently catered to numerous high-profile men, with, most notably, Prince Andrew of the United Kingdom among the accused.[7] None other than Bill Clinton has been named as an Epstein associate, though Clinton has denied any wrongdoing and has not been charged with any crimes (Epstein himself died in prison—his death itself a conspiracy theory re-garding whether it was suicide or an assassination to prevent him from naming powerful names). So, conspiracies *do* sometimes happen. But conspiracy theories persist despite evidence against them, sometimes with evidence against the theory itself being taken as proof of how deep and thorough the plot goes. The Pizzagate conspiracy theory apparently began with a single Facebook account then was amplified by real people and foreign bots alike. Add to this a general sense of societal malaise, and people can become ripe for conspiracy theories.

The Pizzagate conspiracy and its offspring QAnon (an even more vast conspiracy theory involving supposed child sex rings among the powerful, against which none other than Donald Trump is supposedly fighting) demonstrate the propensity for those on the right to fall victim to these kinds of scams. In fairness, the left are far from immune. For instance, the common belief on the far left that the OK hand signal is used to indicate white supremacy is the result of an online trolling campaign that people fell for.[8] I already discussed how Emmanuel Cafferty lost his job over this goofiness in chapter 7. Not exactly a city of people smothered under a volcano to be sure, but still rather catastrophic for him. Not to mention the general chilling effect among a population of folks who now wonder if they're going to get "canceled" if they make a previously innocuous hand sign that only conspiracy theorists find offensive.

There are individual differences in susceptibility, of course. Evidence suggests that the embracing of conspiracy theories is more common among individuals who have experienced setbacks and tend to externalize the fault for those setbacks. Conspiracy theories also appear to create social cohesion among individuals who already feel socially excluded (one reason that shaming people for belief in conspiracy theories tends to backfire). They can also help people feel that their ingroup (those who've identified the conspiracy) are morally superior to the outgroup (those responsible for the conspiracy or the rubes who haven't seen it).[9] To reduce conspiracy theories, we have to understand why people embrace them in the first place. But again, given that perceived social exclusion is often a precursor to conspiracy theories, shaming and blaming tends to backfire, merely reinforcing the motive for engaging in the conspiracy theory. One must approach them with compassion and patience.

SMOLDERING EMBERS

In the end, some conspiracy theories are silly and harmless. One may think the moon landing was faked, but it's unlikely that such an individual is going to try to storm a government building over it. One might reasonably argue that all conspiracy theories come with cost insofar as they decrease trust in authorities. This is a tricky issue. The general untrustworthiness of authorities undoubtedly contributes to conspiracy theories, yet, during times of crisis, it's important to be able to place our trust in authorities who deserve that trust to guide us through the crisis. The COVID-19 epidemic is a classic example of this, revealing both the dodginess of authoritative decision making as well as the squeamishness of much of the general public in trusting authorities, two prongs of a fork that effectively barbecued our response to the epidemic. Even to the extent that some people lionize the authorities or put up "science is real" signs in their yards, this appears to be more culture-war signaling than anything truly rational.

Thus, though some conspiracy theories seem goofy and funny but harmless, others can carry real-world consequences. Not all of these are necessarily as direct as attacking the Capitol with American flags or firing a few rounds of ammunition into marinara sauce. Rather, as with the suspiciousness of vaccines around COVID-19, the cost can come in opportunities lost. People become suspicious of a thing that's actually helpful and fail to put it to good use.

Let's take a look at the seemingly endless controversy over genetically modified organisms (GMOs), some of which end up as food. Now—surprise, surprise—in my training as a clinical psychologist, we didn't get into a lot of detail regarding the use of recombinant DNA technologies in agriculture, so I can't claim to be a GMO expert. Here, like all of us, I must put a fair amount of trust in the "experts" that there's no conspiracy to hide the "real truth" regarding how GMOs are secretly poisoning us and turning us into alien slaves or whatever. But as a psychologist who studies these things, I have insight into how people ignore scientific data once they have a moralistic belief in how something is harmful or evil.

Basically, traditional agriculture involves selectively breeding plants and animals over generations to produce variants that are useful in agriculture (for instance, turning red junglefowl into chickens or converting a bunch of stringy weeds into modern corn, which admittedly, still tastes like stringy weeds to me). By contrast, GMO technology skips a lot of that and simply inserts desirable DNA into plants or animals to create hybrids that are useful. For instance, DNA can be introduced to make plants that are toxic to insect pests or require less water. This can make that crop able to grow in arid conditions or less reliant on poisonous pesticide and herbicides.[10] The advantages of this are pretty evident.

But what about all those weird little squiggly DNA strands in the new critter? If I eat that critter, am I going to develop a third arm or turn into a moth or something? What most people seem to be vaguely worried about is something called *horizontal gene transfer*. Put in simple words, if I eat a plant or animal made with GMO technology, are those bioengineered DNA strands in that product going to enter my DNA and do something unsavory, whether that's getting cancer, growing corn kernels all over my skin, or whatever. Now, this is one of those things that is theoretically possible, so we can't say people are totally crazy for raising the concern. However, the good news is that evidence for horizontal transfer from GMOs to humans is pretty thin.[11] Can I assure you that horizontal transfer could *never* happen? No. But I could tell you that you're more likely to be killed by a stray javelin from the nearest Olympic games. Or, more seriously, you're probably more likely to get sick from salmonella in a "natural" spinach leaf than you are to get sick from the DNA in a spinach leaf bioengineered to resist salmonella in the first place.

This is not to say GMO technology has no downsides. Each GMO product must be tested individually for safety. Just because past GMO products have proven to be safe doesn't mean the next one will. Other risks involve the release of GMO organisms into the wild where, given their advantages, they may replace wild-born species.

But as to the safety of GMOs, here's the rub for conspiracy theorists: in order, as consumers, to be confident in GMOs, we have to have *faith* that the industries producing them are using the highest standards of safety. After all, exactly what they're doing to these plants and animals sounds a bit suspicious, more so given the technology involved sounds like something out of a dystopian sci-fi movie. But so long as we have trust in big business and government, everything's OK, right? It's a good thing there are no examples of big business and government working together to screw over the little guy.

Oh wait, there's lots of examples of exactly that! We can look at stuff like the Ford Pinto (a car known to often explode during collisions yet left on the road because Ford reasoned it would be less expensive to pay out lawsuits than recall all the vehicles[12]) and conclude big business' word on what is "safe" doesn't really mean a lot. Add in the well-known perfidy of politicians and even the sketchy and politicized behavior of science organizations, much as I hate to say it, and is it any wonder that pronouncements that GMOs are safe aren't exactly greeted with widespread sighs of relief?

Thus, even if that GMO-based corn puff isn't *really* going to turn a person into a mutant, suspiciousness about it is kind of understandable (hey, put a little nacho cheese on it, and it may be worth the risk anyway). When the track record of the "authorities"—including scientists—has been rather sketchy, we can begin with some empathy for why people may sometimes seem anti-science.

Unfortunately, this can drive people toward even *worse* sources of information: the legion of idiots, grifters, and psychopaths that occupy the internet and pepper it with nonsense, often for a price. Exactly how this works is a bit more complicated. If someone doesn't believe a scientist with a PhD, why believe this nincompoop who used to be on a popular sitcom and is now screaming on a YouTube channel? This brings us back to confirmation bias: many grifters succeed by not only telling people what they want to hear, but *confirming their suspicions.* "You think the government is filling up your GMO apples with the DNA of Marxists? Well, I've got a video right here showing a space alien and an FBI agent injecting stuff into everything they can find at a GMO orchard. Need I say more? Well, I will for a subscription of $5 a month."

It's easy to make fun, but it works. And before we point and laugh at the rubes with their tinfoil hats, let's remember this works on almost everyone. Remember myside bias? It's easy for liberals to snicker at conservatives with their anti-vaxxing (which actually tended to be bipartisan prior to COVID-19) and beliefs about pedophile kidnapping rings. But many of those same liberals believe we're living in, to quote President Joe Biden, "Jim Crow 2.0" despite enormous evidence to the contrary. Conservatives think we're being overrun by pornographic snowflakes from Mexico, whereas liberals think we're on the verge of becoming a Nazi Russian puppet state. It's always easy to spot the tinfoil on the other side, even as we're tucking our ears under our own aluminum.

The downsides to all this should be obvious. If we're suspicious of GMOs or, say, nuclear energy, this prevents us from using technologies that can help feed people or cut down on pollution. Or people might think that if the government is becoming overrun with soul-stealing Communist spies, we should march on D.C. and take it back, violently if need be.

The good news is that it doesn't seem that belief in conspiracy theories is on the rise.[13] However, most of this data comes prior to the COVID-19 epidemic, and conspiracy theories do have the potential to cause considerable harm, either directly or indirectly.[14] Thus, it's an issue worthy of further thought. So how do we reduce people's belief in conspiracy theories?

REDUCING THE APPEAL OF CONSPIRACY THEORIES

In their review of the research on conspiracy theories, scholars Jan-Willem van Prooijen and Karen Douglas propose four basic motivational components to conspiracy theories. Understanding these may help us enact policies to reduce their spread and impact.[15]

Conspiracy theories are consequential. Put simply, conspiracy theories can help people understand the complexities of the world around them and make decisions based upon them. Granted, the decisions are often bad, but they provide a groundwork for seeing a way past confusion and aligning one's choices along a clear path.

Conspiracy theories are universal. Conspiracy theorizing seems to have evolved as a natural adaptation to be alert for bad motives in others. This was quite adaptive as, oftentimes in our evolutionary history, people absolutely did have poor motives. Conspiracy theories are not specific to our culture or time in history, but likely evolved because they served a function, even if they often cause harm in modern society.

Conspiracy theories are emotional. Ostensibly, conspiracy theories are often put forward with the language of data, analysis, and rationality. Events such as the moon landing are critiqued for the apparent movement of the US flag in moon landing videos, despite there being no wind on the moon (as it has no atmosphere). However, research indicates that those who are susceptible to conspiracy theories tend to be higher in emotional/intuitive thinking rather than being data based (and having a PhD or MD does not make one immune to this). Confirmation bias is typically high among conspiratorial thinkers, whereas curiosity about disconfirmatory evidence is typically low. Conspiracy theories may help people reduce feelings of uncertainty, which can be uncomfortable.

Conspiracy theories are social. Conspiracy theories tend to comport well with two basic social behaviors. First, they tend to draw together members of the ingroup, namely those who believe in the conspiracy. Second, they tend to create clear demarcation lines of ingroup conflict. Thus, if one does not believe the conspiracy, he or she is at best a rube who has been tricked and at worst one of the "enemy." Conspiracy theories often tend to develop a collective belief in the superiority of believers ("We're the enlightened ones!") while also worrying that others (those engaging in the conspiracy) have undue power.

If we look at the two big conspiracy theories roiling through the United States right now—on the right, that there's a left-wing conspiracy to steal elections from conservative politicians and on the left that the United States is a "white supremacist" state on the verge of "Jim Crow 2.0"—we can see similarities. Although both conspiracy theories sometimes point to convenient data, neither is curious in the slightest about inconvenient data. Both pit those who are morally courageous (in their own eyes) against the bad people who either don't understand or deny the conspiracy. Both display a cultural narcissism in that the believers in the conspiracy feel that they are morally superior to those who are not. Both are social, particularly via the spread of memes and posts on social media, but conformity is also enforced in real life, often with social ostracism. And both are consequential, able to drive major decisions, whether election reform or policing reform.

Fixing this scenario is not as simple as waving a magic wand or having a few quick conversations. In my own experience, dealing with even a straightforward moral panic such as the belief that violent video games cause real-life violence can be a fifteen- to twenty-year project. In other words, this is going to require patience. Though some things can be done at the individual level, others must be at the societal level.

WHAT WE CAN DO AS INDIVIDUALS

Listen. As I've mentioned elsewhere, ridiculing people for their conspiratorial beliefs only drives them further into those beliefs. For instance, I've seen some folks on social and news media express glee when antivaxxers die of COVID-19. Not only is this ghoulish and cruel, but it's strategically ineffective. Conspiracy theories are often dependent upon us-versus-them thinking, so reinforcing that backfires.

Instead, listening politely to a person's beliefs can establish trust and rapport. This doesn't mean we need to agree with those beliefs. But being willing to listen communicates respect and breaks down the us-versus-them nature of such paradigms. It can be tough and requires patience, but it's better than indulging in screaming matches that get you nowhere.

Ask what might falsify the theory. Instead of doing a data dump, invite the person to consider and reflect on what kinds of evidence might convince them that the theory is wrong. In some cases, people might then retreat to saying something like, "I'm not here to debate this; the evidence for it is all around!" It can be helpful to politely discuss falsification: that theories survive when people actively try to disprove them rather than assemble evidence for them. Again, keep it cordial.

Data does help. If you really want to tackle a conspiracy theory, having data can help. Now people often get defensive when presented with unfriendly data, so don't expect a thank-you for removing the scales from their eyes. Have the grace to allow them to save face by disagreeing with you in the moment. It's possible they'll reflect on that data at a later time.

Be patient. Unfortunately, persuasion is a long-term game and it's not easy. It's easier and more rewarding to send a snarky meme. Oftentimes when we're persuading someone, it's incremental, and in fact, we may never know the impact we had. People generally won't change their mind amid an exchange, as to do so may feel like losing face. So we don't get rewarded for it in the same sense we do with the likes and applause we get for calling out a "bad person." But persuasion, however unsatisfying it may be for us as individuals in the short term, is far better for the collective good.

Know when to disengage. If a discussion is becoming heated or insults are being used, it's time to back away. Have a disengagement strategy. On social media I usually end conversations that have gone awry by inviting the other person to have an excellent day. You don't need to keep responding. Doing so may only agitate you, undoing whatever incremental persuasion you may have managed to achieve. Ultimately, not everyone is persuadable, so don't expend your energy on those who are not.

WHAT WE CAN DO AS A SOCIETY

For individual actions we can make our own conscious choices. Societal actions require a certain degree of coordination, and this can be more difficult to achieve. Thus, the following strategies are long-term ideas.

Stop rewarding bad behavior in our leaders. Part of the problem we currently face is that our leaders—whether in politics, news media, academia, or entertainment—are rewarded for behaviors that are counterproductive, polarizing, and make conspiracy theories easier to take hold. By contrast, we should reward transparency, honesty, and leaders who are able to acknowledge nuance and complexity rather than just tell us what we want to hear.

Look at how we vote. First, we have a primary system that tends to cater to more extreme voters. Then we're left voting for idiot number one, because we're terrified that idiot number two is worse. I have a radical suggestion: stop voting for idiots at all. Vote for a third candidate or write in "Bugs Bunny." Sure, on the surface, it feels like a throwaway vote, but if enough people do it, politicians will begin to get the message.

Conspiracy theories thrive when distrust in leadership is low, and frankly, there's little reason to trust our current crop of leaders almost anywhere among the "elite." This doesn't mean they're always engaged in rampant conspiracies (though do they generally stack the deck in their own favor? Sure). But they don't inspire confidence and we need people who do.

We also need policies that encourage transparency. One policy that has been interesting is the debate over critical race theory (CRT) being taught in K–12 schools. As we covered in chapter 7, CRT has real problems and there are good reasons to think pedagogies based in it do real harm to kids. This is a view basically shared by many on the right, center, and even left. However, right-leaning politicians often respond by trying to "ban" the teaching of CRT, an approach that raises real free-speech concerns. More recently, some conservative states have instead shifted to laws requiring transparency: making clear to parents what their children are learning in school. This is a much better approach. It's easy to argue that banning even misinformative and harmful speech (as CRT certainly is) is bad, because limiting speech is almost always worse than the speech being limited (which also is certainly true). But transparency is harder to argue about. After all, if schools aren't teaching CRT, or if teaching CRT is no more than teaching the history of slavery and racism in the United States, why argue for hiding it? If we focus on transparency, it's more difficult to argue that the government is hiding something.

Our science and academic institutions need reform. It is now very clear that significant left-wing biases exist in our science and academic institutions. Frankly, being on the left myself, I generally scoffed at this until the past few years, at least in the sense of it being a "really big deal." Sadly, I was wrong.

Now, by reform I don't mean the "defund education" approach that many conservatives seem to endorse, which will just worsen the problem. But there are some concrete steps conservatives can take, mainly in *funding* education. We need more conservative academics, administrators, and people serving on boards of trustees. Conservatives can fund research programs, endowed chairs, and grants specifically related to conservative thought. And sure, conservative donors can use their alumni support to make sure administrators are attuned to free speech and academic freedom concerns when some scholars critique prevailing leftist beliefs. In other words, conservatives can direct their attention toward *protecting* speech and encouraging more conservatives to get involved in academia. That may including nudging their own kids to get PhDs, even if that means having to put up with some "bed-wetting liberals" for a few years (the term isn't mine, but stuck in my head after a friend used it to describe herself). Again, this is a multi-decade process!

By contrast, conservatives need to be wary of indulging in efforts to squash speech they do not like. For instance, they should not threaten to revoke funding if a scholar they do not like gets a promotion. Further, the tenure system should be strengthened, not weakened. The one thing that allows some of us on the left to critique our fellow leftist scholars is the assurance we won't be mobbed out of a job. Without tenure, academia will become *more* leftist, not less.

Of course, academia shouldn't count on conservatives to ride to our rescue. We can take steps ourselves. First, we can commit to free speech and academic freedom principles on a broad scale and push our universities to endorse clear statements of value for free speech. We can work to encourage our universities to hire not just people from diverse social, ethnic, religious, and gender backgrounds, but also those with diverse worldviews, including conservatives.

Second, we need to reduce the administrative bloat that has overtaken universities. College tuitions have soared in the United States and that's not because they're throwing bucketloads of cash at professors. You can't throw a kale salad on a university campus without hitting a vice president of food hygiene or an associate provost of care packages. The trick is that universities hire administrators to cover their asses regarding some perceived social ill. Then when that administrator makes no real impact, the response is that more help is needed, so more administrators are hired ad infinitum, usually with little change in the underlying metrics. This administrative treadmill sucks both resources and authority over pedagogy away from faculty. It sticks students with a higher bill, typically without much to show for it.

Third, we need to stop treating our students like kindergartners in some kind of twenty-four-hour daycare for teens and twentysomethings. This doesn't mean we should be insensitive to students' mental health and social needs, but universities are not mental health centers and are very bad at trying to assume that job. Furthermore, pedagogy and policy should not be framed around students' desires to be shielded from inconvenient facts and opposing worldviews. Students should expect to learn, be challenged, and, indeed, sometimes find themselves exposed to worldviews that offend them. I submit the likelihood that academia's shift to safetyism has *contributed* to young adults' mental health crises, rather than helping them. We are depriving young adults from experiencing the constructive but sometimes challenging environment that builds resilience. As with all things, this means striking a balance. To be clear, I am not arguing for deliberate cruelty or indifference. Rather, academic institutions have lost clarity about their role. As a result, instead of being good at one thing (e.g., teaching facts, developing critical thinking), we're stretched to be involved in many things (mental health, social justice advocacy, etc.), and we've watered down our mission such that we're simply bad at everything.

I've focused on academia here, but we've seen this at science organizations too, whether the World Health Organization (WHO), the American Psychological Association, or the American Medical Association. The more such organizations embrace political orthodoxy on either side (mainly the left at the moment, though the WHO has a strange affinity for carrying China's pail), the more they police language with politically correct language guidelines and such, the less people trust them to be neutral and objective purveyors of fact.

We need to develop social institutions. One issue multiple people point to is a reduction in recent decades of social institutions wherein people might align with others with different worldviews. For instance, attendance at places of worship, social clubs and lodges, even things like bowling leagues have seen significant reductions in membership. These were often places that fostered one sense of shared belonging ("We're both Episcopalians" or "We're both members of the Gutterboyz Bowling League") that made sharing ideas on other dimensions safer and less likely to result in polarization. This exchange of ideas is good. When people become siloed and don't share ideas, this can foster polarization.

Now, I'm the first to point out how aspirational this idea is. Sure, I'll just start up a Dungeons and Dragons club and a bipartisan horde will sign up, we'll put daisies in our hair (or cacti, if conservative), hold hands, and dance in circles around the Maypole. For the ten easy steps to set up your bipartisan social organization, you'll have to wait for my next book. But understanding that these kinds of organizations are culturally important is in and of itself a concrete step. The question becomes then how to incentivize them. This requires both considering the kinds of clubs that people would like today (The Royal Order of Old Geezers is probably not that "cool" anymore) and also understanding the roadblocks that prevent them from forming organically. There may be ways for local and state governments to encourage their development without intruding so far as to make them de facto state arms. This could come in the form of things like tax breaks, start-up funds, and so forth. I'm no policy wonk so I'll leave it up to those smarter than me about these things to mull this over. My point is simply that the deterioration of these types of social organizations has made it easier for people to subdivide into narrower and more aggressive political tribes.

CONCLUDING THOUGHTS

Conspiracy theories are common throughout history and across cultures and worldviews. They obviously provide some kind of function, and if left unchecked, they can cause significant problems. They are fun to mock but doing so often appears to strengthen rather than weaken them. If we want to help prevent another January 6, 2021, we need to understand them better. What would lead so many ostensibly normal people to burn their futures on easily fact-checked misinformation? And before we give the snarky answers—"They're racist bigots"—let's remember that "our side" is just as prone to destructive conspiracy theories, so we need to reach beyond the emotionally and morally satisfying answer to something deeper.

In recent memory alone, whether "Stop the Steal," conspiracies about vaccines, or unquestioned beliefs in "systemic racism," conspiracy theories have resulted in obvious catastrophes. True, none of these has brought our society fully to its knees, but it would be good to get our heads around this phenomenon before one does.

12

DOES EVERYTHING END IN CATASTROPHE?

Well, this has been depressing, hasn't it? By this time, we've traveled quite a journey through human idiocy, folly, and bias. We've seen how often good intentions end in disaster and also how people's intentions often aren't all that good to begin with. We're emotional, aggressive, shortsighted, biased, slow to learn, and quick to deflect blame away from ourselves. It's a wonder we've made it this far. Indeed, as much as we've taken a deep dive in to calamity, it's also amazing to contemplate the catastrophes we've avoided. Despite having nuclear weapons for close to a century, we've managed not to destroy the Earth with them. Previously commonplace phenomena like slavery, conquest by war, misogyny, child exploitation, and unfettered abuse of our natural resources are anathema (though, of course, none of these is entirely eradicated, and some remain all too common). Though the past years have seen the return of autocracy in many parts of the world (including clumsy flirtations with a kind of kleptocracy by Donald Trump in the Unites States), democracy remains widespread where once it was rare. There are, in short, reasons for optimism.

I'm guilty of one thing (maybe many things, but only one thing we'll talk about now) and that's that I find it interesting to focus on human failings. And we have plenty. But there is also much that we do right. Indeed, one thing I *don't* want people to take away from this book is that all is hopeless and humans are entirely irrational and doomed to repeat the same patterns. That often happens, sure, but not always. I'll repeat something I mentioned in the first chapters: for all the flaws of modern society, we are living as close to utopia as people have at any previous point in human history. And although gross inequities remain, particularly related to class, we have made astounding progress and everyone has benefited from this. There is now less disease, war, slavery, mistreatment of women, homicide, poverty, starvation, and so forth than at any previous point in human history. Somehow, we got here working together.

Some of these advances were certainly lucky, fortunate discoveries like penicillin or the location of natural resources. But others were definitely deliberate, the actions of great people and well-designed, data-based policy. Maybe this doesn't happen often enough, but it *does* happen.

I've explored human catastrophes with a goal of better understanding how we get things wrong. By understanding our biases, we can spot when we indulge in them and perhaps reflect a bit more. By knowing how we can make errors, we can learn from them. By understanding human motivation, we can work with it toward desirable policy goals. At the same time, exploring only the negative does not leave us with tools to understand how human potential can be harnessed for good outcomes. So let's take a look to see what humans get right.

PEOPLE DO (SORT OF) LISTEN TO DATA

Wait, you say, didn't I just read a whole book I paid $27.95 for (thanks for that, by the way) telling me that humans *don't* listen to data? We only like information that confirms our prior beliefs and disregard people based on tribalism? Well, all those things are true. There's one important caveat, however, and that's that not everybody has strong opinions on every topic. Where persuasion can occur is within that middle area, namely among folks who don't hold particularly strong views on a topic and don't necessarily view those with opposing views as the enemy.

I'm going to pick on our current president (as of this writing, so maybe don't get too attached) Joe Biden. As I write this, Biden has just crossed the one-year mark of his presidency and it's been brutal. He began his presidency in January 2021 with a 55 percent approval rating (32%

disapproval) according to Reuters.[1] In January 2022, his approval had slipped to 45 percent (50% disapproval). Other polls are even less optimistic, suggesting approval ratings in the 30s.[2] What happened?

What happened is that Joe Biden has often seemed to be far behind the curve on important matters. As we've seen earlier, he's taken to repeating progressive language like he's on a college campus; meanwhile, the US withdrawal from Afghanistan was botched, inflation soared, violent crime remains high in many cities, polarization remains high (and Biden has contributed to it, comparing his opponents to "Jim Crow 2.0" segregationists at times), the COVID-19 virus has raged on, and so on. As to voting laws being debated by Democrats and Republicans, Biden said, "Jim Crow 2.0 is about two insidious things: voter suppression and election subversion" and then added juicily, "It's not hyperbole."[3] If someone has to assure you that something isn't hyperbole, it almost always is. To be fair, the voting laws on both sides of the 2022 debates probably are motivated in part by self-interest, but there's little evidence they roll voting protections back to 1950s-level segregation.[4] Voters sought out Biden in part to reduce this kind of political nonsense and he has not.

Obviously, some voters are sticking with Biden through all of this. Others never liked him in the first place. But a significant number (bad news for Biden) have changed their mind in response to actual circumstances. Of course, Biden has three more years of his term, so perhaps events will change, and things will turn around for him. But the point is that many people are, indeed, persuadable.

Of course, in politics I'm referring to national and world events, not data exactly, but people do respond to numbers and facts. In fact, I've seen it happen in my own area of research. When I began, most psychologists thought video games could be linked to serious acts of violence. Now, whether we're talking about clinicians[5] or scholars who study video games,[6] that's a minority view. That change didn't happen overnight but required multiple studies and continual efforts to present this data to the research community and general public. Obviously, some people still panic over video games, but it's much less common than it was twenty years ago. This highlights related issues: people do listen, but it can take patience and persistence to get the message out there.

PEOPLE MOSTLY WANT TO DO THE RIGHT THING (AT LEAST FOR THEIR SIDE)

Given humans' long history of war, slavery, brutality, genocide, rape, and oppression, it's easy to conclude we're a hopelessly incorrigible species. And it's important to recognize the darkness that makes up part of our motivational structure. We may *think* we're past this, but look how easily, even in the modern age, people happily divide into political camps and gleefully wish each other death if not outright behave in ways to make that happen.

A lot of this is likely left over from previous evolutionary periods when suspiciousness of and hostility toward "them" was rather adaptive. Hell, it was still adaptive right through much of the twentieth century, so we shouldn't be stunned that it didn't suddenly vanish with twenty-first-century moral pretentions. Yet, I'm optimistic we're actually not all that bad.

In fact, people are generally motivated to do the right thing, at least within their own communities. An interesting example of this emerged in the video game *Walking Dead*, based on the television series and graphic novels of the same name. In the game, players are often presented with moral choices wherein they can behave morally or badly. Often, behaving badly is the easier option; doing the right thing comes at more significant cost to the player. Makers of the game, Telltale Games, tracked players' decisions in the games. Overwhelmingly, despite this being a fantasy realm with no real-life ramifications and despite the "bad" choices being better for the players, players tended to choose to do the right thing.[7]

I don't want to be Pollyannaish about this. There are obviously several circumstances in which people will be tempted to do the wrong thing. The first is a scenario in which the benefits of doing the wrong thing are high, the benefits of doing the right thing are low, and the perceived costs of doing the wrong thing are low. This, of course, reflects self-interest. This is a complicated issue but understanding it can help us provide circumstances in which people are more motivated to do the right thing. Transparency can increase the costs of doing the wrong thing. And we can increase incentives and decrease costs of doing the right thing as much as possible.

The second situation is when we assume others will do the right thing, so we don't have to. This is a phenomenon in psychology called the *bystander effect*. Once, I experienced this firsthand. I inherited a medical quirk from my father in which I can have difficulty swallowing, particularly if I eat too fast. Sometimes drinking something can help move the food along. During a restaurant outing with my family some years ago, I found food caught in my throat and decided to drink some lemonade to help wash it down. Apparently, the food was stuck quite high up and the lemonade aspirated into my breathing bits, which promptly slammed shut. This is a normal response to aspirating fluid, but not one I was previously familiar with. It's terrifying! It felt very much like choking to death on food. There I stood in the restaurant, thinking these might be my last seconds, my wife giving me the Heimlich maneuver, while most patrons looked at me like I was quite rude to have interrupted their dinner.

Granted, my wife *was* visibly trying to help me, and the restaurant staff called for an ambulance (though the involuntary reaction goes away after a few seconds and I was not, in fact, dying from anything other than humiliation). Yet I'll always remember the look of indifference on the other diners' faces while I was visibly in distress. The gist of bystander effect is that, unlike when we're alone with a person in need of assistance and more likely to intervene, when we're in groups, we tend to assume someone else will intervene. This makes groups kind of useless in emergencies, since everyone sits around like dummies while someone who needs help perishes. This phenomenon became famous for the story of Kitty Genovese, a young woman murdered in 1964 outside her apartment building. According to legend, dozens of her neighbors heard or watched her die from their apartment buildings without helping or calling the police. In fact, though the murder did happen, the story of the bystanders was made up.[8] Only a few neighbors were able to see the murder and they all called the police; the story was made up by the police chief and a hungry reporter to bury the police's slow response time. To this day, the false parable still shows up in psychology textbooks. Never let the truth get in the way of a good story, I guess.

The third situation is one we've already talked about in this book; namely that we're less likely to help people we perceive as members of an outgroup, particularly if we think of them as outright enemies. That's particularly true in the abstract, when these "others" are amorphous blobs in our imagination rather than real people right before us. The problem here is us-versus-them mentality, tribalism, whatever we want to call it. The solution is to include a wider range of people into "us" and emphasize human universalism. Unfortunately, this process is undone by the xenophobia, sexism, and hostility to diversity on the far right, as well as the identity politics, race essentialism, and weird new forms of sexism (e.g., "toxic masculinity" concepts) on the far left. Indeed, the far right and far left are so similar in their unproductive focus on identity that Canadian comic Ryan Long has a classic bit on YouTube entitled "When Wokes and Racists Actually Agree on Everything."

I'm not trying to delve into the negative again (too late!), but rather to point out that if we understand these limitations, we can see that, within these parameters, most people want to do the right thing. The trick is to understand how to help guide them to that path without instituting some kind of creepy, Orwellian, behavior-modification regime.

WE CAN FIX IT!

One piece of good news is if we can help people understand *why* they make mistakes, we can help them not make those mistakes again in the future. Take, for example, the tragic Air France crash that began our book. A comprehensive analysis went into understanding how the accident occurred. From that investigation, mechanical changes were made to airplanes, but airplane crews also received new training about how to deal with that sort of emergency, and cockpit rules for communication and decision making were clarified to make the kind of confusion in the Air France crash less likely to happen with future flights. We must remember that air flight has become progressively safer over the decades, and much of this comes from learning from prior mistakes, tragic though those mistakes sometimes are.*

Indeed, an entire field of human psychology is devoted to such issues. Called *human factors psychology*, these psychologists try to under-

---

* I say "sometimes" because the majority of airplane emergencies don't end in the kind of complete annihilation of the plane that makes international news. Most are resolved without deaths.

stand how humans interact with machines and how to design better systems to make human errors less probable. Part of this deals with ergonomics, or how to make workplaces more efficient for the humans working in them. For instance, how and where do we best place controls and indicators in a cockpit to give pilots the information they need and allow them to make the best decisions? This field of study also examines how environmental changes can affect user decisions to engage in safer driving behaviors, for instance.

Take the issue of speeding while driving. Many drivers (myself included) have the experience of driving along a road or highway at a comfortable cruising speed. Upon seeing a police speed trap, we look down at our speedometer and only then realize we're quite above the posted speed limit. We slam on our brakes, hoping that's soon enough and the police officer is merciful. The interesting thing about this phenomenon is, unlike the aggressive folks who bob and weave through lanes of traffic, tires squealing, we had no real awareness of or intention to speed (or at least not by as much as we were). Whatever driving speed it was just felt comfortable.

Speeding is a serious issue causing many accidents and deaths each year, so reducing speeding is worthwhile. Deterrence via police patrols can help, but perhaps there are ways of reducing people's sense of comfort while driving at high speeds. Some psychologists have investigated how to design roads to reduce speeding. For instance, some research has indicated that increasing the noisiness of the road, such as by installing blocks of gravel chippings in the pavement, reduces speeding.[9] In effect, by making our brains process more sound, they feel "busier" and less comfortable traveling at higher speeds. Other research has indicated that visual markers can do the trick. For instance, drivers tend to reduce speeds when lanes are narrower and when the road center has repeated visual markings that fly by faster at higher speeds, giving drivers a clearer visual indication of their speed.[10] The placement of guardrails also reduces driving speed.[11] Bottom line, the busier we make roads appear, the more drivers slow down. Roads that are wide, straight, quiet, and with lots of clearance on either side tend to increase speeds. Noisy roads and those with a lot of stuff on the sides—guardrails, even trees—tend to reduce speeds.

So, perception matters regarding how people make decisions. It's also been noticed that people are basically lazy, and this, too, can be used to help people make decisions. In many situations, people may be faced with decisions wherein one choice is the better choice and one choice the worse choice. However, if the worse choice is easier, people tend to pick that one. Nudge theory suggests that if we change that calculus and make the better choice the easier choice, then people will choose that more often. For instance, consider eating healthy. Eating healthy is often more expensive and requires more work from us to prepare our food. By contrast, fast food is cheap, doesn't require preparation (particularly if we're already driving, which is often the case), and is yummy. But eating too much fast food can lead to health problems and obesity. Some changes can be fairly easy (for instance, putting healthier items at eye level in supermarkets and putting naughty choices on higher shelves), but others may require more expensive interventions, such as government investment in subsidizing healthier eating choices. The intent of nudge is to preserve people's freedom of choice while making better decisions easier to make. Particularly for eating choices, nudge theory holds promise.[12]

Nudge theory is controversial, however. Despite the ethos of libertarian paternalism where free will is maintained, it's not too hard to see where nudge theory can become coercive. Governments might use it to guide us toward decisions convenient for them rather than us. And it is not effective for bigger social problems such as global warming.[13] All these types of paternalistic government efforts rely on an assumption of benevolent authorities, and history hasn't always given us a lot of these.

THE CYCLICAL NATURE OF IDIOCY

Right now, certainly in the United States, but elsewhere throughout the world, we've found ourselves in a dark pattern of irrationality and bad decisions. On the political right, we're seeing populism (a tendency to pit "the people" against "corrupt" elites), science denialism, and flirtations with authoritarianism, and, on the left, we're seeing—well—populism, science denialism, and flirtations with authoritarianism. That's horseshoe theory: the more extreme that political positions get on either the left or the right, the more they come to resemble each other. At the very extremes, Nazism and Communism in many respects resembled each other in regard to the practical effects on citizenry than either resembled democracies. On our far right and far left, small but highly vocal, aggressive, and (unfortunately) influential minorities have embraced censorship, eschewed due process, indulged in hate, and pushed our societies in dangerous directions.

The good news is that this has all happened before, and extremism seldom lasts forever. Typically, such things work in a cycle, with extremists overextending themselves to the point that ordinary folks have had enough and demand a return to normalcy. The trick is to hit that inflection point before extremists become firmly entrenched in authoritarian positions (such as in the Soviet Union or other authoritarian regimes throughout the world). At the moment, for many of us, it can seem as if the world has gone mad and that the rational beliefs we once had—that our country is flawed but moving ever toward true egalitarianism, that technology and capitalism have historically abused workers but also have lifted many people out of poverty, starvation, and war, that police sometimes abuse their authority but also provide security, safety, and good governance, that universities and schools can be biased in how they teach youth but also are bastions of knowledge unlike anything we've ever seen before—are now in short supply. It sometimes can seem like perhaps it is us with complex, nuanced, and optimistic views of the world who have somehow been left behind.

But the madness will end or at least subside to a manageable level. This is not a call to passivity, to keep our heads low until it goes away like a passing hurricane. Rather, I am optimistic that if we all raise our heads in ways big and small and demand a return to the core values of our democracy—free speech, due process, rigorous, data-driven, yet civil debate—we can roll back the tides of irrationality currently sweeping so much of the world. It will take bravery, patience, and resilience, but it can be done. In this sense, I end on an optimistic note. During my lifetime, despite all the bad decisions people have made, myself included, things have gotten better and better for almost everyone. This is a global phenomenon. If we manage to keep focused on rationality, this will continue even in the face of major challenges such as climate change. We must calm down and focus on data, not hyperbole. But we've done it before and we can do it again.

That's all I have for you. I hope you've enjoyed this trip down human feebleness. Ideally, you've learned a few things you didn't know before and had a bit of fun along the way. Even better if I've helped you approach your own challenges from a more rational perspective. And, of course, I hope you don't close this book thinking that your decision to buy it was a minor catastrophe.

NOTES

CHAPTER 1

1. Hosford, M., Effron, L., & Battiste, N. (2012). Air France Flight 447 Crash "Didn't Have to Happen," Expert Says. ABC News. Retrieved from: https://abcnews.go.com/Blotter/air-france-flight-447-crash-didnt-happen-expert/story?id=16717404.

2. Bureau d'Enquêtes et d'Analyses. (2012). Final Report on the Accident on 1st June 2009 to the Airbus A330-203 Registered F-GZCP Operated by Air France Flight AF 447 Rio de Janeiro–Paris. Retrieved from: https://bea.aero/docspa/2009/f-cp090601.en/pdf/f-cp090601.en.pdf.

3. Faccini, B. (2013). Four Minutes, Twenty-Three Seconds. *Volare Aviation Monthly*. Retrieved from: http://understandingaf447.com/extras/18-4_minutes__23_seconds_EN.pdf.

4. Pinker, S. (2018). *Enlightenment Now*. New York: Viking.

5. Gallup. (2020). U.S. Church Membership Falls below Majority for First Time. Retrieved from: https://news.gallup.com/poll/341963/church-membership-falls-below-majority-first-time.aspx.

6. Centers for Disease Control. (2021). Retrieved from: https://webapp.cdc.gov/cgi-bin/broker.exe.

7. Beck, A. T. (1976). *Cognitive Therapy and the Emotional Disorders*. New York: International Universities Press.

8. I borrow some of these from the framing of Leahy, who provides a more detailed and comprehensive list. Leahy, R. (2021). Fundamentals of Cognitive

Therapy. Retrieved from: https://cognitivetherapynyc.com/wp-content/up loads/2021/02/arosnonintro.pdf.

9. White, M. (2012). *Atrocities.* New York: W. W. Norton.

10. Stergar, R., & Scheer, T. (2018). Ethnic Boxes: The Unintended Consequences of Habsburg Bureaucratic Classification. *Nationalities Papers, 46,* 575–91.

11. McKeenin, S. (2013). *July 1914: Countdown to War.* New York: Basic Books.

12. Tuchman, B. (2009). *The Guns of August.* New York: Random House.

13. McKeenin. (2013).

14. Asch, S. E. (1956). Studies of Independence and Conformity: A Minority of One against a Unanimous Majority. *Psychological Monographs: General and Applied, 70*(9), 1–70. https://doi-org.stetson.idm.oclc.org /10.1037/h0093718.

15. Torres, J. E. (2020). *The Crucible* Stirs Up Trouble. *School Library Journal, 66*(9), 14.

16. For a contemporary overview, see: Pope, K. S. (1998). Pseudoscience, Cross-Examination, and Scientific Evidence in the Recovered Memory Controversy. *Psychology, Public Policy, and Law, 4*(4), 1160–81.

17. Victor, J. S. (1998). Moral Panics and the Social Construction of Deviant Behavior: A Theory and Application to the Case of Ritual Child Abuse. *Sociological Perspectives, 41*(3), 541–65.

18. Talbot, M. (2001). The Lives They Lived: 01-07-01: Peggy McMartin Buckey, b. 1926; The Devil in The Nursery. *New York Times.* Retrieved from: www.nytimes.com/2001/01/07/magazine/lives-they-lived-01-07-01-peggy-mc martin-buckey-b-1926-devil-nursery.html.

19. Schreiber, N., Bellah, L. D., Martinez, Y., McLaurin, K. A., Strok, R., Garven, S., & Wood, J. M. (2006). Suggestive Interviewing in the McMartin Preschool and Kelly Michaels Daycare Abuse Cases: A Case Study. *Social Influence, 1*(1), 16–47.

CHAPTER 2

1. Shreshtha, S., Swerdlow, D., Borse, R., et al. (2011). Estimating the Burden of 2009 Pandemic Influenza A (H1N1) in the United States (April 2009–April 2010). *Clinical Infectious Disease, 52,* S75–S82.

2. Ponti, C. (2020). All the Ways We've Wiped: The History of Toilet Paper and What Came Before. History.com. Retrieved from: www.history.com/news /toilet-paper-hygiene-ancient-rome-china.

3. BBC. (2020). Coronavirus: Armed Robbers Steal Hundreds of Toilet Rolls in Hong Kong. Retrieved from: www.bbc.com/news/world-asia-china -51527043.

4. Pricenomics. (2014). The Great Toilet Paper Scare of 1973. Retrieved from: priceonomics.com/the-great-toilet-paper-scare-of-1973.

5. Barr, W. B. (2013). An Evidence Based Approach to Sports Concussion: Confronting the Availability Cascade. *Neuropsychology Review, 23*(4), 271–72.

6. Nogami, T. (2019). Negative Misconceptions about Disaster Behaviour through Availability Cascades: An Examination of Secondhand Information and the Moderating Effect of Trait Anxiety on Disaster Myths. *Journal of Community & Applied Social Psychology.* https://doi-org.stetson.idm.oclc.org /10.1002/casp.2441.

7. Cummins, E. (2018). Plane Travel Only Feels Like It's Dangerous. *Popular Science.* Retrieved from: www.popsci.com/plane-risk-safest-travel.

8. Some evidence does suggest that private planes are pretty dangerous, probably because doofuses are piloting them as opposed to professional pilots. See Pappas, S. (2017). Why Private Planes Are Nearly as Deadly as Cars. *LiveScience.* Retrieved from: www.livescience.com/49701-private-planes -safety.html.

9. Winegard, B., & Ferguson, C. J. (2017). The Development of Rampage Shooters: Myths and Uncertainty in the Search for Causes. In L. Wilson (Ed.), *The Wiley Handbook of the Psychology of Mass Shootings.* New York: Wiley Blackwell. http://christopherjferguson.com/WinegardFerguson2017.pdf.

10. Ferguson, C. (2019). Mass Shootings Aren't Growing More Common— And Evidence Contradicts Common Stereotypes about the Killers. *The Conversation.* Retrieved from: https://theconversation.com/mass-shootings-arent -growing-more-common-and-evidence-contradicts-common-stereotypes -about-the-killers-121471.

11. Wheeler, L. (1966). Toward a Theory of Behavioral Contagion. *Psychological Review, 73*(2), 179–92. https://doi-org.stetson.idm.oclc.org/10.1037 /h0023023.

12. Marsden, P. (1998). Memetics & Social Contagion: Two Sides of the Same Coin? *The Journal of Memetics: Evolutionary Models of Information Transmission, 2,* 171–85.

13. Romer, D. (2020). Reanalysis of the Effects of "13 Reasons Why": Response to Bridge et al. *PLoS ONE*. Retrieved from: https://journals.plos.org /plosone/article?id=10.1371/journal.pone.0239574.

14. Ferguson, C. J. (2021). One Less Reason Why: Viewing of Suicide-Themed Fictional Media Is Associated with Lower Depressive Symptoms in Youth. *Mass Communication and Society*. 24(1), 85–105. https://christopher jferguson.com/One%20Less%20Reason%20Why.pdf.

15. Shrier, A. (2020). *Irreversible Damage*. Washington, DC: Regnery Publishing.

16. Madeddu, F., Prunas, A., & Hartmann, D. (2009). Prevalence of Axis II Disorders in a Sample of Clients Undertaking Psychiatric Evaluation for Sex Reassignment Surgery. *Psychiatric Quarterly*, 80(4), 261–67.

17. Van der Miesen, A. I. R., Hurley, H., Bal, A. M., & de Vries, A. L. C. (2018). Prevalence of the Wish to Be of the Opposite Gender in Adolescents and Adults with Autism Spectrum Disorder. *Archives of Sexual Behavior*, 47(8), 2307–17.

18. Cacciola, S., & Deb, S. (2020). N.B.A. Suspends Season after Player Tests Positive for Coronavirus. *New York Times*. Retrieved from: www.nytimes .com/2020/03/11/sports/basketball/nba-season-suspended-coronavirus.html.

19. Lewis, D. (2020). Why Schools Probably Aren't Covid Hotspots. *Nature*. Retrieved from: www.nature.com/articles/d41586-020-02973-3.

20. Guidelines for safely visiting outdoor spaces are provided by the Centers for Disease Control here: www.cdc.gov/coronavirus/2019-ncov/daily-life -coping/visitors.html.

21. Florencio, Joao. (2018). AIDS: Homophobic and Moralistic Images of 1980s Still Haunt Our View of HIV—That Must Change. *The Conversation*. Retrieved from: https://theconversation.com/aids-homophobic-and-moralistic -images-of-1980s-still-haunt-our-view-of-hiv-that-must-change-106580.

22. Ferguson, C. J., Copenhaver, A., & Markey, P. (2020). Re-examining the Findings of the APA's 2015 Task Force on Violent Media: A Meta-Analysis. *Perspectives on Psychological Science* 15(6), 1423–43.

CHAPTER 3

1. Franklin, C. (2021). What's Missing in COVID Conversations? Trust. *Northwest Indiana Times*. Retrieved from: www.nwitimes.com/opinion/col umnists/guest-commentary/guest-commentary-whats-missing-in-covid-conver sations-trust/article_fee7f4e8-75ef-5ebe-ba01-949d937c0462.html.

2. McGraw, M., & Stein, S. (2021). It's Been Exactly One Year since Trump Suggested Injecting Bleach. We've Never Been the Same. *Politico.* Retrieved from: www.politico.com/news/2021/04/23/trump-bleach-one-year-484399.

3. Buckley, C., & Myers, S. (2020). As New Coronavirus Spread, China's Old Habits Delayed Fight. *New York Times.* Retrieved from: www.nytimes .com/2020/02/01/world/asia/china-coronavirus.html.

4. Feldwisch-Drentrup, H. (2020). How WHO Became China's Coronavirus Accomplice. *Foreign Policy.* Retrieved from: https://foreignpolicy.com /2020/04/02/china-coronavirus-who-health-soft-power.

5. BBC. (2020). Coronavirus Declared Global Health Emergency by WHO. Retrieved from: www.bbc.com/news/world-51318246.

6. WHO. (2020). WHO Announces COVID-19 Outbreak a Pandemic. Retrieved from: www.euro.who.int/en/health-topics/health-emergencies/coro navirus-covid-19/news/news/2020/3/who-announces-covid-19-outbreak-a -pandemic.

7. Ferguson, C. J. (2015). "Everybody Knows Psychology Is Not a Real Science": Public Perceptions of Psychology and How We Can Improve Our Relationship with Policymakers, the Scientific Community, and the General Public. *American Psychologist, 70,* 527–42.

8. Gilsinan, K. (2020). How China Deceived the WHO. *The Atlantic.* Retrieved from: www.theatlantic.com/politics/archive/2020/04/world-health -organization-blame-pandemic-coronavirus/609820.

9. Bean, A. M., Nielsen, R. K. L, van Rooij, A. J., & Ferguson, C. J. (2017). Video Game Addiction: The Push to Pathologize Video Games. *Professional Psychology: Research and Practice, 48*(5), 378–89.

10. Thielking, M., & Facher, L. (2020). Health Experts Warn China Travel Ban Will Hinder Coronavirus Response. *Statnews.* Retrieved from: www.stat news.com/2020/01/31/as-far-right-calls-for-china-travel-ban-health-experts -warn-coronavirus-response-would-suffer.

11. Chinazzi, M., Davis, J., Ajelli, M., et al. (2020). The Effect of Travel Restrictions on the Spread of the 2019 Novel Coronavirus (COVID-19) Outbreak. *Science, 368,* 395–400.

12. Richie, S. (2020). Don't Trust the Psychologists on COVID. *Unherd.* Retrieved from: https://unherd.com/2020/03/dont-trust-the-psychologists-on -coronavirus.

13. Granted, they generally don't use the word "junk." See: Open Science Collaboration (2015). Estimating the Reproducibility of Psychological Science. *Science. 349,* 6251. https://doi:10.1126/science.aac4716.

14. Ferguson. (2015).

15. Onraet, E., Van Hiel, A., Dhont, K., et al. (2015). The Association of Cognitive Ability with Right-Wing Ideological Attitudes and Prejudice: A Meta-Analytic Review. *European Journal of Personality, 29*, 599–621.

16. For example, see Kanazawa, S. (2010). Why Liberals Are More Intelligent Than Conservatives. *Psychology Today.* Retrieved from: www.psychologytoday.com/us/blog/the-scientific-fundamentalist/201003/why-liberals-are-more-intelligent-conservatives.

17. This has been well-known for decades. Redding, R. (2001). Sociopolitical Diversity in Psychology: The Case for Pluralism. *American Psychologist, 56*, 205–15.

18. For a nuanced overview, see Zurcher, A. (2014). Ebola, Race and Fear. BBC. Retrieved from: www.bbc.com/news/blogs-echochambers-29714657.

19. See, for example, Tracey, M. (2021). New Documents Show Police Charged Thousands of People for Petty COVID Violations. Retrieved from: https://mtracey.substack.com/p/new-documents-show-police-charged.

20. Howard, J., Huang, A., Li, Z., Tufekci, Z., Zdimal, V., et al. (2021). An Evidence Review of Face Masks against COVID-19. *Proceedings of the National Academy of Sciences, 118.* Retrieved from: www.pnas.org/content/118/4/e2014564118.

21. Drummond, A., Sauer, J. D., & Ferguson, C. J. (2020). Do Longitudinal Studies Support Long-Term Relationships between Aggressive Game Play and Youth Aggressive Behavior? A Meta-Analytic Examination. *Royal Society Open Science.* https://doi.org/10.1098/rsos.200373.

22. State's Attorney for the Judicial District of Dansbury. (2013). Report of the State's Attorney for the Judicial District of Danbury on the Shootings at Sandy Hook Elementary School and 36 Yogananda Street, Newtown, Connecticut on December 14, 2012. Virginia Tech Review Panel. (2007). *Report of the Virginia Tech Review Panel.* Retrieved 08/21/13 from: www.governor.virginia.gov/TempContent/techPanelReport.cfm.

23. Stanovich, K. E., West, R. F., & Toplak, M. E. (2013). Myside Bias, Rational Thinking, and Intelligence. *Current Directions in Psychological Science, 22*(4), 259–64. https://doi-org.stetson.idm.oclc.org/10.1177/0963721413480174.

24. Washburn, A. N., & Skitka, L. J. (2018). Science Denial across the Political Divide: Liberals and Conservatives Are Similarly Motivated to Deny Attitude-Inconsistent Science. *Social Psychological and Personality Science, 9*(8), 972–80. https://doi-org.stetson.idm.oclc.org/10.1177/1948550617731500.

25. Haghtalab, N., Jackson, M., & Procaccia, A. (2021). Belief Polarization in a Complex World: A Learning Theory Perspective. *Proceedings of the*

National Academy of Sciences, 118, e2010144118. https://doi.org/10.1073/pnas.2010144118.

26. You can hear the tape during Paul Rossi's appearance on Megyn Kelly's podcast at: https://podcasts.apple.com/us/podcast/teacher-speaks-out-paul-rossi-on-critical-race-theory/id1532976305?i=1000518301767.

27. Wells, G. L., Malpass, R. S., Lindsay, R. C. L., Fisher, R. P., Turtle, J. W., & Fulero, S. M. (2000). From the Lab to the Police Station: A Successful Application of Eyewitness Research. *American Psychologist, 55*(6), 581–98. https://doi-org.stetson.idm.oclc.org/10.1037/0003-066X.55.6.581.

28. World Health Organization. (2020). Coronavirus Disease (COVID-19) Advice for the Public: When and How to Use Masks. Retrieved from: https://web.archive.org/web/20200410144317/https://www.who.int/emergencies/diseases/novel-coronavirus-2019/advice-for-public/when-and-how-to-use-masks.

29. Centers for Disease Control. (2020). Prevention & Treatment. Retrieved from: https://web.archive.org/web/20200301001825/https://www.cdc.gov/coronavirus/2019-ncov/about/prevention-treatment.html.

30. Jingnan, H. (2020). Why There Are So Many Different Guidelines for Face Masks for the Public. NPR. Retrieved from: www.npr.org/sections/goatsandsoda/2020/04/10/829890635/why-there-so-many-different-guidelines-for-face-masks-for-the-public.

31. Mounk, Y. (2020). Would You Wave the Magic Wand? *Persuasion.* Retrieved from: www.persuasion.community/p/-would-you-wave-the-magic-wand?token=eyJ1c2VyX2lkIjoxNDI5NTk5LCJwb3N0X2lkIjozNjQzMzIyNCwiXyI6IlRXNGdsIiwiaWF0IjoxNjIxNzA1NDY4LCJleHAiOjE2MjE3MDkwNjgsImlzcyI6InB1Yi02MTU3OSIsInN1YiI6InBvc3QtcmVhY3Rpb24ifQ.RxNmn6WIhwOCG4ON6MZwV0vUS6vA9viPgrAHF8HUFLI. Bonilla, X. (2021). Covid19—The Malady of Our Time. *Converging Dialogues.* Retrieved from: https://convergingdialogues.podbean.com/e/32-covid-19-the-malady-of-our-time-a-dialogue-with-nicholas-christakis.

32. Centers for Disease Control. (2021). When You've Been Fully Vaccinated. Retrieved from: www.cdc.gov/coronavirus/2019-ncov/vaccines/fully-vaccinated.html.

33. Stobbe, M. (2021). CDC Says Many Americans Can Now Go Outside Without a Mask. Associated Press. Retrieved from: https://apnews.com/article/cdc-mask-wearing-guidance-d373775ddcf237764c19ff9428b5963.

34. Soave, R. (2020). To Mitigate Racial Inequity, the CDC Wants to Vaccinate Essential Workers before the Elderly. *Reason.* Retrieved from: https://reason.com/2020/12/18/vaccine-cdc-essential-workers-elderly-racial-covid-19.

35. The fleas weren't big winners here, either, and apparently also tended to die. See Eisen, R., Bearden, S., Wilder, A., et al. (2006). Early-Phase Transmission of Yersinia Pestis by Unblocked Fleas as a Mechanism Explaining Rapidly Spreading Plague Epizootics. *Proceedings of the National Academy of Sciences, 103*, 15380–85.

36. Tuchman, B. (1978). *A Distant Mirror: The Calamitous 14th Century.* New York: Ballantine Books.

37. Burke, J., Akinwotu, E., & Kuo, L. (2020). China Fails to Stop Racism against Africans over COVID-19. *The Guardian.* Retrieved from: www.the guardian.com/world/2020/apr/27/china-fails-to-stop-racism-against-africans -over-covid-19.

CHAPTER 4

1. Ackerman, E. (2016). A Brief History of the Microwave Oven. *IEEE Spectrum.* Retrieved from: https://spectrum.ieee.org/tech-history/space-age /a-brief-history-of-the-microwave-oven.

2. BBC. (2011). Gina Robins Cooked Kitten to Death in Microwave. Retrieved from: www.bbc.com/news/uk-england-devon-15856146#:~:text=A%20 woman%20who%20microwaved%20a,then%20a%20%22horrendous%20 screech%22.

3. Klein, C. (2018). The Great Smog of 1952. History.com. Retrieved from: www.history.com/news/the-killer-fog-that-blanketed-london-60-years-ago.

4. For a more nuanced discussion, see Letzter, R. (2019). Are We Really Running Out of Time to Stop Climate Change? *LiveScience.* Retrieved from: www.livescience.com/12-years-to-stop-climate-change.html.

5. Vohra, K., Vodonos, A., Schwartz, J., et al. (2021). Global Mortality from Outdoor Fine Particle Pollution Generated by Fossil Fuel Combustion: Results from GEOS-Chem. *Environmental Research, 195*, 110754.

6. Kharecha, P., & Hansen, J. (2013). Prevented Mortality and Greenhouse Gas Emissions from Historical and Projected Nuclear Power. *Environmental Science and Technology, 47*, 4889–95.

7. Appunn, K. (2021). The History behind Germany's Nuclear Phase-Out. *Clean Energy Wire.* Retrieved from: www.cleanenergywire.org/factsheets /history-behind-germanys-nuclear-phase-out.

8. Wellerstein, A. (2016). The Demon Core and the Strange Death of Louis Slotin. *The New Yorker*. Retrieved from: www.newyorker.com/tech/annals-of-technology/demon-core-the-strange-death-of-louis-slotin.

9. United States Nuclear Regulatory Commission. (2018). Backgrounder on the Three Mile Island Accident. Retrieved from: www.nrc.gov/reading-rm/doc-collections/fact-sheets/3mile-isle.html.

10. Hatch, M., Wallenstein, S., Beyea, J., Nieves, J., & Susser, M. (1991). Cancer Rates after the Three Mile Island Nuclear Accident and Proximity of Residence to the Plant. *American Journal of Public Health, 81*, 719–24.

11. Brady, J. (2019). Three Mile Island Nuclear Plant to Close, Latest Symbol of Struggling Industry. NPR. Retrieved from: www.npr.org/2019/05/08/721514875/three-mile-island-nuclear-plant-to-close-latest-symbol-of-struggling-industry.

12. Lallanilla, M. (2019). Chernobyl: Facts about the Nuclear Disaster. *LiveScience*. Retrieved from: www.livescience.com/39961-chernobyl.html.

13. United Nations Scientific Committee on the Effects of Atomic Radiation. Retrieved from: www.unscear.org/docs/publications/2017/Chernobyl_WP_2017.pdf.

14. Perucchi, J., & Domenighetti, G. (1991). The Chernobyl Accident and Induced Abortions: Only One-Way Information. *Scandinavian Journal of Work, Environment and Health, 16*, 443–44.

15. Becker, K. (1996). Economic, Social and Political Consequences in Western Europe. Retrieved from: www.osti.gov/etdeweb/servlets/purl/603204.

16. Haeusler, M., Berghold, A., Schoel, W., et al. (1992). The Influence of the Post-Chernobyl Fallout on Birth Defects and Abortion Rates in Austria. *American Journal of Obstetrics and Gynecology, 167*, 1025–31.

17. World Nuclear Association. (2021). Fukushima Daiichi Accident. Retrieved from: www.world-nuclear.org/information-library/safety-and-security/safety-of-plants/fukushima-daiichi-accident.aspx.

18. United Nations Scientific Committee on the Effects of Atomic Radiation. (2013). Report of the United Nations Scientific Committee on the Effects of Atomic Radiation to the General Assembly. Retrieved from: www.unscear.org/docs/reports/2013/13-85418_Report_2013_GA_Report.pdf.

19. Larsen, T., & Gravitz, A. (2006). 10 Reasons to Oppose Nuclear Energy. Retrieved from: www.greenamerica.org/fight-dirty-energy/amazon-build-cleaner-cloud/10-reasons-oppose-nuclear-energy.

20. Atkinson, N. (2020). Terrible Luck: The Only Person Ever Killed by a Meteorite—Back in 1888. Retrieved from: https://phys.org/news/2020-04-terrible-luck-person-meteoriteback.html.

21. Eaton, W. W., Bienvenu, O. J., & Miloyan, B. (2018). Specific Phobias. *The Lancet Psychiatry*, 5(8), 678–86. https://doi-org.stetson.idm.oclc.org/10.1016/S2215-0366(18)30169-X.

22. BBC. (2012). Cockroach-Eating Competition Man "Choked to Death." Retrieved from: www.bbc.com/news/world-us-canada-20503586.

23. Healthline. (2020). Are Cockroaches Dangerous? Retrieved from: www.healthline.com/health/are-cockroaches-dangerous.

24. Langley, R., & Morrow, W. (1997). Deaths Resulting from Animal Attacks in the United States. *Wilderness and Environmental Medicine, 8*, 8–16.

25. United States Department of Transportation. (2020). 2019 Fatality Data Show Continued Annual Decline in Traffic Deaths. Retrieved from: www.nhtsa.gov/press-releases/2019-fatality-data-show-continued-annual-decline-traffic-deaths.

26. Centers for Disease Control. (2017). Electrocutions Associated with Consumer Products, 2004–2013. Retrieved from: www.cpsc.gov/s3fs-public/Electrocution-Report-2004-to-2013.pdf?V_9Zl10pv4Wz03uBPRx78IctKRABjYDv.

27. Centers for Disease Control. (1998). Worker Deaths by Electrocution. Retrieved from: www.cdc.gov/niosh/docs/98-131/pdfs/98-131.pdf.

28. Chadee, D., Smith, S., & Ferguson, C. J. (2019). Murder She Watched: Does Watching News or Fictional Media Cultivate Fear of Crime? *Psychology of Popular Media Culture 8*(2), 125–33.

29. McKinlay, C., Vargas, J., Blake, T., et al. (2017). Charge-Altering Releasable Transporters (CARTs) for the Delivery and Release of mRNA in Living Animals. *Proceedings of the National Academy of Sciences, 114*, E448-456.

30. Iyizoba, N. (2016). The Dangers of Genetically Modified Foods. GreenAmerica.com. Retrieved from: www.greenamerica.org/blog/dangers-genetically-modified-foods-guardian.

31. Norris, M. (2015). Will GMOs Hurt My Body? The Public's Concerns and How Scientists Have Addressed Them. Harvard University. Retrieved from: https://sitn.hms.harvard.edu/flash/2015/will-gmos-hurt-my-body.

CHAPTER 5

1. Byman, D. (2015). Comparing Al Qaeda and ISIS: Different Goals, Different Targets. Brookings Institute. Retrieved from: www.brookings.edu/testimonies/comparing-al-qaeda-and-isis-different-goals-different-targets.

2. Federal Bureau of Investigation. (2021). USS Cole Bombing. Retrieved from: www.fbi.gov/history/famous-cases/uss-cole-bombing.

3. As of this writing President Biden appears to be withdrawing most US forces from Afghanistan, ending a twenty-year occupation. The result appears to be a resurgence of the Taliban, once Al Qaeda allies. However, this simply returns things to the pre-9/11 status quo and can hardly be called a victory for either side.

4. Gammon, K. (2012). Can Animals Commit Suicide? *LiveScience.* Retrieved from: www.livescience.com/33805-animals-commit-suicide.html.

5. Arditte, K. A., Morabito, D. M., Shaw, A. M., & Timpano, K. R. (2016). Interpersonal Risk for Suicide in Social Anxiety: The Roles of Shame and Depression. *Psychiatry Research, 239,* 139–44. https://doi-org.stetson .idm.oclc.org/10.1016/j.psychres.2016.03.017.

6. Sheehy, K., Noureen, A., Khaliq, A., Dhingra, K., Husain, N., Pontin, E. E., Cawley, R., & Taylor, P. J. (2019). An Examination of the Relationship between Shame, Guilt and Self-Harm: A Systematic Review and Meta-Analysis. *Clinical Psychology Review, 73.* https://doi-org.stetson.idm.oclc.org/10.1016 /j.cpr.2019.101779.

7. Lankford, A. (2013). A Comparative Analysis of Suicide Terrorists and Rampage, Workplace, and School Shooters in the United States from 1990 to 2010. *Homicide Studies: An Interdisciplinary & International Journal, 17(3),* 255–74. https://doi-org.stetson.idm.oclc.org/10.1177/1088767912462033.

8. Lankford, A., & Cowan, R. G. (2020). Has the Role of Mental Health Problems in Mass Shootings Been Significantly Underestimated? *Journal of Threat Assessment and Management, 7(3–4),* 135–56. https://doi-org.stetson .idm.oclc.org/10.1037/tam0000151.

9. Winegard, B., & Ferguson, C. J. (2017). The Development of Rampage Shooters: Myths and Uncertainty in the Search for Causes. In L. Wilson (Ed.), *The Wiley Handbook of the Psychology of Mass Shootings.* New York: Wiley Blackwell.

10. Hodgins, S. (2008). Criminality among Persons with Severe Mental Illness. In K. Soothill, P. Rogers, & M. Dolan (Eds.), *Handbook of Forensic Mental Health.* (pp. 400–423). Cullompton, UK: Willan.

11. English, R. (2016). *Does Terrorism Work? A History.* London: Oxford University Press.

12. Monahan, J. (2012). The Individual Risk Assessment of Terrorism. *Psychology, Public Policy, and Law, 18(2),* 167–205. https://doi-org.stetson.idm .oclc.org/10.1037/a0025792.

13. Hunter, S. T., Shortland, N. D., Crayne, M. P., & Ligon, G. S. (2017). Recruitment and Selection in Violent Extremist Organizations: Exploring What Industrial and Organizational Psychology Might Contribute. *American Psychologist*, 72(3), 242–54. https://doi-org.stetson.idm.oclc.org/10.1037 /amp0000089.

14. Borum, R., & Patterson, T. D. (2019). Juvenile Radicalization into Violent Extremism: Investigative and Research Perspectives. *Journal of the American Academy of Child & Adolescent Psychiatry*, 58(12), 1142–48. https:// doi-org.stetson.idm.oclc.org/10.1016/j.jaac.2019.07.932.

15. Lotto, D. (2017). On the Origins of Terrorism. *The Journal of Psychohistory*, 45(1), 12–22.

16. Miller, L. (2006). The Terrorist Mind: II Typologies, Psychopathologies, and Practical Guidelines for Investigation. *International Journal of Offender Therapy and Comparative Criminology*, 50(3), 255–68. https://doi-org .stetson.idm.oclc.org/10.1177/0306624X05281406.

17. Jenkins, N. (2015). How Paris Stood with the U.S. after 9/11. *Time*. Retrieved from: time.com/4112746/paris-attacks-us-september-911-terrorism.

18. Blitzer, W. (2003). The Search for the Smoking Gun. CNN. Retrieved from: www.cnn.com/2003/US/01/10/wbr.smoking.gun.

19. Janis, I. L. (1972). *Victims of Groupthink: A Psychological Study of Foreign-Policy Decisions and Fiascoes*. New York: Houghton Mifflin.

20. Harris, B. (2011). From the Sanhedrin to Alan Greenspan, Strategies to Avoid the Perils of Groupthink. *Jewish Standard*. Retrieved from: https:// jewishstandard.timesofisrael.com/from-the-sanhedrin-to-alan-greenspan-strat egies-to-avoid-the-perils-of-groupthink.

21. Esser, J. K., & Lindoerfer, J. S. (1989). Groupthink and the Space Shuttle Challenger Accident: Toward a Quantitative Case Analysis. *Journal of Behavioral Decision Making*, 2(3), 167–77. https://doi-org.stetson.idm.oclc .org/10.1002/bdm.3960020304.

22. Evans, K. (2020). Groupthink: Understanding and Avoiding It. *Product Thinking*. Retrieved from: www.productthinking.cc/p/groupthink-understand ing-and-avoiding.

23. History.com. (2009). The Dixie Chicks Backlash Begins. Retrieved from: www.history.com/this-day-in-history/the-dixie-chicks-backlash-begins.

24. American Civil Liberties Union. (2021). Surveillance under the Patriot Act. Retrieved from: www.aclu.org/issues/national-security/privacy-and-sur veillance/surveillance-under-patriot-act.

25. History.com. (2017). Patriot Act. Retrieved from: www.history.com /topics/21st-century/patriot-act.

26. As any fan of Schoolhouse Rock knows, laws start as bills before being voted into law.

27. Clark, C. (2021). University of California Medical Prof Apologizes for Saying "Pregnant Women." *Daily Wire.* Retrieved from: www.dailywire.com /news/university-of-california-medical-prof-apologizes-for-saying-pregnant -women.

28. Ferguson, C. (2019). Is Gender a Social Construct? *Quillette.* Retrieved from: https://quillette.com/2019/11/30/is-gender-a-social-construct.

CHAPTER 6

1. Zacharek, S. (2019). *Joker* Wants to Be a Movie about the Emptiness of Our Culture. Instead, It's a Prime Example of It. *Time.* Retrieved from: https:// time.com/5666055/venice-joker-review-joaquin-phoenix-not-funny.

2. Adams, S. (2019). Joker's Director Says His Movie Isn't Political. Who's He Trying to Kid? *Slate.* Retrieved from: https://slate.com/culture/2019/09 /joker-movie-joaquin-phoenix-alt-right-hero-incel.html.

3. Ehrlich, D. (2019). "Joker" Review: For Better or Worse, Superhero Movies Will Never Be the Same. *IndieWire.* Retrieved from: www.indiewire.com /2019/08/joker-review-joaquin-phoenix-1202170236.

4. Edelstein, D. (2019). Joker Is One Unpleasant Note Played Louder and Louder. *Vulture.* www.vulture.com/2019/10/joker-movie-review-joaquin -phoenix-as-arthur-fleck.html.

5. Stambaugh, H., & Styron, H. (2003). Special Report: Firefighter Arson. Homeland Security.

6. Marjory Stoneman Douglas High School Public Safety Commission. (2019). Initial Report Submitted to the Governor, Speaker of the House of Representatives and Senate President. Retrieved from: www.fdle.state.fl.us /msdhs/commissionreport.pdf.

7. Frederique, N. (2020). *What Do the Data Reveal about Violence in Schools?* National Institutes of Justice. Retrieved from: https://nij.ojp.gov/topics/articles /what-do-data-reveal-about-violence-schools.

8. Romano, A. (2016). The Great Clown Panic of 2016 Is a Hoax. But the Terrifying Side of Clowns Is Real. *Vox.* Retrieved from: www.vox.com/culture /2016/10/12/13122196/clown-panic-hoax-history.

9. Dickson, E. (2019). What Is the Momo Challenge? *Rolling Stone.* Retrieved from: www.rollingstone.com/culture/culture-news/what-is-momo-challenge-800470.

10. Clark-Flory, T. (2014). Forget about Rainbow Parties, Sex Bracelets and Sexting: Today's Kids Have Not Gone Wild. *Salon.* Retrieved from: www.salon.com/2014/09/01/forget_about_rainbow_parties_sex_bracelets_and_sexting_todays_kids_have_not_gone_wild.

11. Preston, M. I. (1941). Children's Reactions to Movie Horrors and Radio Crime. *The Journal of Pediatrics, 19,* 147–68. https://doi-org.stetson.idm.oclc.org/10.1016/S0022-3476(41)80059-6.

12. As often happens during moral panics, the scholarly community divides, some supporting the panic (which is more profitable in the short term), some decrying it. The work of Amy Orben and Andrew Przybylski is among the most important here and I refer the curious reader to it. For example, Orben, A., & Przybylski, A. (2019). The Association between Adolescent Well-Being and Digital Technology Use. *Nature Human Behavior.* Retrieved from: www.nature.com/articles/s41562-018-0506-1.

13. Parker, L. (2020). Remembering Tom Petty's crazy, controversial "Don't Come around Here No More" Music Video: "This One Took the Cake." Yahoo. Retrieved from: www.yahoo.com/now/tom-pettys-crazy-controversial-dont-come-here-no-more-music-video-233754534.html.

14. Kawai, M. (1965). Newly Acquired Pre-Cultural Behavior of the Natural Troop of Japanese Monkeys on Koshima Islet. *Primates, 6,* 1–30. See also for recent update: Matsuzawa, T. (2015). Sweet-Potato Washing Revisited: 50th Anniversary of the Primates Article. *Primates, 56,* 285–87. https://doi.org/10.1007/s10329-015-0492-0.

15. School Safety Commission. (2018). Final Report of the Federal Commission on School Safety. US Department of Education.

16. She didn't make this up; these kinds of nonsense claims had come, regrettably, from scholars who should have known better. For documentation, see: Markey, P. M., Males, M. A., French, J. E., & Markey, C. N. (2015). Lessons from Markey et al. (2015) and Bushman et al. (2015): Sensationalism and Integrity in Media Research. *Human Communication Research, 41*(2), 184–203. https://doi-org.stetson.idm.oclc.org/10.1111/hcre.12057.

17. United Nations Office on Drugs and Crime. (2021). Retrieved from: https://dataunodc.un.org.

18. Ferguson, C. J., & Smith, S. (in press). Examining Homicides and Suicides Cross-Nationally: Economic Factors, Guns and Video Games. *International Journal of Psychology.*

19. Yee, N., Matheson, S., Korobanova, D., Large, M., Nielssen, O., Carr, V., & Dean, K. (2020). A Meta-Analysis of the Relationship between Psychosis and Any Type of Criminal Offending, in both Men and Women. *Schizophrenia Research*, *220*, 16–24. https://doi-org.stetson.idm.oclc.org/10.1016 /j.schres.2020.04.009.

CHAPTER 7

1. Department of Justice. (2015). Department of Justice Report Regarding the Criminal Investigation into the Shooting Death of Michael Brown by Ferguson, Missouri Police Officer Darren Wilson. Retrieved from: www.justice.gov /sites/default/files/opa/press-releases/attachments/2015/03/04/doj_report_on _shooting_of_michael_brown_1.pdf.

2. Department of Justice. (2015). Investigation of the Ferguson Police Department. Retrieved from: www.justice.gov/sites/default/files/opa/press -releases/attachments/2015/03/04/ferguson_police_department_report.pdf.

3. American Psychological Association. (2020). Mental-Health Leaders: We Must End Pandemic of Racism. Retrieved from: www.apa.org/news/press /op-eds/end-pandemic-racism.

4. Arise Foundation. (2021). Retrieved from: www.arisefdn.org.

5. BBC. (2020). Who Are the Uyghurs and Why Is China Being Accused of Genocide? Retrieved from: www.bbc.com/news/world-asia-china-22278037.

6. Beck, A. (2021). Race and Ethnicity of Violent Crime Offenders and Arrestees, 2018. Bureau of Justice Statistics. Retrieved from: https://bjs.ojp .gov/library/publications/race-and-ethnicity-violent-crime-offenders-and -arrestees-2018.

7. Fessler, D. M. T. (2007). From Appeasement to Conformity: Evolutionary and Cultural Perspectives on Shame, Competition, and Cooperation. In J. L. Tracy, R. W. Robins, & J. P. Tangney (Eds.), *The Self-Conscious Emotions: Theory and Research*. (pp. 174–93). New York: Guilford Press.

8. McDonald, J. (2021). Former SDG&E Worker Sues Utility for Firing Him after White Supremacy Accusation Went Viral. *San Diego Union Tribune*. Retrieved from: www.sandiegouniontribune.com/news/watchdog /story/2021-06-04/former-sdg-e-worker-sues-utility-for-firing-him-after-white -supremacy-accusation-went-viral.

9. Durando, J. (2014). Auschwitz Selfie Girl Defends Actions. *USA Today*. Retrieved from: www.usatoday.com/story/news/nation-now/2014/07/23/selfie -auschwitz-concentration-camp-germany/1303828.

10. See, for example, Eduardo, A. (2021). Stop Calling Me "White" for Having the Wrong Opinions. *Newsweek*. Retrieved from: www.newsweek.com /stop-calling-me-white-having-wrong-opinions-opinion-1624179.

11. *Washington Post*. (2021). *Fatal Force*. Retrieved from: www.washing tonpost.com/graphics/investigations/police-shootings-database.

12. Beck, (2021).

13. Males, M. (2014). Who Are Police Killing? Center for Juvenile and Criminal Justice. Retrieved fromwww.cjcj.org/news/8113.

14. McCaffree, K., & Saide, A. (2021). How Informed Are Americans about Race and Policing? Skeptic Research Center. Retrieved from: www.skeptic .com/research-center/reports/Research-Report-CUPES-007.pdf.

15. Scott, K., Ma, D. S., Sadler, M. S., & Correll, J. (2017). A Social Scientific Approach toward Understanding Racial Disparities in Police Shooting: Data from the Department of Justice (1980–2000). *Journal of Social Issues*, *73*(4), 701–22.

16. Cesario, J., Johnson, D. J., & Terrill, W. (2019). Is There Evidence of Racial Disparity in Police Use of Deadly Force? Analyses of Officer-Involved Fatal Shootings in 2015–2016. *Social Psychological and Personality Science*, *10*(5), 586–95.

17. Hemenway, D., Berrigan, J., Azrael, D., Barber, C., & Miller, M. (2020). Fatal Police Shootings of Civilians, by rurality. *Preventive Medicine: An International Journal Devoted to Practice and Theory, 134*. https://doi-org.stetson .idm.oclc.org/10.1016/j.ypmed.2020.106046.

18. Fryer, R. (2016). An Empirical Analysis of Racial Differences in Police Use of Force. *National Bureau of Economic Research*. Retrieved from: www .nber.org/system/files/working_papers/w22399/w22399.pdf.

19. Zimring, Franklin E. (2017). *When Police Kill*. Cambridge, MA: Harvard University Press.

20. Rohrer, A. J. (2021). Law Enforcement and Persons with Mental Illness: Responding Responsibly. *Journal of Police and Criminal Psychology, 36*, 342–49.

21. Smith, S., Ferguson, C. J., & Henderson, H. (in press). An Exploratory Study of Environmental Stress in Four High Violent Crime Cities: What Sets Them Apart? *Crime and Delinquency*.

22. Gaston, S., Cunningham, J. P., & Gillezeau, R. (2019). A Ferguson Effect, the Drug Epidemic, Both, or Neither? Explaining the 2015 and 2016 US

Homicide Rises by Race and Ethnicity. *Homicide Studies: An Interdisciplinary & International Journal, 23*(3), 285–313.

23. Reilly, W. (2020). *Taboo.* Washington, DC: Regnery Publishing.

24. Lowry, G. (2020). *Why Does Racial Inequality Persist? Culture, Causation, and Responsibility.* Manhattan Institute. Retrieved from: https://media4 .manhattan-institute.org/sites/default/files/R-0519-GL.pdf.

25. Pew Research Center. (2016). Social & Demographic Trends, Demographic Trends and Economic Well-Being. June 27, 2016.

26. Thomas, M., Stumpf, M., & Harke, H. (2006). Evidence for an Apartheid-Like Social Structure in Early Anglo-Saxon England. *Proceedings of the Royal Society: Biological Sciences, 273,* 2651–57.

27. BBC. (2019). South Africa Elections: Who Controls the Country's Business Sector? Retrieved from: www.bbc.com/news/world-africa-48123937.

28. US Census Bureau. (2021). Retrieved from: www.census.gov/content /dam/Census/library/visualizations/2020/demo/p60-270/figure2.pdf.

29. US Census Bureau. (2021). Retrieved from: https://data.census.gov /cedsci. See also Avora, R. (2020). A Peculiar Kind of Racist Patriarchy. *Quillette.* Retrieved from: https://quillette.com/2020/12/22/a-peculiar-kind-of -racist-patriarchy.

30. Turley, J. (2021). Biden's Red Queen Justice: How He Destroyed Both the Investigation and the Reputation of Border Agents. *The Hill.* Retrieved from: https://thehill.com/opinion/judiciary/575007-bidens-red-queen-justice -how-he-destroyed-both-the-investigation-and-the.

31. Delgado, R, & Stefancic, J. (2017). *Critical Race Theory: An Introduction.* New York University Press.

32. Charlesworth, T. E. S., & Banaji, M. R. (2019). Patterns of Implicit and Explicit Attitudes: I. Long-Term Change and Stability from 2007 to 2016. *Psychological Science, 30*(2), 174–92.

33. See, for example, Eduardo. (2021). For all the explicit concern about racism, ostensible progressives often use racist language against ethnic minorities who challenge progressive ideologies.

34. Foundation against Intolerance and Racism. (2021). Grace Church Whistleblower. Retrieved from: www.fairforall.org/grace-church-whistle blower.

35. Cohen, S. (2021). "We're Demonizing White People for Being Born:" Leaked Audio Captures Headmaster of Elite NYC School Agreeing with Teacher Who Was Banned from Classroom for Speaking Out about White-Shaming Students. *Daily Mail.* Retrieved from: www.dailymail.co.uk/news

/article-9491487/Head-NYC-school-punished-outspoken-teacher-admits-de
monizing-white-people.html.

36. Blackwell, M. (2020). Black Lives Matter and the Mechanics of Conformity. *Quillette.* Retrieved from: https://quillette.com/2020/09/17/black-lives
-matter-and-the-mechanics-of-conformity. *Quillette* itself is controversial on the
left for its tendency to puncture progressive shibboleths.

37. Ferguson, C. J. (in press). Negative Perceptions of Race Relations: A
Brief Report Examining the Impact of News Media Coverage of Police Shootings, and Actual Fatal Police Shootings. *The Social Science Journal.*

38. Moore, S. (2021). Will Smith Says "Anybody Who Tries to Debate
Black Lives Matter Looks Ridiculous." *The Independent.* Retrieved from:
www.independent.co.uk/arts-entertainment/films/news/will-smith-black-lives
-matter-b1927916.html.

39. Hess, A. (2020). The Protests Come for "Paw Patrol." *New York Times.*
Retrieved from: https://archive.md/eUwM8.

40. Cassel, P. (2020). Explaining the Recent Homicide Spikes in U.S. Cities: The "Minneapolis Effect" and the Decline in Proactive Policing. *Utah Law
Digital Commons.* Retrieved from: https://dc.law.utah.edu/cgi/viewcontent.cgi
?article=1216&context=scholarship.

41. Smith, Ferguson, & Henderson. (in press).

42. Landgrave, M., & Nowrasteh, A. (2017). Criminal Immigrants: Their
Numbers, Demographics, and Countries of Origin. Cato Institute. Retrieved
from: www.cato.org/publications/immigration-reform-bulletin/criminal-immi
grants-their-numbers-demographics-countries?gclid=CjwKCAjw8KmLBhB8
EiwAQbqNoIy1ysPLvIkRiVAaPTKmtGM1cL3i_npvCtGC-nABwC3ep_Lijj
pHFRoCs34QAvD_BwE.

CHAPTER 8

1. McGuinness, R. (2021). Moment Woman Begs Insulate Britain Climate
Protesters to Allow Her through Blockade to Visit Mother in Hospital. Yahoo News. Retrieved from: https://ca.news.yahoo.com/woman-insulate-britain
-protesters-visiting-mother-hospital-123258494.html.

2. BBC. (2021). What Is Insulate Britain and What Does It Want? Retrieved
from: www.bbc.com/news/uk-58916326.

3. NASA. (2021). It's Cold. Is Global Warming Over? https://climatekids
.nasa.gov/harsh-winter/. And, yes, I cited a kids' page because, let's admit it,

most of us have no idea what's going on in the science—which is one of my points as we'll see.

4. Children's Museum of Indianapolis. (2021). Why Does Air Smell Different after a Storm? Retrieved from: www.childrensmuseum.org/blog/why-does-air-smell-different-after-a-storm. Yep, I'm sticking with kids' references (though these are reputable sources). It seems fitting given how childish people have behaved in this debate.

5. Pinho, B. (2020). Whatever Happened to the Hole in the Ozone Layer? *Discover Magazine.* Retrieved from: www.discovermagazine.com/environment/whatever-happened-to-the-hole-in-the-ozone-layer.

6. Ogden, L. (2019). The Bittersweet Story of How We Stopped Acid Rain. BBC. Retrieved from: www.bbc.com/future/article/20190823-can-lessons-from-acid-rain-help-stop-climate-change.

7. Weidmann, T., Lenzen, M., Keyser, L., & Steinberger, J. (2020). Scientists Warning on Affluence. *Nature Communications, 11.* Retrieved from: www.nature.com/articles/s41467-020-16941-y.

8. Degroot, D., Anchukaitis, K., Bauch, M., Burnham, J., Carnegy, F., Cui, J., de Luna, K., Guzowski, P., Hambrecht, G., Huhtamaa, H., Izdebski, A., Kleemann, K., Moesswilde, E., Neupane, N., Newfield, T., Pei, Q., Xoplaki, E., & Zappia, N. (2021). Towards a Rigorous Understanding of Societal Responses to Climate Change. *Nature, 591*(7851), 539–50.

9. Gifford, R. (2011). The Dragons of Inaction: Psychological Barriers That Limit Climate Change Mitigation and Adaptation. *American Psychologist, 66*(4), 290–302.

10. Pearce, F. (2009). Climategate: Anatomy of a Public Relations Disaster. *Environment 360.* Retrieved from: https://web.archive.org/web/20101125131655/http://e360.yale.edu/content/feature.msp?id=2221.

11. Ferguson, C. J., Copenhaver, A., & Markey, P. (2020). Re-examining the Findings of the APA's 2015 Task Force on Violent Media: A Meta-Analysis. *Perspectives on Psychological Science 15*(6), 1423–43.

12. *Quillette.* (2019). Twelve Scholars Respond to the APA's Guidance for Treating Men and Boys. Retrieved from: https://quillette.com/2019/02/04/psychologists-respond-to-the-apas-guidance-for-treating-men-and-boys.

13. Data from Roff, G., Brown, C., Priest, M., & Mumby, P. (2018). Decline of Coastal Apex Shark Populations over the Past Half Century. *Communications Biology, 1.* Retrieved from: www.nature.com/articles/s42003-018-0233-1.

14. United Nations. (2019). Only 11 Years Left to Prevent Irreversible Damage from Climate Change, Speakers Warn during General Assembly High-Level Meeting. Retrieved from: www.un.org/press/en/2019/ga12131.doc.htm.

15. Bowden, J. (2019). Ocasio-Cortez: "World Will End in 12 Years" If Climate Change Not Addressed." *The Hill.* Retrieved from: https://thehill.com/policy/energy-environment/426353-ocasio-cortez-the-world-will-end-in-12-years-if-we-dont-address.

16. Munger, S. (2018). Avoiding Dispatches from Hell: Communicating Extreme Events in a Persuasive, Proactive Context. In: W. Leal Filho, B. Lackner, H. McGhie (Eds.), *Addressing the Challenges in Communicating Climate Change across Various Audiences.* Cham, Switzerland: Springer. https://doi.org/10.1007/978-3-319-98294-6_8.

17. Weston, E. (2020). Climate Change and the Apocalyptic Narrative: A Critique. The Schumacher Institute. Retrieved from: www.schumacherinstitute.org.uk/download/pubs/res/202009-Climate-Change-and-the-Apocalyptic-Narrative-Ella-Weston.pdf.

18. Carrington, D. (2020). The Four Types of Climate Denier, and Why You Should Ignore Them All. *Guardian.* Retrieved from: www.theguardian.com/commentisfree/2020/jul/30/climate-denier-shill-global-debate.

19. Grossman, A. (2020). Patagonia's "Vote the A**holes Out" Tags Are a Gloriously Direct Message to Climate Change Deniers. *Esquire.* Retrieved from: www.esquire.com/style/mens-fashion/a34039821/patagonia-shorts-vote-tag-message.

20. Aronoff, K. (2018). Denial by a Different Name. *The Intercept.* Retrieved from: https://theintercept.com/2018/04/17/climate-change-denial-trump-germany.

21. Kluger, J. (2014). Americans Flunk Science Again. *Time.* Retrieved from: https://time.com/72080/climate-change-doubters-poll.

22. Ferguson, C. J. (2019). Netflix Has the "Han Shot First" Moment with *13 Reasons Why. Areo.* Retrieved from: https://areomagazine.com/2019/07/24/netflix-has-their-han-shot-first-moment-with-13-reasons-why.

23. Barmann, J. (2021). 31-Year-Old Swimmer Dies after Being Rescued in Rough Surf at Ocean Beach. Retrieved from: https://sfist.com/2020/06/05/31-year-old-swimmer-dies-after-being-rescued-in-rough-surf-at-ocean-beach.

24. Tribou, R. (2021). Man Dies after Being Pulled from Surf in Daytona Beach, Officials Say. *Orlando Sentinel.* Retrieved from: www.orlandosentinel.com/news/breaking-news/os-ne-daytona-beach-drowning-death-20210923-eoxj6i3vkrctdpi7rclhl5zvme-story.html.

25. National Weather Service. (2021). Lightning Fatalities in 2021. Retrieved from: www.weather.gov/safety/lightning-fatalities.

26. Musumeci, N. (2018). Man Mauled to Death by Bear while Taking Selfie with It. *New York Post.* Retrieved from: https://nypost.com/2018/05/04/man -mauled-to-death-by-bear-while-taking-selfie.

27. Wasco, D., & Bullard, S. (2016). An Analysis of Media-Reported Venomous Snakebites in the United States, 2011–2013. *Wilderness and Environmental Medicine, 27,* 219–26.

28. Associated Press. (2007). Man Bit by Rattlesnake after Putting It in His Mouth to Impress Ex-Girlfriend. Retrieved from: www.foxnews.com/story /man-bit-by-rattlesnake-after-putting-it-in-his-mouth-to-impress-ex-girlfriend.

29. Motro, D., & Ellis, A. P. J. (2017). Boys, Don't Cry: Gender and Reactions to Negative Performance Feedback. *Journal of Applied Psychology, 102*(2), 227–35. https://doi-org.stetson.idm.oclc.org/10.1037/apl0000175.

CHAPTER 9

1. Grosshandler, W., Bryner, N., Madrzykowsk, D., & Kuntz, K. (2005). Report of the Technical Investigation of the Station Nightclub Fire. National Institute of Standards and Technology. Retrieved from: https://tsapps.nist.gov /publication/get_pdf.cfm?pub_id=100988.

2. Pemberton, P. (2013). The Great White Nightclub Fire: Ten Years Later. *Rolling Stone.* Retrieved from: www.rollingstone.com/music/music-news/the -great-white-nightclub-fire-ten-years-later-243338.

3. Connor, K. (2016). Classy Lane Fire Resurrects Memories of 2002 Woodbine Blaze. *Toronto Sun.* Retrieved from: https://torontosun.com/2016/01/05 /classy-lane-fire-resurrects-memories-of-2002-woodbine-blaze.

4. Gimenez, R., Woods, J., Dwyer, R., et al. (2008). A Review of Strategies to Prevent and Respond to Barn Fires Affecting the Horse Industry. *AAEP Proceedings, 54,* 160–79.

5. Green, S. (2020). Wash. Firefighters Rescue Girl Hiding in Toy Trunk during Fire. Firerescue1.com. Retrieved from: www.firerescue1.com/search -rescue/articles/wash-firefighters-rescue-girl-hiding-in-toy-trunk-during-fire -d6PX6YkaQ0TNnkZM.

6. Shai, D., & Luppinachi, P. (2003). Fire Fatalities among Children: An Analysis across Philadelphia's Census Tracts. *Public Health Reports, 118,* 115–26.

7. Spicuzza, M. (2015). Milwaukee Townhouse Fire Takes 2 "Precious Little Kids." *Milwaukee Journal Sentinel.* Retrieved from: https://archive

.jsonline.com/news/milwaukee/2-children-killed-in-milwaukee-house-fire
-b99570479z1-324344211.html.

8. Biggs, S. (2006). Extinguish the Threat of Barn Fires. *Horse Illustrated.*
Retrieved from: www.horseillustrated.com/horse-keeping-extinguish-threat-of
-barn-fires.

9. McConnell, C., Leeming, F., & Dwyer, W. (1996). Evaluation of a
Fire-Safety Training Program for Preschool Children. *Journal of Community
Psychology, 24,* 213–27.

10. Huseyin, I., & Satyen, L. (2006). Fire Safety Training: Its Importance
in Enhancing Fire Safety Knowledge and Response to Fire. *The Australian
Journal of Emergency Management, 21,* 48–53.

11. US Fire Administration. (2019). Fire in the United States 2008–2017.
Retrieved from: www.usfa.fema.gov/downloads/pdf/publications/fius20th.pdf.

12. Stromberg, J. (2014). Firefighters Do a Lot Less Firefighting Than
They Used To. Here's What They Do Instead. *Vox.* Retrieved from: www.vox
.com/2014/10/30/7079547/fire-firefighter-decline-medical.

13. BBC. (2020). Gender Reveal Party Couple Face Jail over Deadly California Wildfire. Retrieved from: www.bbc.com/news/world-us-canada-57898993.

14. Balch, J., Bradley, B., Abatzoglu, J., et al. (2017). Human-Started
Wildfires Expand the Fire Niche across the United States. *Proceedings of the
National Academy of Sciences, 114,* 2946–51.

15. Henetz, P. (2004). Boy Scouts Sued over $14 million East Fork Fire.
Caspar Star Tribune. Retrieved from: https://trib.com/news/state-and-regional
/boy-scouts-sued-over-14-million-east-fork-fire/article_4ce356d1-cabb-5c19
-b315-8d84d83db603.html. Also Gephardt, M., & St. Claire, C. (2017).
People Who Accidentally Start Wildfires Face Hefty Fines, Criminal Charges,
Records Show. 2KUTV. Retrieved from: https://kutv.com/news/get-gephardt
/people-who-accidentally-start-wildfires-hefty-face-fines-criminal-charges
-records-show.

16. Enea, J. (2018). Old Time Crime: Contract Firefighter Starts Arizona's
Largest Wildfire to Date in 2002. Retrieved from: www.abc15.com/news/crime
/old-time-crime-contract-firefighter-starts-arizonas-largest-wildfire-in-2002.

17. US Fire Administration. (2003). Special Report: Firefighter Arson.
Retrieved from: www.usfa.fema.gov/downloads/pdf/publications/tr-141.pdf.

18. National Volunteer Fire Council. (2011). Report on the Firefighter
Arson Problem: Context, Considerations, and Best Practices. Retrieved from:
www.nvfc.org/wp-content/uploads/2016/02/FF_Arson_Report_FINAL.pdf.

19. Associated Press. (2014). Woman Who Lit Fire to Help Friends Gets Prison. Retrieved from: www.azcentral.com/story/news/nation/2014/09/03/woman-who-lit-fire-to-give-friends-work-sentenced/15040165.

20. Johnson, R., & Netherson, E. (2016). Fire Setting and the Impulse Control Disorder of Pyromania. *The American Journal of Psychiatry, Residents Journal, 11*, 14–16. Retrieved from: https://psychiatryonline.org/doi/10.1176/appi.ajp-rj.2016.110707.

21. Yorkshire Post. (2009). A City's Memories Branded in Fire of Killer's Reign of Terror 30 Years Ago. Retrieved from: https://web.archive.org/web/20181019135453/https://www.yorkshirepost.co.uk/news/analysis/a-city-s-memories-branded-in-fire-of-killer-s-reign-of-terror-30-years-ago-1-2314856.

22. BBC. (2021). Confessed Hull Arsonist Peter Tredget in New Appeal over 26 Deaths. Retrieved from: www.bbc.com/news/uk-england-humber-58876813. Note: Tredget also used the name Dinsdale at times. I've stuck to Dinsdale in the narrative.

23. Colarossi, N. (2021). Just 2 Percent of Hispanics Use the Term "Latinx," 40 Percent Find It Offensive: Poll. *Newsweek*. Retrieved from: www.newsweek.com/just-2-percent-hispanics-use-term-latinx-40-percent-find-it-offensive-poll-1656412.

24. Beda, S. (2020). Climate Change and Forest Management Have Both Fueled Today's Epic Western Wildfires. *The Conversation*. Retrieved from: https://theconversation.com/climate-change-and-forest-management-have-both-fueled-todays-epic-western-wildfires-146247.

25. Baumeister, R. F., Campbell, J. D., Krueger, J. I., & Vohs, K. D. (2003). Does High Self-Esteem Cause Better Performance, Interpersonal Success, Happiness, or Healthier Lifestyles? *Psychological Science in the Public Interest, 4*(1), 1–44.

CHAPTER 10

1. Concannon, C. (2019). Immigration: How Ancient Rome Dealt with the Barbarians at the Gate. *The Conversation*. Retrieved from: https://theconversation.com/immigration-how-ancient-rome-dealt-with-the-barbarians-at-the-gate-109933.

2. Gershon, E., & Segman, R. (2021). Perceptions of the Other—A Continuity of Racism by Anatomically Modern Humans against Neanderthals and against Jews. *Journal of Anthropology and Archaeology, 9*, 17–27.

3. Spierenburg P. (2012) Long-Term Historical Trends of Homicide in Europe. In: M. Liem & W. Pridemore (Eds.), *Handbook of European Homicide Research*. New York: Springer. https://doi.org/10.1007/978-1-4614-0466-8_3.

4. McCall, G., & Shields, N. (2008). Examining the Evidence from Small-Scale Societies and Early Prehistory and Implications for Modern Theories of Aggression and Violence. *Aggression and Violent Behavior, 13*, 1–9.

5. Spierenburg, P. (2001). Violence and the Civilizing Process. Does It Work? *Crime, Histoire & Sociétés, 5*(2), 87–105.

6. Sherif, M. (2001). Superordinate Goals in the Reduction of Intergroup Conflict. In M. A. Hogg & D. Abrams (Eds.), *Intergroup Relations: Essential Readings.* (pp. 64–70). Philadelphia: Psychology Press.

7. Simply do an internet search for "racism," "economics," and "immigration."

8. United States Commission on Civil Rights. (2008). Impact of Illegal Immigration on the Wages & Employment of Black Workers. Retrieved from: www.usccr.gov/files/pubs/docs/IllegImmig_10-14-10_430pm.pdf.

9. Borjas, G. (2016). Yes, Immigration Hurts American Workers. *Politico.* Retrieved from: www.politico.com/magazine/story/2016/09/trump-clinton-immigration-economy-unemployment-jobs-214216.

10. Schaffner, B., Macwilliams, M., Nteta, T. (2018). Understanding White Polarization in the 2016 Vote for President: The Sobering Role of Racism and Sexism. *Political Science Quarterly, 133*, 9–34.

11. Stanovich, K. (2021). *The Bias That Divides Us.* Cambridge, MA: MIT Press.

12. Maxouris, C., & Watts, A. (2020). Immigrant Acquitted of Murder in Kate Steinle Shooting Is Not Competent to Stand Trial Due to Mental Illness, Evaluator Says. CNN. Retrieved from: www.cnn.com/2020/02/15/us/kate-steinle-immigrant-mental-illness/index.html.

13. Light, M., He, J., & Robey, J. (2020). Comparing Crime Rates between Undocumented Immigrants, Legal Immigrants, and Native-Born US Citizens in Texas. *Proceedings of the National Academy of Science.* Retrieved from: www.pnas.org/content/117/51/3234.

14. Nowrasteh, A. (2020). New Research on Illegal Immigration and Crime. Cato Institute. Retrieved from: www.cato.org/blog/new-research-illegal-immigration-crime-0.

15. Lopez, M., Gonzalez-Barrera, A., & Lopez, G. (2017). Hispanic Identity Fades across Generations as Immigrant Connections Fall Away. Pew Research Center. Retrieved from: www.pewresearch.org/hispanic/2017/12/20/hispanic-identity-fades-across-generations-as-immigrant-connections-fall-away.

16. Zitner, A. (2021). Hispanic Voters Now Evenly Split between Parties, WSJ Poll Finds. *Wall Street Journal.* Retrieved from: www.wsj.com/articles/hispanic-voters-now-evenly-split-between-parties-wsj-poll-finds-11638972769.

17. Sanchez, G. (2021). Immigration and the Latino Vote: A Golden Opportunity for Democrats in 2022. Brookings Institute. Retrieved from: www.brookings.edu/blog/how-we-rise/2021/06/17/immigration-and-the-latino-vote-a-golden-opportunity-for-democrats-in-2022.

18. Kelly, C. (2019). Ocasio-Cortez on Calling Detention Centers 'Concentration Camps': We Have to "Learn from Our History." CNN. Retrieved from: www.cnn.com/2019/06/27/politics/alexandria-ocasio-cortez-concentration-camps-the-lead-cnntv/index.html.

19. Skodo, A. (2019). How Immigration Detention Compares around the World. *The Conversation.* Retrieved from: https://theconversation.com/how-immigration-detention-compares-around-the-world-76067.

20. Adams, B. (2021). Biden Promised an Investigation of that Border "Whipping" Incident. It's Not Happening. *Washington Examiner.* Retrieved from: www.washingtonexaminer.com/opinion/biden-promised-an-investigation-of-that-border-whipping-incident-its-not-happening.

21. Yglesias, M. (2021). *One Billion Americans.* New York: Portfolio.

CHAPTER 11

1. Bacon, J. (2021). 6 US Capitol Police Officers Recommended for Discipline in Jan. 6 Riot Ahead of "Justice for J6" Rally. *USA Today.* Retrieved from: www.usatoday.com/story/news/nation/2021/09/12/6-us-capitol-police-officers-recommended-discipline-jan-6-riot/8307721002.

2. Massimo, R. (2021). Medical Examiner: Capitol Police Officer Sicknick Died of Stroke; Death Ruled "Natural." WTOP. Retrieved from: https://wtop.com/dc/2021/04/medical-examiner-capitol-police-officer-sicknick-died-of-stroke-death-ruled-natural.

3. Steer, J. (2021). Timeline: How the Attack on the U.S. Capitol Unfolded on Jan. 6, 2021. Fox8. Retrieved from: https://fox8.com/news/timeline-how-the-attack-on-the-u-s-capitol-unfolded-on-jan-6-2021.

4. Dickson, C. (2021). Poll: Two-thirds of Republicans Still Think the 2020 Election Was Rigged. Yahoo News. Retrieved from: https://news .yahoo.com/poll-two-thirds-of-republicans-still-think-the-2020-election-was -rigged-165934695.html.

5. Leonnig, C. (2021). *Zero Fail: The Rise and Fall of the Secret Service.* New York: Random House.

6. Robb, A. (2017). Anatomy of a Fake News Scandal. *Rolling Stone.* Retrieved from: www.rollingstone.com/feature/anatomy-of-a-fake-news-scandal -125877.

7. Haroun, A. (2022). Prince Andrew's Ex-girlfriend Says in a New Documentary That Jeffrey Epstein and Bill Clinton "Were Like Brothers." Yahoo News. Retrieved from: https://news.yahoo.com/prince-andrews-ex-girlfriend -says-222750055.html.

8. Anti-Defamation League. (2022). OK Hand Gesture. Retrieved from: www.adl.org/education/references/hate-symbols/okay-hand-gesture.

9. Biddlestone, M., Green, R., Cichocka, A., Sutton, R., & Douglas, K. (2021). Conspiracy Beliefs and the Individual, Relational, and Collective Selves. *Social and Personality Psychology Compass, 15*(10). https://doi-org .stetson.idm.oclc.org/10.1111/spc3.12639.

10. Mariani, A. (2007). The Science behind GMOs. In *The Intersection of International Law, Agricultural Biotechnology, and Infectious Disease.* Leiden: Martinus Nijhoff.

11. Phillips, T. (2008). Genetically Modified Organisms (GMOs): Transgenic Crops and Recombinant DNA Technology. *Nature Education, 1.* Retrieved from: www.nature.com/scitable/topicpage/genetically-modified-organ isms-gmos-transgenic-crops-and-732. Keese, P. (2008). Risks from GMOs Due to Horizontal Gene Transfer. *Environmental Biosafety Research*, 7, 123–49.

12. American Museum of Tort Law. (2022). Grimshaw v. Ford Motor Company, 1981. Retrieved from: www.tortmuseum.org/ford-pinto.

13. Vittert, L. (2019). Are Conspiracy Theories on the Rise in the US? *The Conversation.* Retrieved from: https://theconversation.com/are-conspiracy -theories-on-the-rise-in-the-us-121968.

14. Leonard, M., & Philippe, F. (2021). Conspiracy Theories: A Public Health Concern and How to Address It. *Frontiers in Psychology.* Retrieved from: www.frontiersin.org/articles/10.3389/fpsyg.2021.682931/full.

15. Van Pooijen, J., & Douglas, K. (2018). Belief in Conspiracy Theories: Basic Principles of an Emerging Research Domain. *European Journal of Social Psychology, 48*, 897–908.

CHAPTER 12

1. Reuters. (2022). *50% of Americans Disapprove of the President.* Retrieved from: https://graphics.reuters.com/USA-BIDEN/POLL/nmopagnqapa/.

2. Monmouth University. (2022). GOP Has Congress Edge by Default. Retrieved from: www.monmouth.edu/polling-institute/reports/monmouth poll_US_012622.

3. The White House. (2022). Remarks by President Biden on Protecting the Right to Vote. Retrieved from: www.whitehouse.gov/briefing-room /speeches-remarks/2022/01/11/remarks-by-president-biden-on-protecting -the-right-to-vote.

4. Hogan, L. (2022). This Isn't Jim Crow 2.0. *The Atlantic.* Retrieved from: www.theatlantic.com/ideas/archive/2022/01/challenge-americas-electoral -system-college-count-act/621333.

5. Ferguson, C. J. (2015). Clinicians' Attitudes toward Video Games Vary as a Function of Age, Gender and Negative Beliefs about Youth: A Sociology of Media Research Approach. *Computers in Human Behavior, 52,* 379–86.

6. Ferguson, C. J., & Colwell, J. (2017) Understanding Why Scholars Hold Different Views on the Influences of Video Games on Public Health. *Journal of Communication, 67*(3), 305–27.

7. Fogel, S. (2015). Telltale Games: The Majority of *The Walking Dead* Players Try to Do the Right Thing. *Venture Beat.* Retrieved from: https:// venturebeat.com/2012/08/15/telltale-games-the-walking-dead-statistics-trailer.

8. Manning, R., Levine, M., & Collins, A. (2007). The Kitty Genovese Murder and the Social Psychology of Helping: The Parable of the 38 Witnesses. *American Psychologist, 62*(6), 555–62. https://doi-org.stetson.idm.oclc .org/10.1037/0003-066X.62.6.555.

9. De Waard, D., Jessurun, M., Steyvers, F. J. J. M., Reggatt, P. T. F., & Brookhuis, K. A. (1995). Effect of Road Layout and Road Environment on Driving Performance, Drivers' Physiology and Road Appreciation. *Ergonomics, 38*(7), 1395–1407.

10. Godley, S. T., Triggs, T. J., & Fildes, B. N. (2004). Perceptual Lane Width, Wide Perceptual Road Centre Markings and Driving Speeds. *Ergonomics, 47*(3), 237–56.

11. Ben-Bassat, T., & Shinar, D. (2011). Effect of Shoulder Width, Guardrail and Roadway Geometry on Driver Perception and Behavior. *Accident Analysis and Prevention, 43*(6), 2142–52.

12. Arno, A., & Thomas, S. (2016). The Efficacy of Nudge Theory Strategies in Influencing Adult Dietary Behaviour: A Systematic Review and

Meta-Analysis. *BMC Public Health*. Retrieved from: https://bmcpublichealth .biomedcentral.com/articles/10.1186/s12889-016-3272-x.

13. Goodwin, T. (2012). Why We Should Reject "Nudge." *Politics, 32,* 85–92.

INDEX

abortions, 64–65
academia, reform of, 201–3
accidental fires, 164–65
accountability of leaders, 36
acid rain, 143–44
Adams, Sam, 95
administrative bloat in colleges, 202
advocacy groups, 93, 108–9, 167–68
affective forecasting, 10, 14, 15–16
airplane crashes, 1–5, 27–28, 35, 210
air pollution, 60, 73
alligator populations, 150
all-or-nothing cognitive error, 68
al Qaeda, 78–80, 86. *See also*
    September 11 attacks
American Medical Association, 203
American Psychological Association
    (APA), 43, 55, 147, 203
ancient Greeks, 96, 101
anecdotes, 27–28, 47–48, 73, 138,
    178
animal attacks, 69–70
APA (American Psychological
    Association), 43, 55, 147, 203

apartheid, 115, 118, 127–28, 130
Armageddon claims, 150–51
arsonists, 165–67
Asch, Solomon, 17–18
Austria-Hungary, 11–14
authoritarian governments, 94
availability cascade: about, 27–29;
    characteristics of, 33–34, 37;
    comparisons, 31, 34; conditions
    for, 29; examples of, 31, 32–35,
    73; news media and, 73, 134–36;
    responding to, 35–37; shaming
    nature of, 136–37

Babbitt, Ashli, 188
barn fires, 161, 162
Beck, Aaron, 8
Beda, Stephen, 169
Bengkulu Indonesia, 117
Biden, Joe, 131, 181, 183, 184–85,
    206–7, 225n3
bin Laden, Osama, 78–80, 82–84, 88
black death, 53
Black Lives Matter, 136–37

Blackwell, Matthew, 134
blaming tendency, 10, 14
Border Patrol agents, 131, 185
Borjas, George, 176
Brown, Michael, 113–14, 124–25
Brown v. EMA court case, 107
Buckey, Ray, 20–21
bullshit asymmetry factor, 49
Bureau of Justice statistics, 119, 120
Bush, George W., 87, 90–91
bystander effect, 209

Cafferty, Emmanuel, 117
cancel culture, 44, 117–18
Capitol riot, 187–89
car crashes, 28, 70–71, 211
Carson, Johnny, 26
catastrophizing bias, 8–9, 16
CDC (Centers for Disease Control
    and Prevention), 7, 50–51
Challenger space shuttle disaster,
    89–90
Chauvin, Derek, 131–32
Chernobyl disaster, 62–65
child sex ring conspiracies, 191–93
Chinese government, 41–42
Churchill, Ward, 85–86
church membership, 6
civil liberties, 91–94
civil rights era, 121–22
climate change: all-the-time activism
    for, 59; Armageddon trap,
    150–51; finding a solution to,
    144–48, 153; good intentions and,
    75; history of environmentalism,
    142–44; Insulate Britain response
    to, 141; name-calling trap, 150,
    152–53; resistance to, 144. *See
    also* nuclear power

Climategate, 146–47
Clinton, Hillary, 107, 181
clown sightings, 102
coal, 58–59, 73
Coca-Cola fiasco, 90
cockroaches, fear of, 69–70
cognitive biases, 8–10, 14–16. *See
    also specific biases*
cognitive dissonance, 169
cognitive limitations, 145
coincidence, 74
concentration camps, 182–84
confirmation bias, 19–20, 46, 47–48,
    169, 198
conformity, 17–19, 116–18, 152. *See
    also* social contagion
conspiracy theories: about, 189–
    93; child sex rings, 191–93;
    genetically modified organisms,
    71–73, 194–95, 196; individual
    actions for countering, 199–200;
    reducing the appeal of, 197–98;
    societal actions for countering,
    200–204; stolen election claims,
    187–89, 204; trust and, 194
COVID-19: about, 23–24, 40,
    44–46; devastation of, 39; mask
    wearing, 21–22, 40, 44–46,
    50–53; NBA game cancellations,
    32–33; partisanship and, 94;
    public health messaging, 40–44,
    52, 53–56, 194; successes of, 56;
    swine flu compared to, 23; toilet
    paper panics, 24–26
crime and immigrants, 177–78
critical race theory (CRT) debate,
    48–49, 132, 133–34, 200–201
The Crucible, 19
cultivation theory, 71–73

culture: contributing to income disparities, 130; COVID-19 as culture war, 40, 44–46, 55–56; fears primed by, 71–73; "Great Replacement" concerns, 178–80; solidarity after 9/11 attacks, 40. *See also* the political and social left; the political and social right

Daghlian, Harry, 61
dark, fear of, 69
data: conspiracy theories and, 199; focusing on, 36–37, 213–14; health officials' politicizing, 54; persuasion with, 206–7; scrutinizing, 45–46
decision making: conformity in, 17–19; constraints on, 16; emotions and, 2–4, 111; nudge theory, 211–12; threat identification and, 69–71, 73–75; training and experience helping with, 100–101. *See also* evidence
"defund the police" efforts, 137
deinstitutionalization movement, 110
demographics: of immigrants, 178–79; median household income, 128–29; of police shootings, 118–25; poverty rates, 127
depression (national), 5–8
detention facilities, 182–84
Devos, Betsy, 106
dichotomous thinking, 9, 14
Dinsdale, Peter, 166–67
disasters and availability cascade, 27–29
disconfirm, inability to, 9, 16
discrimination against outsiders, 53. *See also* immigration

disengagement strategy, 200
Dixie Chicks, 91
documentaries, 47
Douglas, Karen, 197–98

East Asian groups, 128–29
eating choices, 212
Ebola breakout, 43–44
echo chambers, 48–49
economics of racism/immigration, 126–30, 175–76
educational reform, 201–3
Ehrlich, David, 96
elections and conspiracy theories, 187–90, 198, 204
Electrical Safety First, 58
electrocution deaths, 70–71
emotion: conspiracy theories appealing to, 197–98; decision making and, 2–4, 111; desensitization of, 100–101; evidence and, 19–20; flight or fight, 4–5; irrationality of, 74; systemic racism and, 21–22; vaccines and, 74. *See also* fears
"The Emperor's New Clothes" effect, 116, 133
energy sources: coal, 58–59, 73; fossil fuels, 58–60, 66–68, 73; renewable energy sources, 66–68. *See also* nuclear power
England's racial apartheid, 127–28
environmentalism, 67–68, 142–44, 169–70. *See also* climate change
Espinosa Garcés, María Fernanda, 150
essential workers, 50–52
European countries' alliances, 13

evidence: anecdotes as, 27–28, 47–48, 73, 138, 178; availability cascades and, 37; emotion and, 19–20; eyewitness testimony, 49; interpreting with cognitive biases, 8–10, 14–16. *See also* data

evolutionary history: conspiracy theories as universal, 197; fears as threats, 69–71; hostility toward "them," 173–75, 178, 208; male risk taking, 156–57

experts, 71–73

"explicit lyrics" sticker, 103

extrapolation bias, 44

extremism, cycles of, 212–13

eyewitness testimony, 49

falsification, 199

fears: culture contributing to, 71–73; evolutionary advantages of, 69–71; of "Great Replacement," 178–80; of microwave ovens, 57–58; of nuclear power, 61, 73–76. *See also* availability cascade

Ferdinand, Franz, 11–13, 85

Ferguson (Missouri) police shooting, 113–14

Fessler, Daniel, 117

firefighter arsonists, 98, 165–66

fires: attraction to and terror of, 160–62; bad decisions leading to, 163–67; dangers of suppressing, 169–70; decreases in residential fires, 163; at gender reveal parties, 163–64; Great White show, 159–60; increases in wildfires, 168–70; safety training, 162–63

Floyd, George, 115, 131–32

Ford Pinto, 195–96

fossil fuels, 59–60, 66–68, 73

Freedom Act, 92

Froelich, Harold V., 26

Fukushima disaster, 65–66

fundamentalist recruitment, 82, 83

Garcia Zarate, Jose, 177–78

generalization, 8

generational concerns and moral panics, 101, 103–5

genetically modified organisms (GMOs), 71–73, 194–95, 196

Genovese, Kitty, 209

German tribes and Roman Empire, 171–72

Germany in World War I, 15–16

Gifford, Robert, 145–48

GMOs (genetically modified organisms), 71–73, 194–95, 196

Gobert, Rudy, 32

Gore, Tipper, 102–3

Goths and Roman Empire, 171–72

government-sponsored mental health care, 109–11

"Great Replacement" fears, 178–80

Great Smog, 59

Great White show, 159–60

Green America, 67–68, 72

Gregg, Leonard, 165–66

groupthink, 88–91, 94

gun control issues, 54, 106–7, 108

Haitian immigrants, 131, 185

hand sanitizers, 23

Hispanic identity, 180, 181–82

HIV (human immunodeficiency virus), 33–34, 35

hoarding of resources, 26–27

horizontal gene transfer, 195
How Madness Shaped History
   (Ferguson), 110
human factors psychology, 210–11
human immunodeficiency virus
   (HIV), 33–34, 35
humiliation, 84
hunter-gatherer societies, 156–57
Hussein, Saddam, 87–88, 91

ideological capture, 93
immigration: changing demographics
   of, 179–80; complexity of issue,
   185; costs and benefits of, 175–
   77; historical perspective, 171–
   72; origins of prejudice, 173–
   75; violence and, 138–39;
   wrong ideas from the left, 180–
   84; wrong ideas from the right,
   178–80
Imo (Japanese snow monkey), 105
"incels," 95–96
information sources. *See* anecdotes;
   data; evidence; news media
"injustice collectors," 82
Insulate Britain, 141
intent of others, 9
involuntary celibates, 95–96
Iraq War, 86–89, 90–91
Irreversible Damage (Shrier), 30–
   31

Jaws (film), 149–50
Johnson, Sadie, 166
Joker (film), 95–96
July Ultimatum, 13–14
"june bug" incident, 30

"Knockout Game," 102, 135

Lankford, Adam, 81
Latino identity, 180, 181–82
Latinx terminology, 168
lightning dangers, 155
"lived experiences," 47–48. *See also*
   anecdotes
Long, Ryan, 210
Longely, Ty, 159–60
Lowry, Glenn, 127

March of Dimes, 168
mask wearing, 21–22, 40, 44–46,
   50–53
mass homicides: mental health of
   perpetrators, 80–82, 97, 109;
   violent video games and, 28–29,
   47, 105–6. *See also* Parkland
   (Florida) school shooting
McConnell, Mitch, 187
McMartin Preschool case, 20–21
media, 95–97, 102. *See also* news
   media; violent video games
mental illness: government-sponsored
   care, 109–11; mass homicides
   and, 80–82, 97, 109; police
   shootings and, 124; violent crime
   and, 108–9
microwave ovens, 57–58
mind reading, 9, 16
mob mentality. *See* groupthink
"Momo Challenge," 102
morality: availability cascades and,
   33–34, 35; groupthink and, 89;
   rational *versus* moral thinking, 19
moral panics, 21–22, 101–5
motte-and-bailey arguments, 136–37
music lyrics, 102–3
myside bias, 20, 48–49, 52–53, 152,
   196

name-calling, 150, 152–53
narcissism, 83–84
NASA, 89–90
National Volunteer Fire Council
   (NVFC), 165
Neanderthals, 172
negativity bias, 5, 8
news media: availability heuristic
   and, 73; fears supported by,
   27–28, 73; groupthink and,
   91; highlighting stories of
   shootings, 120–21, 134–36;
   mental health solutions not
   reported by, 110–11
nuclear power: Chernobyl disaster,
   62–65; as clean energy, 67;
   concerns about, 61–62, 73–76;
   difficulty of changing minds
   about, 73–75; Fukushima disaster,
   65–66; safety of, 58–60, 66–68,
   73, 75; Three Mile Island disaster,
   62, 63
nudge theory, 212
NVFC (National Volunteer Fire
   Council), 165

Obama, Barack, 92, 113, 183
Ocasio-Cortez, Alexandria, 150
opiod epidemic, 125
optimism: cause for, 22, 205–6;
   cyclical nature of idiocy, 212–13;
   learning from mistakes and, 210–
   12; need for data focus, 213–14;
   people doing the right thing,
   208–10
Orr, John, 98
Our World in Data, 66–67
outsiders, 53, 209–10
ozone layer depletion, 143–44

pandemics, 53. See also COVID-19
paranoia, 84
Parents Music Resource Center
   (PMRC), 102–3, 104
Parkland (Florida) school shooting:
   about, 97–98; gun control and,
   107–8; mental illness and violent
   crime, 108–11; school resource
   officer's actions, 98–101; violent
   video games and, 105–7, 108
Patriot Act, 91–92
Pazoozles example, 74
perseverative errors, 4
personal freedoms, 93–94
personalizing behavior, 9, 14
persuasion, 150, 152–53, 199–200
Peterson, Scot, 98–101
Pew Research Center, 127
Pizzagate, 191–93
PMRC (Parents Music Resource
   Center), 102–3, 104
police shootings: delegitimizing
   policing, 124–25; mental illness
   and, 125; perceptions of, 122–23;
   socioeconomic class and, 125. See
   also race and policing
the political and social left:
   availability cascades, 131–37;
   conspiracy theories, 193;
   progressive's views on racism,
   176–77; resembling the right,
   212–13; virtue signaling, 44. See
   also specific politicians on the left
the political and social right:
   availability cascades, 138–39;
   conspiracy theories, 193; race-
   baiting, 131; resembling the left,
   212–13; virtue signaling, 44. See
   also specific politicians on the right

politics: COVID-19 and, 41–42, 94; culture wars and, 55–56; polarization from lack of social institutions, 203–4; propaganda, 91–94; science not mixing with, 54; social cohesion after 9/11, 85–87; "systemic racism" terminology and, 132–33; of video games, 106–7; of voting blocs, 181–82; of WHO, 42. *See also* the political and social left; the political and social right; worldviews

poverty, 110, 127

power struggles, 104–5

Pripyat (Soviet Union), 63–64, 65

pro-dodo movement, 167–68

public health messaging, 40–44, 52, 53–56, 194

pyromania, 166

QAnon, 193

Quillete, 134

race and policing: anti-cop sentiment, 137; demographics of police shootings, 118–25; "Ferguson effect," 124–25; murder of George Floyd, 115, 131–32; news coverage of police killings, 120–21, 134–36; shooting of Michael Brown, 113–14

racism: apartheid, 115, 118, 127–28, 130; cancel culture and, 117–18; Ebola outbreak narrative and, 43–44; explicit racism decreasing, 132–33; immigration and, 175–76, 180–81; mass homicide and, 29; perceptions of, 6, 7; progressives' views on race and,

176–77; rhetoric ratcheting up, 139; slavery's legacy, 115–16, 126, 129, 130; wealth and income disparities and, 126–30. *See also* critical race theory (CRT) debate; systemic racism

radiation exposure, 61–62. *See also* nuclear power

"Rainbow Sex Parties," 102

Reilly, Wilfred, 127

religiosity, 6

renewable energy sources, 66–68

Resurrect the Dodo movement, 167–68

Rice, Condoleezza, 88

Richie, Stuart, 42–43

ridicule, 35–36

risk assessment, 68–73, 147, 154–57

Robber's Cave experiment, 174–75

Roman Empire, fall of, 171–72

Rossi, Paul, 48–49, 133–34

Salem witch trials, 19

"sanctuary city" law, 177–78

satanic ritual abuse panic, 20

school resource officers (SROs), 98–101

school shooters, 81–82

science. *See* data

self-esteem movement, 169–70

self-interest, 208

self-serving bias, 49

September 11 attacks: author's memories, 77; cultural solidarity following, 40; groupthink and Iraq War, 90–91; mental health of suicide terrorists, 80–82; responses to, 79, 85–89, 91–94;

terrorists' goals, 78–80, 82–84; trust in narrative of, 190

Serbian state, 11–14

shame: cancel culture and, 117–18; moral availability cascade and, 136–37; propaganda effects and, 92–93; race relations and, 116–18; social exclusion as precursor to conspiracy theories, 193; suicide and, 81

shark depopulation, 149–50

Shrier, Abigail, 30–31

Skeptic Research Center, 122

slavery, historical legacy of, 115–16, 126, 129, 130

Slotin, Louis, 61

Smith, Will, 136–37

smog, 59

snakes, 69, 70, 156

Snider, Dee, 102–3

social advantages to myside bias, 48–49

social comparisons and climate change, 145–46

social contagion, 30–31

social institutions, 203–4

social media and suicide, 102

societal malaise, 8

socioeconomic status and race, 123–24, 125, 127

South African apartheid, 128

South Asian groups, 128–29

speeding while driving, 211

SRO (school resource officers), 98–101

standpoint epistemology, 133

Stanovich, Keith, 177

Station club fire, 159–60

Steinle, Kate, 177–78

stolen election claims, 187–90, 198, 204

suicide rates, 7, 30

suicide terrorists, 80–82

summer camp experiment, 174–75

"sunk costs" effect, 55, 75, 146, 155

swimming dangers, 154–55

swine flu, 23–24

systemic racism: all disparities not due to, 126–30; culture wars and, 55–56; data not supporting, 118–25; economics and, 126–30; emotional processing of, 21–22; open letter against, 52; protests and riots reacting to claims of, 132; terminology of, 132–33. See also race and policing; racism

Taboo (Reilly), 127

Telltale Games, 208

tenure system, 202

terrorist leaders, 84. See also September 11 attacks

threats. See fears

Three Mile Island disaster, 62, 63

toilet paper panics, 24–26, 29, 34

trans identification, 30–31

transparency, 200–201, 208

travel restrictions, 42

tribal virtue signaling, 44, 45

Trump, Donald J.: factors associated with voting for, 176–77; on immigration, 181, 183; race-baiting, 131, 132; on violent video games, 97, 105, 107

trust of the public: authority figures needing, 190; conspiracy theories and, 194, 195; public erosion of, 146–47; public health messaging and, 40–44, 52, 53–56, 194; scientific data and, 153

unarmed individuals in shootings, 120–24
US Capitol riot, 187–89
US Fire Administration, 163
Uyghur minority, 116

vaccine controversy, 74. *See also* COVID-19
van Prooijen, Jan-Willem, 197–98
violent crime: between cultural groups, 173–74; firearm access and, 108; homicide spike, 137, 138; perpetrators of, 108–11, 119–20, 138; riots and stolen election claims, 187–89, 204; school shooters, 81–82. *See also* mass homicides; race and policing
violent video games: APA on, 55, 147; changing views of, 35, 207; hearings on, 97; mass homicides and, 28–29, 47, 105–6; news media supporting fears of, 73
voters and political parties, 181–82

Walking Dead video game, 208
Wall Street Journal, 181
warning fatigue, 151–52
Washington Post data, 121, 122
weather events, 154–55
Welch, Edgar, 191–92
white supremacist hand signs, 117, 193
"white supremacy" in the US, 52, 126, 128, 132, 191, 198
WHO (World Health Organization), 41–42, 50–51, 203
wildlife dangers, 156
Wilson, Darren, 113–14
witch hunts, 19
Woodbine Racetrack fire, 161
World Health Organization (WHO), 41–42, 50–51, 203
worldviews: anecdotes supporting, 47, 48; of bin Laden, 83–85; climate change and, 145; progressives on race, 176–77; students needing exposure to, 202–3. *See also* the political and social left; the political and social right; politics
World War I, 10–16
World War II, 10

Zacharek, Stephanie, 95